You want to kn...
Condemned to ... with you
It's some kind of daily suicide
Some phase that I outgrew
I ain't sadistic, masochistic
You and me we're through
I'm sick to death of everything you do
And if I'm gonna puke
Babe I'm gonna puke on you

"Sick On You"
The Hollywood Brats, 1973

from what it's like

Sick On You

The Disastrous Story of
THE HOLLYWOOD BRATS,
the Greatest Band
You've Never Heard Of

Andrew Matheson

BLUE RIDER PRESS
New York

blue
rider
press

BLUE RIDER PRESS
An imprint of Penguin Random House LLC
375 Hudson Street
New York, New York 10014

First published in Great Britain by Ebury Press in 2015

Library of Congress Cataloging-in-Publication Data
Names: Matheson, Andrew.
Title: Sick on you : the disastrous story of the Hollywood Brats, the
greatest band you've never heard of / Andrew Matheson.
Description: New York : Blue Rider Press, [2016]
Identifiers: LCCN 2015047029 (print) | LCCN 2015047709 (ebook) | ISBN
9780399185335 (trade pbk.) | ISBN 9780399185342 (eBook)
Subjects: LCSH: Hollywood Brats (Musical group) | Rock
musicians—England—Biography.
Classification: LCC ML421.H654 M38 2016 (print) | LCC ML421.H654 (ebook) |
DDC 782.42166092/2—dc23
LC record available at http://lccn.loc.gov/2015047029

Printed in the United States of America
1   3   5   7   9   10   8   6   4   2

For Kerry

Sick On You

Introduction

This tale comes via memory, reel-to-reel, diary, acetate, journal, and cassette.

I was eighteen years old, six feet tall, 148 pounds, sopping wet, and, like Dylan's farmhand on "Maggie's Farm," I had a head full of ideas that were driving me insane. Most of those ideas revolved around starting a band.

I was driven by the purest of all the emotions: hatred. I hated absolutely everything I heard in the charts. Music needed to be grabbed by the lapels and shaken up.

So I got some cash, a suitcase, and a guitar, and off I went to London where legend had it the streets were paved with gold records. I also took with me a set of rules. Five rules chiseled in granite, sacrosanct and unbreakable. Follow these rules and I would create the perfect band.

Rules for a Rock 'N' Roll Band
~ The Template ~

1. Four or five members maximum. No sax, no horn section, no keyboards, no Moog-synthesizer boffin, no backup chanteuses, no nothing. Two guitars, a bass, drums, and singer, that's it. Think the Beatles, Kinks, and Who for four, Stones for five.

2. The singer sings. That's it. No hanging a guitar around his neck mid-show and strumming a few cowboy chords to show he can play, no sitting at the piano for a poignant ballad or two, and definitely no tambourine bashing. And for Christ's sake, no standing on one leg and sucking and wheezing into a flute like that hobo in Jethro Tull. At a pinch a shake of maracas but

just for a portion of a song then toss them aside. If a singer can't think what
to do with himself during a bandmate's solo he should consider a career as
a bank teller.

3.   Great hair, straight hair, is a must and is nonnegotiable. If a member starts
      going thin on top put an ad in the *Melody Maker* immediately. If he has
      too tight a natural curl or, saints preserve, a perm, well, shame on you for
      hiring him in the first place. Be firm about this; a hat won't work.

4.   No facial hair. Girls, or at least girls you'd ever deign to paw, do not swoon
      over the Grateful Dead. Jerry Garcia is no sane, recently showered girl's
      idea of a pinup.

5.   No girlfriends. They are cancerous for the esprit de corps. They lower the
      band's collective sexual currency and can twist a measly bass player's brain
      until he thinks he should get a triple-album solo deal and headline Vegas.
          Two words: Yoko and Ono.

I still believe in these rules but as fate would have it we broke most of them.

Prologue

Staring up. Standing in steel-toed rubber boots and filth-encrusted overalls; standing in the mud and the crud, staring up. Standing in crypt-like total darkness pierced only by the beam from the lamp on my hard hat, a beam growing weaker by the minute as the battery pack on my belt dies. Staring up, waiting for, praying for, the cage.

The cage, the chariot comin' for to carry me home, at long last descends into this stinkhole. Clanking, juddering, the jail-cell-on-cables crashes to a halt. The chainlink guillotine door rises. I climb aboard. The guillotine crashes down and I get yanked up to the blessed, sunlit surface, never to go down a mine again, I pray, for the rest of my life.

In the shower I lather up in terror as usual, eyes wide open and stinging from soap. Keeping a sharp lookout because these Canadian nickel miners are a tribe of knuckle-dragging, grunting, violent troglodytes. They know it's my last day and they've been making noises about cutting my hair.

Twenty hours later and I've escaped. I've got a blue cardboard suitcase with white leatherette piping in my hand and a black Vox Mark VI teardrop guitar at my feet.

I'm eighteen years old.

I've got a thousand bucks in my pocket.

I'm standing on the cobbles of Carnaby Street.

London, that great cesspool into which all the loungers and idlers of the Empire are irresistibly drained.

Arthur Conan Doyle

1971

I

London. What's it like, this town in July 1971? This town just past the fag end of the sixties? This so-called Swinging London? Let me tell you, it's bloody marvelous. It is tawdry and garish, filthy and littered and chokingly diesel perfumed. It is filled with a thousand hucksters and shysters and gypsy girls in Piccadilly with sprigs of heather already pinned to your lapel before you can protest, palms held out and a "cross my palm with silver, for luck," the veiled, unsubtle threat of misfortune should you not, with coin, comply. It is teeming with girls and the girls are stunning, teetering around in stack-heeled, knee-high boots, in suede micro-miniskirts with gossamer scarves, Cleopatra eyeliner underlining fluttering Twiggy lashes.

Union Jacks are everywhere, flapping amid the gargoyles on the stone buildings, hanging in whipping-in-the-wind plastic rows on the shops and stalls, on T-shirts, knickers, tea towels, socks, ashtrays, salt and pepper shakers, bowler hats, bobbies' hats.

Rule Britannia.

Britannia rules the airwaves.

Maybe.

"Chirpy Chirpy Cheep Cheep" by Middle of the Road, a song that makes you want to drive spikes into your ears and crucify your brain, hits number one in the charts and stays there.

The Beatles are dead. Poor, pure, blond, bitchy Brian drowned. Jimi choked. Morrison, reduced from a pretentious West Coast pseudo-poet, albeit with great hair and a svelte physique, to a bloated, bearded metaphor, soon to float, barely, in a Paris bathtub.

Hippies run the show: beards and denim and crap music with mind-numbing guitar solos and daft, boring, nonsensical lyrics; drummers allowed to thump their stupid tubs alone on stage for fifteen minutes while everyone else takes a break. Gongs, for Christ's sake. Gongs. Incense. Double bass drums.

Who looks good? Nobody looks good. Who sounds good? Nobody sounds good. My grand plan is to create a band to rectify that situation. Wipe the slate clean.

But first I must find some digs. I haven't been in London since my parents kidnapped me as a child, dragging me, kicking and screaming in a sack, to Northern Ontario. Word is that an agency is the best bet so there I go. The Greek lady behind the desk says that what I am seeking in terms of accommodation (not much) will cost between six and ten quid a week. No sweat, I've got the grand in hand. She reaches over her shoulder and sells me a London *A–Z*, slips a few addresses in my hand, and sends me all over town to see bedsits. But none do I see. As soon as the prospective landlords clap peepers on my guitar case it is case closed. Time after time I knock. Time after time it happens.

This becomes tiresome and demoralizing. I am hot and tired and jetlagged and hungry and dying of thirst.

Six o'clock. The buses and Tubes and streets are jammed with commuters on the move. This is tough and it's getting late. There is just one more address in my pocket: Finborough Road, Earls Court, London SW10.

"Kangaroo Valley, mate," says the guy wedged near me on the stifling Tube, reading over my shoulder.

"Kangaroo Valley?"

"Fuckin' Aussie ghetto, innit?"

So, it's a fucking Aussie ghetto. What does that mean to me? Nothing. Off I get at Earls Court station, turn right, and, with the *A–Z* as my guide, I set off for Finborough Road. I pass two pubs adjacent to one another, busy with the after-work crowd. At least I assume that's what they are. Actually, the customers all seem to be men. They *are* all men, but I'd lay a quid or two that these specimens don't actually come from Australia. They've spilled out onto the street, standing in studied poses wearing leather chaps, Brando *Wild One* hats, silver wallet chains, and white singlets, mustaches apparently mandatory. They mew and whistle as I walk by.

The building I'm looking for is triangular, at the point where Finborough Road and Ifield Road converge. P'raps I should stash the guitar in a hedge or something. Make a better impression. Perish the thought. Stash my black Vox Mark VI teardrop? Not a chance. This guitar is not leaving my white-knuckled grip.

It's the same guitar I saw Brian Jones play on *The Ed Sullivan Show* when I was thirteen. It's the only guitar I have ever wanted and I worked down that stinking nickel mine to get the $263 it took to buy it. I had it custom-painted black. Brian's was white, mine's black, and I'm never going to part with it, and I'm certainly not going to stash it in a hedge.

Number 119. I press the buzzer and wait.

The old chap who answers the door is garbed in slippers and smoking jacket, with a polka-dot scarf knotted nattily around his neck. He is tall, slightly stooped, and leaning on a silver-tipped cane, snow-white hair combed straight back, military 'tache. Quite a look, actually. He gives me the twice-over and politely asks me to follow him up the stairs.

Over strong tea he tells me the bedsit is mine if I want it, £6.50 a week, two weeks in advance. The small room is on the top floor. It is shopworn but clean, with threadbare carpet, single bed, rattan armchair, sink, wee cooker thing with a tiny electric element, and window facing west over Ifield Road. Down the hall is the bathroom, shared with the two other top-floor tenants. Want a bath? Shilling in the meter.

I pay the man. I take the room. I unpack my suitcase. It contains clothes and five LPs.

Beggars Banquet—Rolling Stones
Get Yer Ya-Ya's Out!—Rolling Stones
Let It Be—Beatles
Something Else—Kinks
Back Door Men—Shadows of Knight

Next day I hit the town and I keep hitting it. I buy clothes up and down the King's Road. I have a smooth drink in the Chelsea Drugstore and a cold one in the Markham Arms, and another here and another there. Chelsea Potter? Why not? I buy a black sweater with "Rock 'n' Roll" stitched in yellow across the front. I buy a wine-red velvet jacket and tight, black velvet strides.

I head to Savile Row where I stand across the street from the blessed number 3, home of Apple Corps, center of the Holy Fief of Beatledom. Rooted to the spot, I'm gawking up like a rube at the roof where, not so long ago, his hands were getting a bit too cold to play the chords. It is a hot, humid afternoon in London in July, but I've got chills.

Shaking it off and putting it back in my trousers, I head anywhere, which happens to be south. Where Savile Row meets Clifford Street, I pop into Mr Fish, purveyor of the most dazzling shirts known to man. I order and am measured for two custom-made, hand-stitched stunners with all the attendant and requisite "Yes, sirs" and "Quite right, sirs" a chap could possibly want. A lilac dress shirt with "le cuff Français" at an extravagant £15 and a white chemise featuring an explosion of lace at the front and on the cuffs for a ludicrous £35 strike my fancy. Each will bear a label stating "Peculiar to Mr Fish."

When the sun goes down I make my way to Wardour Street and the Marquee. The stage at the Marquee is hallowed ground. The Stones, the Who, and on and on played here, trod these very boards. And tonight, who is on? Some Irish guitarist named Rory Gallagher. Nothing but twelve-bar blues and denim, everything I detest: the tortured grimacing during the guitar solos, the nods of approval and shoe-staring during the drum solo, the shamrock Delta accent. But I don't care. I'm not really watching. I'm leaning on the bar and it's the Marquee.

I'm back nights later too, girlishly giddy with excitement that is all too damply extinguished because who is on? Arthur Brown's Kingdom Come, that's who, with his beard (the matted focal point of a general revolting hairiness) and his chronic, faux-demonic makeup and his "I am the God of Hellfire" routine.

You've been telling us that since '68, mate. We were enthralled then and we are utterly rapt now. Press on.

It's a daft show. He moves like a drunk hippy uncle and he looks mildly demented, especially during his showstopper when he sets his hat on fire. But I don't care. I'm here at the world-famous Marquee.

The manager of the Marquee, Jack, an over-friendly, unctuous type sporting a shiny suit, black horn-rims, and a clunking gold pinkie ring, takes a shine to me, asking increasingly personal questions. I tell him I'm going to start a rock 'n' roll band and I intend to wipe the floor with the competition. This throws him, and it's the moment when I get the first indication that the term rock 'n' roll has an entirely different connotation here in the mother country.

You mention rock 'n' roll and immediately English brains think of Jerry Lee Lewis, Eddie Cochran, Chuck Berry, Gene Vincent, Little Richard, Bill Haley, and all the rest. Brylcreem, duck's arse hairdos, Teddy Boys, drape coats, winklepickers, brothel creepers, and leather jackets—in short, the fifties. Rock 'n' roll in Britain is for those who never got over Elvis joining the army. Well, that's not the way it is for me, chaps. Those guys did their bit but they're from the Middle Ages as far as I'm concerned.

First I heard of Chuck Berry, I was on my bike crunching the gravel at Larchwood Public School, holding a Hitachi transistor up to my ear when "No Particular Place to Go" came on. I liked it. I really wanted to "park way out on the kokomo," but not enough to go out and buy the vinyl. I was a kid on a bike. It took the Fabs with George singing "Roll Over Beethoven" and the Stones doing "Carol" for an entity called Chuck Berry to get into my skull.

As for Eddie Cochran, well, as far as I'm concerned, "Summertime Blues" is by the Who from *Live at Leeds*. And Little Richard? It took Paul singing "Long Tall Sally" and the Swinging Blue Jeans doing "Good Golly Miss Molly" for me to get that tutti-frutti picture. So that's what I find myself up against here, elbow on the bar, at the Marquee. You say you're going to create a new, wild rock 'n' roll band in July 1971 and everybody thinks quiffs and pomade.

Midway through one night, while I'm leaning on the bar drinking light and bitter, surveying the possibilities, Jack sidles up and invites me back to his pad after closing. I came in on a Pan Am flight, not a turnip truck, so I've seen it coming and I deflect the overture with what I hope is grace and humor. After all, I want to play here some day.

A pretty blonde girl, miniskirt and white stockings, butter-wouldn't-melt mouth, corners me at the bar, says she's got tickets to the Tyrannosaurus Rex gig at the Roundhouse in Chalk Farm, and next thing I know we're riding the Northern Line en route. I've heard these pixies on the radio doing some fairy drivel titled, if you can believe it, "Ride a White Swan." What the hell does that mean? Apparently they are comprised of some curly-haired, chubby-faced elf on acoustic and a tall, skinny drink of milk on congas. With that lineup my expectations are subterranean. But it's just the miniskirt that's got me in its sway.

We arrive late and, Hello, hello? The joint is positively rocking. This is no knee-staring acoustic hippy duo; they've plugged in, cranked up the decibels, and shanghaied a bass player and drummer. Not sure what the conga player in the white suit is contributing to proceedings, but he's got good hair and seems harmless enough. Anyway, it's all about the little guy up front with the Jheri curls and elevator shoes. He plays a Les Paul, all crunching chords and lots of posing. He's clomping around, sticking his lips out like an inflatable Jagger sex doll.

Our seats are great but there is no sitting down—the atmosphere is sticky-hot and throbbing. The sound is fantastic, crunching out of Orange amps and stacks of WEM speakers. They end with something called "Hot Love" and it's not bad, considering.

Next morning the sweet little thing catches the train back to Sheffield and, touchingly, she has left me a little parting gift, something to remember her by. Something of which I am entirely and blissfully unaware.

I need an amp. Shaftesbury Avenue and Charing Cross Road, winding up from Leicester Square to Denmark Street, is Candy Cane Lane for a musician. Music shops are everywhere, brimming with instruments and gear I've only seen in films and magazines. Vox with its AC-30s, Super Beatles, Phantoms, and Marauders; Gibson Firebirds, Flying Vs, Explorers, Les Pauls, J-200s; Fender Strats and Precisions, Jazzmasters and Telecasters, and dozens more. Gretsch, Ludwig, Hofner, Premier, Zildjian, Martin, Shure, Marshall, Rickenbacker: names I can recite like a confessing Catholic while my eyes pop out of my skull like a snot-nosed Dickensian Christmas orphan as I stare in the windows and walk the aisles.

Macari's is my favorite shop, with its redolent-of-Beatles Vox sign beckoning. Come on in, it says, we've got that AC-30 you know you can't live without. In I go, carrying my Mark VI into Aladdin's cave. Musicians are everywhere, trying and buying, tuning and strumming, tightening snares, smacking tambourines, and twiddling with amps—a jumble of noise and music.

Then a middle-aged guy in a blue checked shirt, with coiffed, white rockabilly hair comes over and introduces himself as the real Macari. His jaw must be in peak physical condition because the thing doesn't cease clopping up and down for at least an hour. This guy can talk, and sell. He doesn't stop talking.

Next thing I know, my beautiful Vox Mark VI teardrop, with the custom jet-black paint job, the one I vowed to keep and cherish for the rest of my life, the one I worked 3,000 feet below the earth's surface in a stinking, wet, dark, dank mine to be able to afford, is hanging on Macari's wall and I am walking out the door with a beat-up, chipped, metallic-blue Fender Stratocaster and a Vox AC-30.

How did that happen?

II

For a musician, Thursday is the most important day of the week. At dawn on Thursdays, Fleet Street vans disgorge the bales of the music press, the rags that report and advertise and fuel the biz of music. These papers are stuffed with who's doing what, who's wearing what, who smells like money, who stinks of failure, who's new, who's old, who's in a snit, who's suing who, who's number one, whose number's up, who's in, who's out, who's shaking it all about.

And it's all there in black and white under the splash red headlines. Every eagerly awaited Thursday the newspaper nests are festooned with the *New Musical Express*, *Sounds*, *Record Mirror*, *Disk*, and the rest. But the most read, revered, and necessary of all is the *Melody Maker*.

It's been around for donkeys', dealing in jazz, big bands, and bebop, but since "Love Me Do" it has become more and more the tribune and mouthpiece of the pop and rock community. But, more than the gossip, the features, the rubbish tawdry tales of popdom, the *Melody Maker* is the conduit, the message board, the lonely hearts club. For the *Melody Maker* features that most essential element—the lifeblood of singers, guitarists, bass players, keyboardists, drummers, tuba players—in fact, any musician that makes a noise and wants a gig—in its back pages. It is the famous "Classifieds" section, and it is here that we all learn to turn every Thursday.

I lie on my bed and scan the "Vocalists Wanted" column, trying to find an ad that just might fit my bill. Nothing ever screams out at me. None mention rock 'n' roll, or at least none that don't want the new Buddy Holly or the new Danny for the new "& the Juniors." They just say "Rock," with all the plodding, Cro-Magnon, drum-solo indulgence that word, in my mind, has come to entail.

Nevertheless, I do stock up on 2p pieces and walk to the phone box in Redcliffe Square and make calls to a few circled ads that I, sort of, just maybe, if you squint your eyes, might fit.

And get this straight. I'm no rookie, no dabbling dilettante. I've been singing in bands since I was thirteen. First band I was in was with sixteen- and seventeen-year-olds. They seemed like grizzled pensioners to me. They smoked. They steamed up windows with chicks in the backseats of Chevy 427s. They shaved.

"Night, Mum. Night, Dad."

"You off, son? Seems a bit early."

"Yeah, I'm tired. Got that history test tomorrow, too."

"Oh, of course. All right then. Sleep tight, love."

Into my bedroom, lock door, grab clothes, out the window. Back through the window at 1 a.m., conk out with $11 in my pocket.

I've played high-school dances, community centers, roller-skating rinks, wedding receptions, TV talent shows, Christmas telethons, youth clubs. I've been there.

Now I whip off on the buses or Tube, directions in hand, to all over London, to unfamiliar locales: Wapping, Tooting Broadway, Walthamstow, Mile End, Tufnell Park. To rehearsal studios, back rooms, cellars, pubs, factories, churches. And I audition.

A dozen auditions. Then a dozen more. And so it goes. They don't like me and I return the sentiment. This is going to be more difficult than I thought, bruising too. Every Thursday, same as thousands of other musicians across Britain, I lie on my bed with a pen scanning the ads in the *Melody Maker*.

I hear the other tenants as they pass my door, heading to the communal loo. The most we've all shared is a glance and a nod. They seem to be an English woman of indeterminate vintage, a Dutch woman, early twenties, and an English man, possibly a student, wispy attempt at a beard, National Health specs. On my social stepladder students are perched on the rung one down from hippies.

Sitting at the small wooden table, I look out at the relentless Wednesday rain. On the other side of Ifield Road, two floors down, an attractive lady sits at a dressing table near the window brushing her shoulder-length hair. She is starkers.

III

The grand is gone. A thousand bucks. Where did it go? Clothes and clubs and Strats and all sorts. But it is undeniably gone, with the exception of a lone tenner.

I have to get a job, there's no alternative. So I brush all my teeth and drag my zero qualifications down to the Labour Exchange, where a kindly, bored woman gives me forms to fill out and suggests three employment opportunities. The first two make my eyes glaze over but the third seems worth a shot. Moss Bros, famous apparently though I know not of it, needs a chap to work in the department of formal rentals. Off I go to Covent Garden, and upon arrival at Moss Bros I am put in a lift, sent down into the bowels of the building, and placed under the tutelage of one Goolam Assenge, pronounced Goolam Assenge.

According to Goolam, this is the job. Gentlemen come into Moss Bros to hire formal attire—morning coats, gloves, toppers, and such. The attending salesman ascertains the customer's requirements, bends slightly at the waist, backs obsequiously away, then turns and sprints down to the lower floor where there are row upon row of shelves and hangers containing all the garments in all the sizes. He grabs three or four pairs of trousers that he feels are within his customer's general size range, and hares off up the stairs with them. Fifteen or so minutes later he clatters back down, throws the trousers in a heap in the corner, grabs four top hats, and tears off back up the stairs again. My job, explains Goolam, is to pick up the garments, fold them neatly, and put them back where they came from.

Now, multiply that salesman by ten, multiply that customer by a hundred, add the fact that this is the racing season, consider that a percentage of the salesmen are psychotics, factor in the piles of rental returns, and you'll still not come remotely close to comprehending the volume, the madness, the bitchiness, the chaos, the stacks and never-ending stacks of pin-striped toff-wear I have to deal with in my new position. I will work from nine in the morning until five in the afternoon, half day on Saturday, for the princely sum of £11.50 a week. I am to start the next morning.

On the way home I decide to stock my larder, or at least the narrow shelf above my cooker, and attempt to wring as much as possible out of my lone remaining £10 note. From a small shop where the proprietor is the spitting image of Gandhi's more emaciated brother, I buy a loaf of bread, a small box of tea bags, a tiny white jar of fish paste, a plastic container of chocolate spread, two tins of spaghetti, and a bottle of milk. At home I heat up one of the tins of spaghetti, and for dessert I eat three chocolate-spread sandwiches. I nod off reading H.G. Wells's *A Short History of the World*.

Next morning, shilling in the meter followed by a tepid, shallow bath, and I'm off. By about the tenth minute my new job starts to drive me nuts. By the end of the day I want to murder the salesmen in creatively brutish ways. They treat me as though I do not exist. As far as they are concerned, the piles of clothes they throw on the floor get put back neatly and in an organized fashion by magic.

Goolam is at the cleaning end of the Moss Bros equation: dry cleaning, repairs, ironing, nothing fazes him. He is the voice of cheerful, calm reason. He laughs, he smiles, he sings ditties. He tells tales about the salesmen. Goolam does go on a bit but he gets me through my first few days, then a week, then ten days.

With my £11.50 I must pay for twelve Tube journeys, to and from Moss Bros, per week. Home sweet bedsit costs £6.50 per week. Even seven baths a week costs seven shillings.

I begin to go hungry at about the same time as my crotch begins to itch.

More Thursday trips to the red phone box in Redcliffe Square, more auditions, more failures—some abject and embarrassing. Most of these bands are bluesy combos, with big perms or auburn Afros, playing "Rock Me Baby" till my marrow aches. The big, harsh, scratchy, ersatz Delta vocal they want is just not my forte. Other bands flaunt their delusions of prog grandeur. Sweeping arrangements, ludicrous lyrics, excruciating non-melodies that I'm expected to grasp in five minutes. I keep reminding myself, Groucho Marx fashion, that if I got one of these gigs I wouldn't want it anyway. But there's no escaping the fact that these auditions hurt and gnaw at the confidence.

The routine at Moss Bros, Goolam notwithstanding, is grinding me down too. The job never gets done, not even for five minutes. All those hours of picking up clothes, folding them, putting them neatly away . . . same clothes, same shelves, ad infinitum.

At home of an evening I'm nearly out of food. Just two stale heels of bread and some chocolate spread remain on my shelf. I try to convince myself that stale bread is just white toast. In my Redcliffe phone box, spending a precious 2p calling for yet another audition, someone has left behind a copy of Jean-Paul Sartre's *Nausea*. I give it a go later at home. It's hardly a page-turner.

And what's with this itch? I remind myself of a straw-chewing yokel the way I'm constantly scratching at my nethers. At work I've started ducking into nooks or the loo to claw away at my groin like an ape. On the Piccadilly Line I hang on to the hand strap and cross my legs, my eyes watering, fighting the impulse to grope myself in public. What's going on? I'm the most fastidiously clean guy in town.

Then, one night in the bathtub, driven to utter distraction by the discomfort, I am aghast to spy a gruesome little black critter ridin' the range on my nuts. Hey, what do I mean "a"? This is a full-on invasion. They look like scuttling seabed crustaceans and there appear to be dozens of them.

Gradually, my mind obviously dulled from lack of nourishment, I grasp the disgusting reality and am repulsed beyond belief. Christ, I've had fifty baths since that Tyrannosaurus Rex night. Wouldn't the little bastards drown? I spray my most cherished accoutrements with shaving cream, grab my Gillette razor, and one minute later my bits look like a plucked chicken in a Chinatown window on a chilly day. On the windowsill I spy a nailbrush left by some former tenant, bristles bent into twisted little J shapes. I apply it to the offending area with vigor, to the point of pain. I've never actually scrubbed my balls before and I won't be recommending it anytime soon. God, this is awful. I dry off and inspect myself with a mirror held at mostly unattractive angles.

In bed later I am so revolted that I lie awake all night cursing Sheffield and fiddling with my new lower-tonsorial arrangement. Saturday dawns and there's no denying it: I still itch.

12:01: I'm out the door of Moss Bros and into the nearest library. The librarian offers assistance but I demur. She persists helpfully. I demur emphatically. It takes me just under an hour and I blush every time my research leads me to another book that I furtively pull from the shelves, but finally I have my answer. That answer is, apparently, something called Dettol.

Out the library door, avoiding eye contact, I scour the streets until I locate the nearest chemist. Dettol is cheap, mercifully, so, flushed of cheek, I purchase a big bottle and attempt to saunter suavely out of the shop the way I imagine Jean-Paul Belmondo would in similar circumstances.

Back to Finborough Road. In the bathroom I strip and glance at the label: isopropanol, pine oil, chloroxylenol, castor oil, other ingredients I'm too impatient to read. I climb in the tub, take the top off the bottle, upend it, and splash the contents liberally all over my infested formerly erogenous zone. One second later I am leaping out of the tub and bouncing around on tiptoes, legs spread as wide as I can get them, cupping my balls and screaming, "Aaahhh, aaahh, ahhhh!" interspersed with curses of the "oh fucking god" variety. There is a knock at the door. With Herculean effort I stop jumping and manage to momentarily stifle the yelping.

"Yes?" I respond. Too high a pitch, too frightened; get a grip. Got one, as it happens.

"Is everything all right?" It is the Dutch girl from down the hall. We haven't even been introduced.

"Yes. Yes, everything's fine."

"Are you certain?"

Am I certain? No, I'm not fucking certain, truth be told, which it won't be, not now, not ever. "Yes, yes. Fine, thank you. I . . . ah . . . scalded my . . . toe. Hot water."

"Your toe?"

Go away, woman.

"Yes, my bloody toe. But it's fine now. Thank you."

"You are welcome. Would you like bandage? I have it."

"What? Bandage? Why would I . . . no, thank you very much."

"But your toe is bloody."

"My toe is not bloody. I just . . . just stubbed it, that's all. No, scalded it. Thank you, though."

"You are welcome."

I pause and listen, my groin on fire. All quiet on the Dutch front. She must be gone, surely. Seconds pass with nary a floorboard squeak. I need to be sure.

"Good-bye," I say.

"Good-bye," she replies cheerily, and I hear her footsteps go down the hall, her door closing.

Back to the inferno. I climb into the empty tub, lie down, and wriggle like an upside-down lobster toward the tap end. Draping my legs over the edge of the tub and arching my pelvis upward, I maneuver my sizzling, frying balls to just underneath the tap and turn on the cold water full blast.

"AAAAIIIEEEEE!"

The cold water is not the blissful relief I had envisioned; in fact it has created some sort of chemical reaction that is not only beyond pain, at least as I have previously experienced it, but has also left my most prized apparatus steaming and, as I see in the mirror while leaping out of the tub, a ghastly puce color. I am further dismayed to note that my penis, in shock no doubt at the unprecedented torture, has shrunk to embarrassingly minuscule proportions. Is there no end to this ignominy? Of course there isn't. I lie on the floor, fetal and whimpering, waiting for the knock. It arrives on schedule, with a Dutch accent.

"Hello? Hello? Is everything okay? Hello?"

"Hello," I answer in a voice I do not recognize, twisting my neck to try to make it sound as though it's not coming from the floor. "Yes, it's just . . . just . . . the water was too hot. Everything is fine. Please go away."

"Are you certain? You screamed so oddly, like a girl. I was worried."

Like a girl, she said. I am lying on the floor, nude, clutching my terrified, shriveled dong, having unadvisedly doused my pestilence-ridden undercarriage with napalm, and a strange woman outside the bathroom door is telling me I screamed like a girl. Is this the absolute nadir of my existence? God, I hope so.

I do know that I've rather had it with the nosy Netherlands Florence bloody Nightingale.

"I'm fine. Leave me alone."

"Are you certain?"

Am I certain, again? This defies belief. Where did she learn that phrase? And why? So she could say to some passing guy, "Please, which way to the train station?" And the guy tells her and she replies, "Are you certain?" She could get a punch in the nose with that carry-on. Get a refund on your Fodor's, lady. You're wasting your guilders at Berlitz.

"Yes, I am certain. I've never been more certain of anything in my entire life. Now for Christ's sake, bugger off and let a man wash his balls in peace."

Silence, then a snort, then footsteps and a door closing. She has gone. I wait for a few seconds then clamber delicately back into the tub. I turn the taps so that a soothingly cool pool eventually envelops my dangling tackle and slightly relieves what feels like the sting of a hundred especially spiteful bees.

Half an hour later, wrapped in a towel and after much peering down the hallway to make sure the coast is clear of meddling Dutchwomen, I waddle back to my room with as much dignity as I can muster. On my back, on the bed, legs spread wide, fanning my groin with the *Let It Be* cover, I reach out for the Dettol bottle on the bedside table and study the label. Among the many words printed on it are these: cleaning floors, sinks, unblocking drains. Do not apply directly to skin. Serious injury may occur. Dilute ten parts water to one part Dettol.

Oh.

The next few days are a painful blur. I go to work, moving gingerly, dealing with the hailstorm of trousers, coats, and toppers under a duress that, of course, must be kept private.

On top of that, the food situation is becoming critical. I quite simply can't afford to eat. The canteen at Moss Bros is rather good, with mouth-watering shepherd's pies, stews, egg and chips, and the like, cheap too, but I just can't squeeze any coins out of my budget to buy a morsel.

The reigning Miss Moss Bros 1971, voted by management and staff and well worthy of the title, takes pity on me and, without asking, buys me lunch one day. Next day, after work, she takes me home on the train to Kent for tea with her mum. For obvious, private reasons I must remain chaste. In fumbling hallway encounters I deflect her advances under the pretext of being noble and respectful of her mother. This drives her even madder with desire.

An ad in the *Melody Maker* announces a huge sale this Saturday at the Orange shop in Denmark Street. The "Biggest Sale in the History of Orange," it blares. Presumably that's big. Doors open at 8 a.m. I'm going to have a look. I arrange for a couple of hours off at Moss Bros.

I'm up early on Saturday and arrive at Denmark Street at a quarter to eight to find a lineup of musicians three deep, stretching over a hundred yards along the pavement. And this early in the morning that's not an attractive sight. Oh well, in for a penny. I join the line.

The chap in front of me looks like one of the Three Musketeers (a lesser one but by definition it's a small club): skinny and slight of frame, sporting shoulder-length auburn hair parted in the middle, a pointy goatee attempt, and a twirled mustache. We start to chat and establish a surprisingly immediate rapport. He's Irish, from Dublin, and he's a guitarist. He says he has been in London for a couple of years, playing in bands and such. His name is Eunan and he lives in Cricklewood.

The doors at Orange open and a mob scene erupts. A herd of fat women at a bake sale are better behaved than this bunch. Pushing, shoving, elbowing, swearing, and for what? For a load of rubbish, that's what. Everything on sale appears to be broken. Speakers dangling from split cabinets, amplifiers dented beyond recognition.

What a gyp. Mostly what's on offer seems to consist of dozens of cardboard boxes overflowing with old leads, tubes, plugs, assorted knobs, circuit boards, and bits of unidentifiable plastic. I fight my way back out the door and head toward Shaftesbury Avenue. I'll get a cup of tea and wait for Foyles to open. What a chronic waste of time.

Wonder what happened to the Irish guy?

IV

In the Moss Bros canteen, nursing my salesmen grievances and my recently napalmed nethers (the crabicide was a success), I notice a box on the wall, over which is the word "Suggestions."

I write a suggestion.

> *I suggest that I be issued with a cricket bat to smash the salesmen in the teeth and teach them some manners.*
> *Sincerely,*
> *Andrew Matheson*

I pop it into the suggestion box.

My freedom of movement gradually returns and the day I no longer walk like John Wayne with a hernia I resume the audition process. It's a Wednesday and I read for the tenth time last week's *Melody Maker*, trying to spy that one ad I missed, the one that screams out at me, "Here we are." But none do.

It is getting depressing. Hungry and lonely are the predominant themes of the evenings I spend up in my tidy eyrie. The starkers lady across Ifield Road has not, to my knowledge, played a return engagement at her dressing table. I check every fifteen minutes so I'm reasonably sure. I can't plug in the AC-30 because of Dutchy and the other two down the hall, so I plink, plinkety, plink on my chipped blue Strat, hour after hour, trying, in vain, to forget my beautiful Vox Mark VI.

Morning: a glass of water, a cold bath, and I'm off on the Tube to Covent

Garden. Goolam is kind and gives me a cup of horrible tea from a flask he brings in every day. He hails from the island of Mauritius and is the first Muslim I have ever met. He sings:

> *This is my island in the sun*
> *Given to me by an Englishman*

The manager of the lower level of Moss Bros is a sour, humorless individual with a thousand crushed aspirations typed all over his gray face. He's not mad about me and makes this obvious with looks, sneers, tuts, and sighs every time we cross paths. So it must be killing him to have to track me down in my tucked-away little corner of chaos, and even worse to have to hand me an envelope with my name on it and a gold-embossed message in the top-left corner: From the desk of Harry Moss.

I know he is waiting for me to open it, and that the curiosity is gnawing away at him like a bowel maggot, so I just stand there looking down at the envelope, smiling and nodding. Finally, I stick it in my inner coat pocket. "Thank you," I say, and turn back to my tasks.

"Hrrmph," he replies charmingly.

Later, in private, I open the envelope. Stark raving wonder of wonders, it is an invitation to take tea with Harry Moss tomorrow afternoon at three o'clock.

The next day I'm in a good mood. I'm famished, of course, but I feel fab. I'm in black velvet strides and a purple polo neck. Not even the idiot salesmen can get me down today.

Just before three o'clock I get in the lift and tell the operator to take me to the top floor.

A lady is waiting who ushers me in to the inner sanctum of the Moss Bros empire. And there he is, sitting behind his desk, white haired and about as dignified looking as a gentleman who isn't my landlord can possibly get. Harry Moss, the great man himself, wearing an eye-popping suit and ascot. Wonder where he shops.

"Do sit down, oh, and would you care for . . . ?" Harry indicates a food-laden cart the size of a hay wagon being wheeled over to us by the lady who escorted me in. There are crustless sandwiches of at least a half-dozen varieties, the puffiest of pastries, silver pots of tea and coffee, the creamiest of creams, sugar-cube pyramids, cakes and crumpets and all manner of other unidentifiable edibles. It is all I can do to concentrate, mind my manners, and stop myself from diving in like a fat boy at a county-fair pie-eating contest.

Harry sips tea while I tread the tightrope between gorging my starving self and being a polite, forelock-tugging employee.

"So Andrew, I . . . I, um . . . received your *suggestion* yesterday."

He distinctly raises an eyebrow when he says the word "suggestion."

"You did?"

"Yes," says Harry. "Yes, it was brought to my attention and I must say it did give me quite a chuckle. I was most amused. Cricket bat?" Here, he balls his right hand into a soft fist and allows himself a quiet "Heh, heh, heh" into it.

What follows is a surprisingly comfortable and frank discussion of life deep in the depths of Moss Bros, and Harry Moss himself seems sincerely interested. After pouring us each a second cup of tea Harry poses a question.

"So, tell me, Andrew, if you don't mind me asking. What is it you earn on, shall we say, a weekly basis here at Moss Bros?"

The manners. The manners in the marrow, the sheer born-in-the-bone politeness of that question. This man is the supreme being at Moss Bros. He has but to press a button and some minion will all too readily impart the information regarding precisely what pittance this lesser minion is earning. Harry Moss is no doubt already well aware of what I earn. And yet the status-conferring question.

"Eleven pounds fifty a week, sir."

"Hmm. Well, let me just say that while I can't, heh, heh, condone this *cricket bat* business, I do applaud your attitude."

"Well, thank you, sir. I just . . ."

"And so I thought I would authorize a rise to fifteen pounds per week, effective immediately. Would that suit?"

Would it suit? Would it ever. That's a massive £3.50 increase and effective immediately, which means I get paid that sum tomorrow, Friday, payday.

Harry and I wrap things up with smiles and a handshake and I'm back in the lift, heading down but feeling up.

Walking home from Earls Court station, I stop in at Gandhi's brother's joint for a celebratory tin of spaghetti, some fish paste, and a loaf of bread. A little further on I buy the *Melody Maker*. Money no longer being an object.

That night I am full of food and optimism. I read the *Melody Maker*, looking for that ad that screams. Then, oddly, one does jump out at me. It doesn't exactly scream but it does raise its voice. It nags.

Violent, extrovert vocalist
Rock 'n' roll band. Semi-pro?
Must be happy
Reasonable gear
01-427-1001
6:30 pm

It says rock 'n' roll but I'm suspicious. What do they mean "Semi-pro"? That's a dreary sign. And, confusingly, they want a "happy" "violent" guy. Do I qualify as happy and violent? I don't feel overly happy. And what constitutes "reasonable gear"?

I almost don't call. On the Thursday night I don't. On the Friday I don't. But on the Saturday I read the ad again and gather a pocketful of two-pence pieces. Standing in the phone box in Redcliffe Square, I dial the number, the receiver is picked up, and I rock the coin right into the slot. I speak to a chap with the non–rock 'n' roll name Tim. The band sounds promising, no whiff of Brylcreem at all really. He did mention that he once played with Screaming Lord Sutch, but I'm only dimly aware of what that means in musical terms. Tim says they auditioned some singers earlier that afternoon but none worked out.

The "reasonable gear" they want me to have is a microphone, an amp, and a couple of PA columns. I tell him about my Strat and AC-30, and he says a swap should be easy. Tim and his bass player are coming to Earls Court to see me Monday night. So that's that, then. Maybe I'm on my way.

On Monday night Tim and his bass-player pal Roger arrive on schedule. Both are older than me by at least three or four years. Tim, the guitarist, is a rumpled sort, jeans and T-shirt, stocky build, mid-length hair, a bit thin on top. Roger is the complete opposite. Stylish in a dance-palace lad sort of way, thin, wearing a yellow-and-gray checked jacket with lapels like twin ironing boards pinned to his chest, black trousers with a crease that could slice bread, black shoes, serious platform soles. Dark shoulder-length hair, and he's got a distinctly sardonic look wrapped around his boat. Looks-wise, he's not a million miles removed from Bill Wyman.

We talk and they plug in the amp and check out the Stratocaster, sighting down the neck and yanking on the tremolo. Tim twiddles the knobs of the AC-30 like a safecracker, listening for hiss or buzz. None, as it happens. He nods his approval, plugs in the guitar, and launches into a raunchy snarl of a twelve-bar. After thirty seconds or so he stops, props the Strat against the amp, and, sticking his chin out like a grizzled doorstop, he decrees, "Not bad, not bad." Which, oddly enough, is exactly what I am thinking about them.

An audition is set for Saturday.

Next day, I check out of Moss Bros early and take my Strat and AC-30 back to Macari's. The man himself seems pleased as Punch to see me again and, one nonstop chatter-fest and two backslaps later, the trade is made. I am now the proud possessor of an Electro-Voice amplifier, two scratched and scuffed speaker columns of suspicious pedigree, a mic stand, and a Shure microphone. Well, sort of a Shure microphone. Shure-ish at least. Yeah, Shure.

Macari helps me carry the equipment out to the street, hails a cab, and helps me load it in. As the taxi pulls away from the curb he waves good-bye. That is such a cheery smile on his face.

Later in the evening, as if to cap off an eventful day, the lady on Ifield Road reappears, nude at her dressing table, brushing her hair. I watch for minute after minute until she turns quickly, looks up, and catches me spying. I jump back, almost knocking over the speaker columns that now dominate the room. I've been caught in the act, exposed as a peeping Andrew.

Lights out, into bed. I lie there in the dark thinking about the naked lady, my upcoming audition, my ravaged though healing genitalia, and a gray swirl of other random thoughts and fears. Just before I fall asleep, it occurs to me.

At Macari's my Mark VI was no longer hanging on the wall.

V

It's Saturday. I'm excited and nervous but acting cool, riding in a blue Humber van. Tim has come to Earls Court to snag me and the gear and haul us to somewhere called Stanmore for the audition. The gear seems to have passed his inspection. Macari's has cachet. Tim is chatty and gruffly cordial, weaving expertly in and out of traffic, telling tales of Screaming Lord Sutch, and Jerry Lee Lewis, whom he also played with somewhere back down the line. As previously mentioned, I'm not a paleontologist, but I try to hang in there with the details. Talk turns to the Stones and the Pretty Things. I don't know much about the Pretty Things but I can hold my own with the Stones chat.

Truth be told, I have a positively encyclopedic knowledge of all things related to British pop music from at least February 9, 1964 (Fabs/*Sullivan Show*) onward. And who came before then, anyway? Cliff, Frank Ifield, and Helen Shapiro? Come on. Ask me who the bass player is for the Dave Clark Five and I'll spout out Rick Huxley. Ask me what was the third single released by the Yardbirds and I will tell you "For Your Love," of course. Ask me if Dave Dee, Dozy, Beaky, Mick & Tich are any good and I'll say, "Of course not."

It's a forty-five-minute drive and we cover a variety of subjects. I ask about the ad.

"So, did you have a lot of response?"

"Yeah, a bit. Tried out a few last Saturday, mostly wankers."

"Well, I'll give it a go."

"I know you will."

Such assurance. What a boost. Maybe I can start to feel a little less nervous. Tim continues.

"We got a call from a piano player."

"Oh, yeah?" Who needs a piano player?

"Yeah, but I've lost his number, actually. Norwegian guy, called Gorvan or something. Maybe he'll call back."

"Norwegian?"

"Yeah, I know."

Stanmore in Middlesex is Pinewood Studios beautiful. Leafy, cobbled in parts, picture-postcard perfect, and the antithesis of anywhere any rock 'n' roll band has ever rehearsed. The church hall, for it is a church hall, where the audition will be held, is just south of magical. Small, redbrick exterior, worn wooden floor, arched ceilings, spooky acoustics, small kitchen off the main room—I've never seen anywhere better to set up and plug in.

Tim and I lug in my gear. Roger is there and already set up. He says hi, sitting back in a chair reading *Mayfair* magazine. He doesn't seem bothered about a thing in the world. His Fender Jazz bass leans against a wall. In the middle of the room is a Premier drum kit. Beside it, on his knees, is a stocky roadie fiddling with something underneath the ride cymbal. I am pleasantly surprised that they have a roadie.

We plonk down a column and Tim gestures toward the roadie. "Andrew, this is Nigel, our drummer. Nige, Andrew."

Our drummer? Not a roadie? He's got frizzy hair, his clothes are wrinkled, his jacket is tatty tweed with worn suede elbow patches. This is not a drummer; this is a geography teacher. Anyway, we set up, we plug in, we get ready—ready teddy to rock 'n' roll. But what shall we start with? How about "Johnny B. Goode"? All right with me, mateys, because I've learned the lyrics. I grab the microphone and right away I'm deep down in Looziana.

We're moving now. Against all odds, I'm having fun. Tim knows his way around a Fender Tele. Roger's the shining star of this outfit. He plays fine, looks great, and throws in a backing vocal every now and again. It's ragtag, but it's all right.

But there's something happening here. What it is is exactly clear.

The drummer is more than slightly off. Nigel's timing is scattershot, his rolls and fills haphazard and unpredictable. And if they are out then the whole equation is iffy. And iffy is useless and useless won't get you anywhere.

If you don't have a drummer you have nothing. That's gospel. That's how important they are. Any other part of the band can be squidgy. The bass can wander, the guitar can be out of tune and time, the singer can wail away off-key, but if the drummer is on the money then the show rolls merrily along. It's bad when they know this, of course, because then they quickly develop all the charm and modesty of Buddy Rich or Ginger Baker.

But that's just the way it is.

On the Tube back to Earls Court I am positively aglow. Roger and Tim gave me the thumbs-up. I'm in. But now to reshape this thing into what I want it to be. The pros are that it is an actual band, with a van, rehearsal facilities, rock 'n' roll roots, and Roger and Tim seem like good sorts.

The negs are, number one, the drummer, number two, the fact that only one guy looks what I would call right for my band—that's Roger—and, number three, that we need one more musician. I know it's nowhere near "my band," but now I'm on the inside and, as everybody knows, that's where all the best revolutions start.

A pattern develops. I work all week at Moss Bros. I rehearse Saturdays and Sundays in Stanmore. At nights during the week I write, read, or skulk around with the lights off, trying to see the naked lady on Ifield Road.

When the church hall is unavailable the band decamps to a couple of other places for rehearsal. The first is a huge room in Brunel University that Nigel (a student, apparently, not a geography teacher) somehow finagled. He says this joint is famous for the most suicides of students per annum of any university in the UK. I'm not surprised. It has cold, concrete-bunker esthetics with all the elegance and style of a women's prison in Murmansk.

Our rehearsals here are enough to send me suicidal, though. We grind through a torturous hour trying, for some reason, to wrestle "Morning Dew" into submission, and spend another on the relentlessly plodding blues dreck of "Rock Me Baby." This bunch have obviously been spinning the *Truth* LP by the Jeff Beck Group this last week. The lyrics are killing me. Take "Morning Dew." Yeah? You're walking in the morning dew? Right. You apparently heard a young girl cry. No kidding? What happened, then? Why is she crying? What's the story? Nothing, there is no story, just this plodding, melody-deprived, monotonous drone.

Then there's "Rock Me Baby." The writer wants her to rock him, I get that. And the length of time he wants her to rock him for is, imaginatively, all night long.

Sheesh.

The blues. I just don't get it. The repetition utterly baffles me. Why do they always repeat the first line? It drives me nuts—it's eye-rollingly boring.

Afterward, driving me back to the Tube at Harrow on the Hill, Tim sighs and says, "Too bad you don't sing like Rod Stewart."

It's a long ride home.

The lads have a third rehearsal space. This one is frigid cool. Through some connection of Tim's we get to rehearse at the Railway Hotel in Harrow. This being the venue made famous—fabulously famous—by the Who when Pete Townshend accidentally stuck his guitar into the ceiling during a particularly flamboyant move, yanked it out, and, for the first time ever, smashed it to smithereens in front of a frothing mod mob.

The room is a narrow rectangle, the stage a mere ten inches off the floor, and there, above center stage, is a hole in the ceiling. Tim points to it. That's the hole, he says.

Roger and I begin to develop a bit of an affinity. We go out for a pint or two. We crumble up hashish, stick a chunk on the end of a pin, and take turns inhaling the junior dragon tails curling upward. He's a japester and a quipster and delivers both in an arid, droll style that has me convulsing with laughter. He is a bachelor with sharp suits and a job at Boosey & Hawkes in North London, putting saxophones together. He drives a green Zephyr. He takes me under his wing. Back at his dad's place in Hatch End he teaches me how to iron that lethal crease in my trousers. He takes me to clubs. And he's always got flocks of girls around him. In his presence I feel a bit of a green Zephyr myself. But I do all right.

I ask Tim, the de facto leader, "What's the name of our band? We don't have a name."

Tim suggests I make a move from Earls Court to Harrow. Says there's a place for rent on Blawith Road, just down the street from him, and also he's got the inside track on a job for me. Makes sense. The band's here, rehearsals are

here, the clubs Roger and I frequent are here, and it's a long, noddy haul back
to the old Aussie ghetto after a night out.

One Thursday night I am lying on my bed reading a biography of Napoleon
when there is a knock at my door. It is a middle-aged chap with a sad look and
a sadder voice.

He tells me his dad is dead, and his dad was my landlord. Back on my bed
with Napoleon on my chest I think of my landlord, whom I've only met once,
his interesting flat, his open nature, and his gentlemanly bearing. I wish I had
spoken with him again.

Next morning, I do a runner.

On Friday I give my five-hour notice at Moss Bros. Goolam seems sincerely sad.
"Mister Andrew, what will I do? What will Miss Moss Bros do?"

"What about Miss Moss Bros?"

"Oh, don't be silly. We all know."

"Know what? I had a cup of tea. And who is 'we all'?"

"Your workmates, you silly, silly man. And you will go to play music in
Harrow. Do you know what is in Harrow? Do you?"

"No. What's in Harrow, Goolam?"

"Skinheads, you silly. Don't you know? With their boots and their braces."

Goolam is exasperated with me. It seems he'll sincerely miss me. In truth,
I will miss him too. He walks me out to the street and shakes my hand, and
then waves me good-bye.

When I get to the corner I turn back. Goolam is still there, waving. "I will
see you on *Top of the Pops*," he shouts. I smile and salute, then turn and go.

VI

I move into 52 Blawith Road in Harrow, a semidetached house owned by an Indian family. The husband is a short man with a wide smile, blue teeth, and hair like Roy Orbison. Tim has arranged a job for me at the NATO base in Northwood as a gardener. You get security clearance and you're buzzed in to mow around all the nose cones of the intercontinental ballistic things. It's a doddle, really, and I get paid £21 a week.

The first flush of being in a band has worn off and I'm worried about the sound. Not only does the drummer stink, the whole affair sounds decidedly thin. We need another musician. I don't know where these boys got their keyboard fetish. Personally, I'd like another guitarist.

You see, the situation is a bit pressing because Tim has set up a gig in three weeks' time at a club in Ware, Hertfordshire.

Two weeks and a dozen rehearsals later, we've got a couple of sets worked out, basic blues rock with a splash of grease. Not horrible, not great. But we still haven't found a guitarist and we still haven't got a name.

Tim comes up with a stopgap guitar solution, which involves driving to the guy from Mungo Jerry's house in Harrow and begging some guitarist parading around with the moniker Snowy White* to help us out. Snowy is a blond guy (who'd have guessed?), about twenty-three, and comes fully equipped with a Les Paul, a Marshall stack, and the cutest little ego you've ever seen.

We stand there, in the front room of 32 Mungo Jerry Drive, with caps

---

* Mr. White went on to a career of some renown with Thin Lizzy and, not remotely as thin, Pink Floyd.

metaphorically, except in Tim's case, in hand. Tim plights our troth as Snowy reclines on his sofa like a bored, mid-limbo limbo dancer, playing elaborate guitar figures, complete with grimaces, on his unplugged gold Les Paul while staring at *Opportunity Knocks* on the telly. Finally, reluctantly dragging his eyeballs away from Hughie Green, Snowy agrees to one whole rehearsal and the gig itself with the bored magnanimity of an Arab potentate. Gee, thanks, oh mighty Snowy.

The rehearsal has its pros and cons. On the pro side, we've never sounded better. A plodding rock yawner like "Rock Me Baby" is now exciting, with structure and real dynamics. Snowy's solos are excellent in that fifty-note-per-bar, ridiculous-pained-facial-expression way that people seem to love in modern guitarists. On the con side, he of course susses the Nigel problem instantly, and also shortly afterward decides that he can't stand me, which gets on my wick. One more eye-roll and he'll have a fake Shure rammed in his yap.

While driving home from rehearsal with Roger and Tim, "Itchycoo Park" by the Small Faces comes on the radio. For some non-drug-induced reason they decide to call us Itchy Coo.

On the day of the gig the members of the newly minted Itchy Coo load the gear and pile into the Humber van for the drive up the M1 to Ware. I've got a wire hanger with stage clothes: red velvet jacket, Mr Fish shirt, black strides, and stack-heeled daisies. Needless to report, I am the only band member with "stage clothes."

We're buoyant, we're kickin' the stall, we're ready to strut whatever stuff we think we have. We are joking and laughing. I'm lounging in the back, stretched out on one elbow on a PA column, gabbing with Roger and Nigel. And I'm grateful because I'm miles away from the exalted Snowy sitting up front in the passenger seat, talking guitar chops with our chauffeur for the evening, Tim.

Finally, we're there. Where? Ware. Now we have to find the place. We drive down one street then another. We have to back out of a tight cul-de-sac. We find ourselves driving down a street we've already gone down. We drive down a one-way street and, lordy, we see two good-looking babes walking on the pavement toward us on the passenger side.

"Ask them, ask them," comes the chorus from the boys in the back to the boys up front.

Tim pulls up beside the girls, who react with giggling wariness, stopping and holding on to each other's arm. Snowy rolls down the window.

"Uh, hi. I was just . . . we . . . do you . . . uh—"

"Are you a band?" interrupts one of them mercifully. They are both great-looking, close up: fab hair, pink lips, legs way up to their afterthought miniskirts.

Too bad the "eloquent" Snowy is our front man at this delicate moment. Anybody else would be preferable. Roger would be perfect and he's almost clambering over the seats to get to the front line. Too bad Snowy's the man to answer.

"Uh, yeah . . . yeah, we're playing here tonight."

"You are?" The girls perk up. They've unlinked arms. They're leaning on the van, ducking and peering in to see the rest of us in the back. One strokes the van's aerial up and down, suggestively. Well, suggestively to those of us sporting a below-the-belt brush cut, whose sex life of late has consisted of nothing save groinal infestation and amateur voyeurism. She pings the aerial back and forth with languid forefinger flicks. Snowy continues in sparkling vein.

"Yeah. Yeah, we are."

"Where are you playing?" asks one.

"Can we come?" asks the other.

Snowy, clearly unused to interest from anyone other than fellow blues aficionados, stutters, "Yeah . . . uh . . . yeah, sure," while from the back of the van Roger leads the choir in variations on the theme of, "Yes indeed, come to the gig."

"So, where are you playing?" asks babe number one, flicking her locks over her shoulder.

"The Youth Club," says Roger.

The girls recoil from the van as though they've touched a hot stove. "The Youth Club?" says babe number one. "The Youth Club?" says babe number two, looking aghast at babe number one. Then both stagger off down the street, bent over and laughing hysterically.

Evidently in Ware, among local hipsters, the Youth Club is not quite the preferred venue du jour. Abashed but intrepid, we eventually find the place, set up, and play the gig. Surprise, surprise, it goes quite well judging by those out front who, in truth, don't seem to expect much. Everybody in the band rises to the occasion, even Nigel. The place is packed, albeit with "youths," but we do get them hopping.

On the long drive back to Harrow I think to myself that it's not a bad start, but I don't delude myself about the long slog ahead.

Coming into London on a lonely stretch of highway, we run over a rabbit with a soft, slithery *thump*—despite Snowy's desperate warning scream. At three in the morning, as I'm dropped off bleary-eyed at Blawith Road, Tim gives me a couple of quid, my share of the gig money. Chickenfeed. Cluck cluck. Most of the gig dosh goes to the Snowman.

Tyrannosaurus Rex are now called T. Rex, a saving of four syllables, and they've got a new single out, "Get It On." Its skeleton is "Little Queenie," the Stones version from *Ya-Ya's*. I can't believe nobody in the press is mentioning it. Just goes to show that risible lyrics need not be a deterrent. This thing is rocketing up the charts.

I spend most of my time in my room writing and reading, with towels and T-shirts stuffed in the cracks around the door to keep out the stench of Indian food. In a used bookshop on Harrow Road I spy a novel that I buy just because of the author's name: Richard Matheson. I've always liked the name Richard. It costs 40p. The title is *I Am Legend*.

Roger and I go out to pubs and clubs, especially one club we've discovered in Watford: the New Penny. It is always packed and throbbing, plus it has a decent restaurant serving great steak and chips. The main barmaid is a pretty girl, a friendly sort, by the name of Carole.

Nigel the drummer finally gets the hint, packs up his kit, and takes his elbow patches back to where they belong, to Brunel, academia's concrete suicide hot spot. Tim puts another ad in the *Melody Maker*, for a guitarist this time and a drummer.

Next Saturday, and what shows up in Stanmore in response to the ad but, of all things, a couple of Australians. Mal, the guitarist, is ten feet tall, skinny as a coatrack, with hair like a big ball of tumbleweed scotch-taped to his skull. Martin, the drummer, is not what I would call classically good-looking; rather, he's the absolute spitting image of Yosemite Sam. You know, that *Looney Tunes*,

Bugs Bunny—nemesis cowboy chap? The resemblance is uncanny, right down to the handlebar mustache. Every time he does a drum roll I keep expecting a "Yee-haw!" Still, he is a slight improvement in the timekeeping department.

Mal's got a black Stratocaster and a Marshall stack and he can play, in a tame, tentative kind of way. His playing seems a natural extension of himself, quiet and thin. I turn up his amp when he's not looking. We plug in and give it a go. It's not so bad. We're a few planets away from a great-looking band dressing sharp, playing fast and nasty. But it's a start. Again.

One day after rehearsal, driving back to Blawith Road in the van with Tim, he asks me if I've got any ideas for lyrics. Do I have ideas for lyrics? I've been doing nothing else in my Harrow garret. Night after night I've been writing away until I nod off. I dash into the house and emerge with a sheaf of things I've written lately. I hand them through the van window.

He puts it into first gear. I watch the blue Humber exit down Blawith with my lyrics. I plunge my hands into my pockets and slink off back into the house of Roy and Mrs. Orbison.

Two days later Tim hands them back, saying, "I can't do anything with these, too many words."

In the New Penny, for the sixth night in the last ten days, I'm standing at the bar with Roger, knocking 'em back, when a song comes on that is the best thing I've heard for months. I'd be willing to bet my life there is not a beard or gong involved in the band that's making this noise. As soon as it ends I actually squirm my way through the dancing mob to ask the DJ what it was. It's "Get Down and Get with It" by some bunch called Slade.

It's October. "Maggie May" by Rod Stewart is number one. I get laid off. No reason, I'm just invited to get lost. No more money, no more Yankee grub—this is serious. A week goes by, a week of peanut butter sandwiches and Roy Orbison hanging around the front door asking for the rent. I've only got maybe eleven quid to my name. What to do? Roger and I go out to the New Penny.

Carole overhears my tale of woe in the way that barmaids do, from the other side of the bar I'm propping up at the end of the evening. No problem, she says, come and stay at her house. Her man won't mind and they've got loads of room. Next day, I exit the house in Blawith Road early and lurk in the bushes across the street until Roy goes to wherever it is he goes, then I sprint up the stairs, throw the clothes, the records, and the peanut butter in the cardboard suitcase and hare off to Harrow & Wealdstone station.

Another runner.

One hour later, I'm knockin' on the door of 112 Bradshaw Road in Watford.

"Hello, Andrew, lovely to see you, come on in," says Carole. "Pop your suitcase in the front room. I've got to dash but Bruno will be here any minute. Actually, now that I think of it, I forgot to tell him about you." And with that she's gone.

She hasn't told him? I'm sitting on the couch, suitcase at my feet, waiting for Bruno, whom I've never met, to come home so I can tell him I've been invited by his woman to move in. And, truth be told, I don't even really know Carole. I'm already terrified of Bruno. This is his castle, after all, and that's a knuckle-dragger of a name if ever I heard one.

If I were a nail biter my fingers would have been bloody stubs in the near hour it takes Bruno to get home. Only it's not Bruno; it's Brillo. I misheard his missus. This guy is named Brillo for the visually obvious reason that you could quite easily use his head to scrub burned pots and pans. Add some Vim and rub his bonce back and forth across a countertop and you could remove even the most stubborn stains. I've never seen a white chap with such a hairdo.

Turns out he's a great lad. Sense of humor well intact, looks a bit like John Cleese from the Pythons.

The house is a two-up two-down wreck, freezing and damp. The loo is outside. Trains to Euston and the North rattle past the rotting back fence every twenty minutes. Black smoke rises in a thin, acrid spiral from a permanent rubbish fire smoldering inside the backyard air-raid shelter, the curved corrugated-iron roof barely visible amid a jungle of stinging nettles, automobile skeletons, broken glass, and rusty tin cans.

There's no place like home.

VII

Kit Lambert, the Who's manager, called it "a version of Hell." Pete Townshend's schoolmate described it more succinctly as "a dump." It is a pile of chipped bricks and crumbling mortar leaning out over railway tracks, held together on the outside by moss and soot, and on the inside by stained wallpaper and reeking red carpets. When the trains rumble by, the bones of the building rattle, and plaster stained from the smoke of a million cigarettes falls in puffs and chunks like yellowed snow from the ceilings.

It is the Railway Hotel in Harrow and, yeah, it might be a bit on the decrepit side, but we think it's rather fab.

Tim sets up a rehearsal and we give it a bash. Since Roger, Tim, and I have been at this for a bit now and the Aussies are, of course, familiar with each other, the band has a cohesion it has never had before and in parts is sounding, dare I say it, a scintilla of a percentage point above average.

There's a pub upstairs, a prior visit to which may account for the warmth of my assessment and definitely accounts for the people that show up from time to time to watch us go through our moves. This turns out all right, as you tend to give it that little extra kick when half a dozen girls walk in and linger while draining their Babychams.

During a break, one girl comes up to me and says she works for CBS Records. "Do you have a tape?" she asks. No, we don't. Truth is, fuzzy warm assessments aside, we're not that good. We're nowhere near where I want us to be. She's in the record biz so there's a good chance she is on mind-altering pharmaceuticals.

* * *

At the church hall in Stanmore on the next drizzly Saturday, Tim says that Gorvan, the Norwegian keyboard player, has called again, out of the blue. Lost our number for a month or so then found it, apparently. Bright boy. Tim says the three of us, sans Mal and Yosemite, are going to Paddington on Monday night to meet him.

Why we need a keyboard player, I don't know. We are just starting to sound half-decent. Besides, it would make us a six-piece, which doesn't fit my template. What are we, the Nashville Teens? Georgie Fame and the Blue Flames? I ask you.

Monday night. London Street, Paddington—where the bear comes from. Seventeen London Street, to be precise. Drizzle as usual and there's a pile of rags with a filthy, dented bowler hat and cantankerous personality slumped against the wall outside Ladbrokes. We step kindly over him and locate the address. Tim pokes a forefinger in the buzzer and we wait. Finally, we hear him clomping down the stairs, this keyboard player. There are lots of stairs. The clomping gets progressively louder. The door swings open. Good Lord. He looks bloody amazing. Well, aside from the *Sgt. Pepper*–era mustache.

He's wearing tight white jeans, absolutely sprayed-on tight at the hips and flaring at the bottom like an Apollo rocket at liftoff. The guy's perched atop high heels, wearing a silver-studded leather wristband, more rings than is strictly necessary, and a necklace dangling down over his skintight, black-and-white, horizontal-striped jumper.

But the main eye-popper is without doubt the hair. It's thick, it's straight, it's wild, it's dishwater blond, and it's down to the bottom of the boy's rib cage. My mind is in overdrive; my band template just ran out into traffic and got knocked over.

We go for a pint in the Sussex Arms down the street: Who do you like? Where are you from? What have you done? What gear do you have? He likes the Stones and the Pretty Things; he's from Norway; he's been auditioning; he doesn't have any gear.

As the minutes go by, in the way that the subtle dynamic of dialogue engineers these things, Tim and Roger become more and more surplus to requirements. In mere minutes they are secondary, peripheral. It's nothing personal, it's just that Gorvan and I see eye to eye; we're weirdly in sync on some *Twilight Zone* level.

Tim arranges for Gorvan to come to rehearsal in Stanmore on Saturday. Doesn't matter that he hasn't got any gear—there's an old, kicked-around upright piano in the hall, and it's surprisingly only a mile out of tune. I'm revved up about the possibilities now and I can't wait to see him play. I know he's going to be perfect.

Oh yeah, and his name isn't Gorvan.

It's Stein Groven.

Saturday. Stein shows up in Stanmore looking as fab as I had expected, a picture in white and pale blue, carrying four small, black ovals with wires on the ends. In the middle of each oval is a volume knob. They turn out to be a sort of black noise-sperm. For the uninitiated, which is me, he explains that they are pickups. He climbs aboard the upright piano, sticks his arms deep into the guts, and places these pickups, like sabotage mines, where they can do the most damage, and then asks if he can plug into an amp. His wish is someone's command, and soon he's got volume and soon we tune.

Stein sits on the wooden piano stool facing away from the band, toward the wall. Above his piano is an arched stained-glass window, the afternoon sun shining through. I can't see his face but I do see him take a deep breath.

We decide on, what else, that ode to the boy with the gunny-sack guitar case from deep down in Louisiana. Tim rips into the intro, Yosemite, Mal, and Roger hit the three downbeats, and the boys are just about to tumble in on the fourth, when out of the speakers pours a sound we've never heard before. It's a lightning waterfall of piano notes as Stein executes a cool glissando with one upturned thumb scraping down the upper keys, perfectly timed to end with Yosemite's crash.

Well, sir, if this ain't the magic it is at least mixing the potions. The band is immediately elevated to another level. We get to the first solo and the guitar boys are fighting over who takes it. With a bow and a sweep of the arm I give the nod to Tim, seniority trumping the mild colonial boy. Tim shakes off his Screaming Lord cobwebs and attacks his upper frets with menace. Out of the corner of my eye I see Mal turn up his Marshall, sneaky boy. Next time around it's his turn, and undeniably something new has been unleashed in Melbourne Mal. He makes some moves. He crouches and makes his Strat squeal. He nods his head and his corkscrew haystack hair wobbles to the beat. Roger and I look at each other and raise all four of our collective eyebrows. Then we hit the last verse. Time to go Johnny go.

We're at maximum volume, everybody's in, and we're rocking, whipping this nag down the final furlong. I'm twirling the mic stand around above my head like a cheerleader when a piano stool whips past my shins and goes flying, spinning across the wooden floor. Turning to my left I see Stein on his feet and bent over, pounding on the keys, head down, twin curtains of hair tossing, flying, grazing his wrists.

We build to a furious finish, bringing proceedings to a halt with three emphatic power chords. On the last one Stein doesn't even make a pretense of playing the chord; he just smashes his palms down on the keyboard.

When the last feedback-drenched note dies we all start laughing and yelling. We've never been remotely close to sounding this good. Who is the idiot that said we didn't need a keyboard player?

During a break in proceedings Stein and I knock back a beer in the kitchen. I like this Norwegian guy. This Norwegian guy is a relief. The thing is that he emphatically *gets it*. I don't have to twist his arm or plead or buttonhole him or grab him by the lapels or talk him into anything. Everything I say he gets, and vice versa. Also, he looks great and, like me, he's thinking way beyond this rehearsal hall in Stanmore. He's thinking of making waves, making trouble, making records, making his mark and looking sharp while he's doing it— playing fast and nasty. It's a shame about the upper-lip toupee but without a doubt, now that he and I are together, we've got the nucleus.*

Now, what do we do with the rest of these chumps?

One day goes by and the phone rings in Watford. Stein asks, "Do you have any lyrics?" Do I? A train ride to hand over a sheaf and the next day the phone rings again in Watford. He says, "I love these. Let's write."

I start spending time at Stein's place in London Street and he becomes a

---

* Stein Groven aka Gorvan, Oslo, 2013

"I had been to many hopeless auditions, including one for Status Quo with about four hundred other keyboard players. I had met a thousand wankers and Yes fans. Andrew rode in like Sir Galahad on a white horse."

regular visitor to 112 Bradshaw. We play records and talk and talk and talk until our jaws ache. In Watford, Carole feeds us; in London Street I meet Sonja, Stein's girlfriend. Wow. She's a nice girl, a bit shy about her command of the English language, but she doesn't have to talk. She's six feet tall and a classic Nordic blonde. Another Rock 'n' Roll Rule down the drain.

Stein and I learn about each other and plot the future. He is a Stones fanatic. I love the Kinks. He tries to sell me on the Pretty Things but it doesn't work. Like me, he hates everything that is going on at the moment in music.

We tune up a couple of guitars. It's as though we've been doing this forever. Stein has my sheaf of lyrics and the first thing he takes out and puts on the coffee table is my attempt at mimicking the brown-eyed handsome man. A couple of months ago I barely knew three Chuck Berry songs, now I'm doing my best to copy him.

Stein plays what he has come up with. Crap acoustic, dead strings maybe, but his music delivers. Fifteen minutes later we've moved this, changed that, and written our first song, "Southern Belles."

The pub is rowdy and cheery, decorated for Christmas with little twinkling red-and-green lights, almost believable plastic holly, and fake frost sprayed on the windows. It's Christmas Eve, and I've met Roger late this afternoon, after his shift at Boosey & Hawkes. The jukebox is cranked but it is drowned out by carols sung in happy voices by various drunken off-key choirs. Blackouts, strikes, the IRA: all forgotten in the spirit of the season. Next Yule pub, same Yule scene.

The third pub on the path to Watford is a carbon copy of the first two, except the patrons are more soused and, if possible, even more off-key. It's crammed, elbow to elbow: a cheery, beery throng handing pints overhead from front to back.

Then, out of nowhere and nothing, violence erupts—instantaneous, nasty, and a hair away from lethal. A pint glass is broken, the jagged edge shoved full in the face of a chap standing at the bar not four feet from where we stand. Girls start screaming, glasses are hurled from all sides. Madness ensues, with people thrown to the floor and crushed underfoot. More smashing glass, chairs flying through the air, and the floor slippery with blood and beer.

I stand still on the periphery, dangerously transfixed and gaping wide-eyed, until Roger grabs my collar, yanks me through a side door, and pushes me toward the car. An hour later we are wrapped in the calm, cool disco chaos of Christmas at the New Penny in Watford.

Happy Christmas, everybody.

Food comes first,
then morals.

Bertolt Brecht

1972

I

Tim informs us that he has lined up a gig in Southend-on-Sea. The trick is that it's for this Friday, a mere two days hence. Some band canceled at the last moment so he was asked and said yes. He bumped up the fee accordingly, real cash, nearly thirty quid each.

This time it's pure Brylcreem. Some kind of severe rock 'n' roll emporium for duck-tailed die hards and Teds. There will be no flashes of "Jumpin' Jack" at this gig. No feathered-haired blues-pop hybrid stabs at modernity need apply. This is strictly Elvis, Bill Haley, Carl Perkins, Jerry Lee Lewis territory. And this presents a problem.

Tim and Roger can play this stuff in their sleep and Stein seems surprisingly familiar with the Jerry Lee Lewis catalog. But Mal, Yosemite, and I haven't got a clue. During rehearsal Mal tries to grasp the chords, his wide eyes glued to Tim's fingers on the fretboard, and Roger plays facing Yosemite, tutoring him on the stops and starts. Me? I've got two hours' worth of fifties grease lyrics to learn.

Ballpoint pens scratch frantically, with Tim and Roger dredging up and writing down the lyrics to all these ancient rockers: "Whole Lotta Shakin' Goin' On," "Great Balls of Fire," "Blue Suede Shoes," "Heartbreak Hotel." And what's with the mathematics? It's always one for the money, one o'clock, two o'clock, one-eyed cat peeking in a seafood store, twenty-flight rock, numbers everywhere.

Speaking of numbers, have you counted the cast of characters in "Jailhouse

Rock"? You've got the Warden, Shifty Henry, the Purple Gang, Spider Murphy, the Prison Band, Number 47, Sad Sack, Number 3, Little Joe, and a drummer boy from Illinois all doing things to one another (as apparently happens in the slammer), and I've got to sort it out and sing it. Do *you* know what Bugsy said to Shifty? Me neither. Turns out to be, "Nix, nix." Who'd have guessed?

In the back of the van, as we fight traffic on the long slog from Harrow to Southend, Roger plays acoustic and puts me through my paces. Tim yaps back over his shoulder from the front seat when I screw up "Breathless" and "Somethin' Else." It's too much, man.

Due to traffic we arrive at the gig way too late for a soundcheck and are forced to lug the gear in under the gaze of many an evil eye. The joint is full and getting fuller. Black leather and chains and jeans, brothel creepers, winklepickers, pretend Hells Angels, real ones, Teddy Boys, and tarts in poodle skirts and red chiffon scarves.

A pall in the hall of cigarette smoke, lager, sweat, hairspray, Old Spice, Evening in Paris, Brut—all the good ones. Malevolence too. The patrons ain't patient and they make it apparent that they do not like what they see strolling in.

Onstage, Stein surveys the upright piano and climbs aboard, up top, lifting the lid, reaching in, and placing, with care, his stick-on pickups. He's brought along another toy today as well: a tool that looks like a candle snuffer, a wooden handle with a ratchet on the end for tuning the piano. He and Roger set about playing notes over and over—"Give me an E"—until things sound reasonably in tune. Naturally, the punters are enthralled.

A knot of horrible, rough-looking womanish types, a chromosome or two short of alluring, are gathered around the front of the stage, already yelping nasty things at us.

This is a foreign country. I don't speak the language and I don't know the customs. The tight blue strides and red kimono I'm wearing don't seem to be helping matters, either. There's a bad feeling to this. You'd swear hate was hanging in the air, an almost palpable red fog of the stuff rolling in, from them to us. Altamont on the Estuary. What kind of greaseballs were these yokels expecting? Orange-glowing cigarette ends bob up and down out there in the darkness.

Roger seems resigned and taciturn as ever, busy plugging things in and tuning, but he's wary, keeping an eye on the enemy. Mal is whiter than ever, bleach white, with fear. Yosemite's holed up behind his kit, screwing with his hi-hat, in siege mode already. Stein seems implacable, outwardly calm, facing the wall, fingers on the keys, playing along with the records coming out of the hall's loudspeakers. But I catch his eye and he's nervous. He's hiding behind his hair.

Tim, though, is at ease—eager as Vince, a native, prodigal sonny boy returning home to his people. He's got his thinning hair combed back, black denim trousers, white T-shirt, and leather biker's jacket. Stick him in a museum. He's tuned and plugged in. He flips a switch on his amp and, presto, he's got some of what he calls "Duane Eddy reverb" going and he's itching to unleash it.

Me, I'm knocking back cans of warm lager. I've untied the kimono at the front and I'm ready.

Soundcheck? We don't need no stinkin' soundcheck.

We kick off with "Blue Suede Shoes." The balance is awful—I can't hear Stein or Mal—but, wonder of wonders, the black leather seas part to open up some hardwood floor space, and within seconds factions of the mob are dancing. They're bopping around like extras from some *Gidget* movie, Von Zipper's gang on bennies and bitter. They're jiving, they're twisting, they're doing some strange dance where they stand, legs spread, feet planted, hands on hips while they bend at the waist and shake their shoulders at each other.

First set lasts just over an hour. I'm doing my best with this glut of fifties lyrics, making some up as I go to the obvious and audible disgust of the prowling purists out there in the dark. Still, we get through it unscathed and the whiff of applause at the end of the set almost offsets the hecklers.

These include the pack at the back, the heaving, swaying herd crushing in around the bar. They are monumentally unappreciative of our efforts, and their proximity to the intoxicants isn't improving their mood. As Yosemite and Roger bring each number to a halt we hear catcalls and insults from this cashew gallery.

And the weird-gendered gaggle at the front, stage right, with their conical, rancid-pink, fairground candyfloss hairdos, their leather and chains and their miserable Easter Island faces, are starting to give me the willies. A couple of times during the first set I try to engage these creatures at the lip of the stage. I try charm and inclusion. "Hey, don't you chicks dance? C'mon, shake a tail-feather."

No response. Just sneers, a general tilting of their beehives together and minutes spent muttering.

Sheesh. Tough crowd.

The second set starts with the clock just nudging 11 p.m. and the crowd just nudging completely drunk. Tim decrees a shot of Jerry Lee Lewis, so it's over to Stein Lee Groven and away we go with "Great Balls of Fire," something about shaking my nerves and rattling my brain. Shame I can't remember the rest.

I get drunker, the songs get dodgier, the night gets edgier. Some short, greasy rider with "Hells Angels—Essex" on his jacket and a German helmet plonked on his fat skull starts flicking lit cigarette butts at me. Mal decides discretion is the better part of retreat and backs up until he's almost behind his Marshall stack. Roger, though, doesn't stand for this cigarette flicking. He's up front and giving lip. Von Ribbenflick responds with two fingers and a couple of syllables but the butt flicking stops.

We serve up a "Summertime Blues"/"Shakin' All Over" combo, Tim twanging all over the place, and the room starts jumping. A couple of scuffles erupt at the back near the bar. What's the cause? Who knows? Girls and drinks probably, same combination that's been causing grief since the dawn of time. Again, I try to work my magic on the stage creatures.

"Good lookin' chicks here in Southend."

I massacre "Jailhouse Rock," completely messing up the mathematics and who's doing what to whom, which upsets the local Elvis Presley Immaculate Lyric Preservation Society, whose members start howling from all corners when the song ends.

Finally, mercifully for all concerned, it's time for the last number. We decide to hit 'em hard then slink off into the night. Two minutes, twenty seconds of Chuck's "Sweet Little Sixteen" should do nicely.

One black-leathered stage-slag, neither sweet nor little nor sixteen, glowering under a brittle blonde hair-sprayed hive, waves an empty beer mug in my direction. "Oi, oi, poofter! You in the fuckin' frock. Yeah, you. You fuckin' call us 'chicks' one more time and we'll fuckin' glass ya."

As Tim rips into the opening of "Sweet Little Sixteen," my rejoinder is lager-slurred and delivered through a grin. "Sure thing, baby. Go lean up against that wall. It's plastered too."

I'm not allowed to enjoy the hilarity of my Henny Youngman riposte for more than a millisecond, due to the pint glass whizzing past my face and smashing just behind Yosemite's drum kit.

And after that? Well, after that it's a fascinating blur really. Glasses smashing, scary womenoids climbing onstage, microphone stands kicked over, punches, kicks. My hair gets pulled by the clutching fistful, I am punched and scratched. The kimono, which I nicked from Carole's wardrobe, is in shreds, and all this courtesy of a strange breed of wild-eyed drunken skag who, judging by their choice of shrieked insult, seem convinced that I am a homosexual.

Not for the first time it's Roger who comes to the rescue. He yanks me out of the scrum and shoves me down the back steps. A couple of the other lads show up and together they stuff me in the back of the van, right up against the front seats. Two cabinets are bounced down the steps, pushed in after me, and, bravely, I choose to stay hidden behind them. More equipment is thrown in. I keep my head down, listening to the shouting and shrieking getting louder outside, wincing at each pound on the side of the van.

Tim, with all his blessed Lord Sutch clout, is standing at the back of the van, arms crossed, negotiating and lying like mad. He tells them I'm not here, nobody knows where I am, I'm back in the hall, I ran off down the road, I'm at the pub around the corner, good riddance to bad rubbish.

And it works. Gradually, over the course of fifteen or twenty minutes, things calm down. Seems like hours, though, to Sir Prancelot, cowering in his torn kimono behind a fortress of amplifiers in the van.

Finally, we are all piled into the Humber. Tim palms it into gear, hits the gas, and, thank the god of one-night stands, we're headed down the highway. There is no room in the back of the van. In the panic nothing was packed right. Cymbals were thrown in still on their stands, guitar cables are dangling from amps, black spaghetti cables and wires are everywhere, a hi-hat foot pedal digging in someone's back, gear stacked to the roof, musicians jammed in wherever they can fit. But we're out of there. All that's missing from this frenetic exit is a banjo soundtrack.

Gradually, as the miles and minutes roll by, hearts stop pounding and things calm down until each musician is left alone with his thoughts, staring out the window at the outskirts of the metropolis rising up around us.

A huge red neon sign advertising a brand of bitter spells out "TAKE COURAGE" on the London skyline. I will. This is it. History lessons and rock 'n' roll archeology are over. This is not what I set out to do and this stops tonight.

It's nearly three in the morning when we pull into Paddington and roll up to 17 London Street. Stein disentangles himself from the cables wrapped around his boots and climbs out through the back doors into the drizzly, gray street. The derelict is tucked in for the night, bowler hat poking out under his cardboard blanket on the doorstep of Ladbrokes. I get out of the van to have a word with Stein. I take off my torn kimino, ball it up, and throw it into a bin. I've got scratches on my face and chest, raccoon eyes, and mascara streaks down my cheeks.

"I'm coming to see you tomorrow."

Stein nods. "I know."

Next day, Stein and I have a summit in London Street. It's time to take over. Time to slip into another gear:

Boot out Tim.

Boot out Yosemite.

Absolutely no more greaser "rock 'n' roll."

Get a new name.

Stein has to shave off that mustache.

Afterward, on the way to Paddington station, I notice the derelict leaning on a lamppost, perusing *The Times*, resplendent in a torn kimono.

II

Stein and I spend days together scheming, building this thing in our heads. The sound we hear in our joint 45-rpm cerebral cortex is a guitar with six Vietnamese razor-wire strings played by a great-looking madman whipped on by a rhythm section playing at blitzkrieg speed behind a mouthy vocal screeching the gospel.

We hole up in his bedsit with a guitar and a couple of cans of lager, and edit "Southern Belles," "The Boys in Blue," "Son of the Wizard," and "Melinda Lee."

But the months drag by. Nobody wants us, nobody books us; rehearsals are a sulky drag. The revolution, though, is under way.

By June 22, 1972, Tim is gone and Yosemite's days are numbered. They are numbered "2." He and his mustache are shown the door. They leave together, muttering at the injustice and swearing revenge.

Roger informs us that we've been offered a gig at Stanmore Town Hall on July 1, eight whole days away. A tenner each. Drummer panic breaks out. We put an ad in, where else, the *Melody Maker*.

DRUMMER WANTED
Young, slim
Must look, act & think like a star
No beards, no chrome-domes, no fatties
723-0759 (after 5 pm)

Thursday, ad in *Melody Maker*. Friday, auditions in the church hall. Saturday, play the gig. It's all about the planning.

* * *

Answering the phone is not for the faint of heart. It entails a flat-out sprint upon hearing the first ring, down three stairs and along ten yards of rickety, uneven hallway, snag-ends of worn carpet snatching at your shoes, in order to beat the overweight, but surprisingly fleet, Portuguese lady in Flat 2 to the receiver. It seems London is, all of a sudden, bursting at the seams with young, good-looking drummers.

Again, the phone rings. Another drummer, of course. Oh no, he's from Canada. That blasts ack-ack into his fuselage for a start. He jabbers away about Led Zep and Cream, and I'd like to tell him he's blowing the interview but I can't get a syllable in sideways. This guy can talk. He chatters away like Groucho Marx on helium and I tune out. I'm just about to hang up when I hear him say, "at the 100 Club with Memphis Slim."

"Hey, wait. What did you say?"

He screeches to a desert-dust halt like the *Looney Tunes'* Road Runner. "What's that? Oh, Memphis Slim? Yeah, one night down at the 100 Club he was playing and his drummer didn't show up, so he asked, 'Can anybody play drums?' and I said, 'Yeah.' Got up and helped him out."

Well, I couldn't tell the difference between Memphis Slim and Chattanooga Chubby and, as previously mentioned, I'm not interested in the blues and wouldn't cross a goat trail to see any Memphis, Muddy, Howlin', Blind, Lightning, Wee, Asthmatic, or any of the rest, but a certain amount of respect nonetheless must be accorded. And, by extension, same goes for anyone, even a drummer, who has accompanied one of these relics onstage.

So this drummer, incessant chirp and all, is given the benefit of the doubt along with directions to the church hall in Stanmore.

Friday afternoon in the church hall, all of twenty-eight hours before the gig. I'm sitting on the floor beside my microphone stand, trying for the second or third time to get into *Nausea* by Sartre. This bilge has got vanity press written all over it.

We've scheduled the drummers to arrive at twenty-minute intervals but, being drummers, their timing is off and nine arrive at once. They all look hopeless, not a shred of style. Roger and Stein do the cordials and the choreography, saying hello, lining them up. They each get a couple of songs. Seven go by; this is grim. Lest we forget, we have a gig tomorrow.

Up next is a Brummie, head-shop threads, army-surplus face, that accent. He gets to give "Johnny B. Goode" a shot and it is as bad as I'd feared. Stops pop up where they shouldn't and the tempo is all over the place. It ends and I call out "Next."

Brummie looks up like a particularly dull beagle, head to one side. "What's next?"

"Him there," I say, pointing to the next drummer in line.

"What the fuck?" He stands up, drumsticks gripped like weapons.

Roger intervenes with minimum verbals and maximum leather jacket. I head to the kitchen while it blows over. Stein joins me. We've got a sink full of cold water bobbing with cans of Long Life lager.

"It's bad," says Stein, popping a top. "Think one of them will do, just for tomorrow?"

"Not a chance. Listen."

Roger and Mal are running another drummer through his paces and it is dire. I open the door a crack and take a peek. Apparently, Che Guevara's dad is on drums, wearing that stupid T-shirt of his son's that you see everywhere. I close the door and turn to Stein. "We're doomed, mate."

No sooner is it closed than the door smacks into my back and in pushes this guy: skinny, thick black shoulder-length hair, and a pale, animated face somewhere between *Mad* magazine and cherub.

"Hi. Sorry, didn't mean to bop you. Hey, is that beer? Can I have one?" And before we can say, "Get stuffed," he steps to the sink and plucks a Long Life out of the water. Head thrown back, the pointiest Adam's apple I've ever seen bobbing up and down—blissfully, rudely unselfconscious. This has to be the Memphis Slim guy.

He is wearing the tightest jeans I've seen on anyone not bubbling with estrogen, along with a black tank top, black plimsolls, a pair of Ludwig drumsticks sticking out of his back pocket, and an annoyingly cheery grin. He's next up on the hot seat. Five minutes and one song later, Lou Sparks is in the band. And he has joined a band with a new name. When Stein arrived at the auditions he took me to one side. "I've got it," he said, very conspiratorial.

"Yeah, well don't give it to me."

"A name for the band."

"Do tell," I said, not expecting much.

He smiled and leaned in closer. "The Queen."

"The Queen?"

"The Queen."

I try it out now: "The Queen."

"Imagine the headlines in the *NME* and *Melody Maker*," says Stein. " 'The Queen in Riot at Hammersmith Odeon,' 'The Queen Pukes on Arrival at Heathrow,' 'The Queen in Scuffle with Fluff Freeman on *Top of the Pops*.' Can you imagine?"

I can imagine. In fact, I'm imagining like crazy. I like it. We run it by Roger. His enthusiasm doesn't quite match ours, but he agrees too.

So that's it. We are the Queen.

And we've got a gig in twenty-four hours.

III

We've been set up and soundchecked since the afternoon and, insanely enough, we feel ready for this gig. This drummer, Lou Sparks, has given the band a jolt. His manic energy and humor, not to mention his playing, have given us the belief that, even with no rehearsal, we might actually pull this off, which is good because we've got no choice and the place is packed.

It's an early start, though, 7 p.m., and the organizer, a lovely lady in a blue wide-brimmed hat with a veil hanging down the front and feathers protruding therefrom, for some reason asks if we can start the show with a couple of acoustic songs.

Short notice, but no sweat. Stein and I grab acoustic guitars, sit on a couple of stools center stage like refugees from Woodstock, and dish up the first public performance ever of "The Boys in Blue," which goes down a treat, and "Wild Horses" by the Stones, which doesn't. In retrospect, "Wild Horses" *is* a thuddingly boring song when not being done by the Stones. Still, you live and wince.

Then, jacked up, under-rehearsed, and newly christened the Queen, we come on for our world premiere and, without over-egging the soufflé, we kill 'em. We play until 1 a.m., and even though half the time we don't know what we're doing it doesn't seem to matter. Even though every hour, on the hour, we repeat songs we've already done, they love it. We've rebuilt the engine, cranked up the tempo, volume, and attitude, and it works.

Lou looks and plays great, like he's been part of the band forever.

A woman of indeterminate vintage has been gyrating at the front of the stage since the first note of the second set, and she keeps giving me alluring looks borrowed for the evening from a Pola Negri film. At around midnight she takes the belt off her dress and starts whipping the floor almost to the beat. An excessive response, perhaps, and not entirely befitting the social status implied by her eye-popping jewelry, but there you have it. She's dancing dead in front of my microphone, and on the backswing of one ferocious flog the buckle slices the back of my hand, drawing blood. Yeow!

After the last song she wraps my hand in a silk scarf. She mentions that she is the ex-wife of Roger Moore. Who would lie about that? Good gig, though. Stein and I and Roger and now Lou just might have something going.

Back in Watford, I'm getting on Carole's nerves. It's a mystery to me. After all, I'm not exactly underfoot. I sleep until three in the afternoon then drink coffee and read the paper until Brillo gets home from work. Then the two of us watch TV—cartoons, *Blue Peter*, whatever—and have a laugh, then we pop down to the pub for a pint.

She has somehow got it into her head that I am a lazy waste of space leading her husband astray. Sometimes I can't even take an hour-long bath without detecting a distinct chill in the air and a certain heavy heel-to-floor ratio when she walks around. Plus, there's the kimono situation. She's tearing the house apart looking for the damn thing, last seen in shreds on a *Times*-reading derelict in Paddington.

Under pressure from Carole to hit the road, I answer an ad in the local rag and find a room in a house in Bushey, right next door to Watford: 32 Cross Road, £17.50 a month. I've got nineteen quid to my name and I pay a month in advance. I leave Bradshaw Road the same way I entered Bradshaw Road, a cardboard suitcase in my hand and a faintly baffled expression on my face.

Cross Road is a quiet, leafy street—the word "bucolic" springs to mind. The joint is occupied by three guys, two of which, Angus and Ewen, are students. I don't know if I mentioned this, but I can't stand students. Students are nothing more than hippies with pens. But it's the third chap, Dick, whom I can't take my eyes off. Where have I seen him before? He stares out through Coke-bottle specs and is tall, rail thin, and bald as a boiled egg. Well, bald except for a frankly pointless straggly fringe wrapped monk-like around his lower skull from ear to shining ear. How do I know this guy?

They take me down to their local, the Rifle Volunteer, for a pint. We walk in and, bloody hell, they've all got their own private pewter tankards up on a shelf behind the bar.

It's a good English pub, though. Oak beams, red velvet seats, smoke-yellowed paint, ridiculous pattern amid the stains on the carpet, the works. But I sense a definite thuggish element among the denizens. Blokes like extras from *Straw Dogs* hunched over their personal tankards, eyes shifting back and forth, hod-carrier knuckles poking out of the frayed sleeves of donkey jackets.

My eyes are shifting too, back and forth, checking out the surprising sprinkling of quite attractive girls; real girls with real lives, as it turns out: teachers, nurses, secretaries, soon-to-be lawyers in the making. Names come and go: Susan, Christine, Briar, Ada, Jen.

After four pints and no food my interior noggin is swirling and twirling. Off to my left I see lamplight gleaming off Dick's shiny, hairless pate. That does it. It hits me. Mystery solved. I remember where I've seen him before. There is an eight-foot-high, black-and-white poster of him at every Tube stop in London. The poster is divided in two: on the left side is Dick, forlorn, lonely, a bald man; on the right is a new Dick in hipster threads, flashing a toothy smile, confident, cool, a swingin' Dick, as it were. And why? The transformation is due to one immutable fact. Perched atop the second Dick's skull is a luxuriant, shoulder-length thatch of hair—hair that any Pink Floyd roadie would be proud to sport and shampoo once a month.

He's a toupee model. And here he is, my new housemate.

It's only September but already there is a chill lurking around my toes in the mornings, and I'm constantly famished beyond belief. Everyone else in the house leaves in the morning to go to work or to protest in front of the American Embassy or whatever it is these types do. In their absence I ransack the cupboards and the fridge. It's Mother Hubbard time. Find a match, light the stove, put on the kettle. Nick a tea bag. In a tin I find a quarter of a bag of crusted sugar that I take to the living room and eat with a spoon while waiting for the water to boil.

Roger brings word that something has happened to our church hall in Stanmore. Well, nothing has happened to the actual church hall, it is more to do with our status there, which appears to have been downgraded; we can no longer rehearse there. It is mysterious and smacks of intrigue, vengeance, and ghosts of guitarists past.

Meanwhile, Stein comes into close personal contact with a fiver, so the two of us limbo under the turnstiles and make our way to Wardour Street, and from there, inevitably, we wander to the portals of the Marquee. Standing in the bar section we nurse our pints, sneering at the band through the glass partition and generally bemoaning our fate.

But fate is a funny thing. One minute you are brimful of bile, awash in dark thoughts and contemplating the doing of foul deeds, and the next you could be in baggy shorts of a tropical flower pattern hanging ten on the crest of a gigantic wave of optimism, at one with the world and contemplating a modest but heartfelt donation to some African scam charity.

And so it transpires that, from the nursing and the snarling, we are instantly thrust into a tumult of grinning and slurping by the simple miracle of Oily Jack, the manager of the Marquee, sashaying over to us, buying us pints, and offering us a gig on September 30.

There are two clubs in town, the Marquee and the Speakeasy. But the Speak is out. Play there? We can't even go there. It is the forbidden kingdom, home of the famous, the fatuous, the fabulous, where we would be as non grata as five personas could ever be. Then there's the glorious, exalted, celebrated Marquee. The greatest club in the history of clubs. The undefeated, undisputed King of Clubs. Bring on the contenders. What have you got? Los Angeles, what have you got? You've got the Troubadour, home to every knee-staring, bearded, Martin-strumming folkie who ever whined his way into the charts. And you've got the Whisky a Go Go. New York has something called CBGB, so they say. Where else? What else? Nowhere and nothing.

Absolutely everybody has played the Marquee. The Stones, the Who, Hendrix, Yardbirds, Animals, Cream, as well as more recent affronts to the sensibilities like Yes, Jethro Tull, Pink Floyd, and Strawbs.

Now, out of the blue, it is our turn. We are beyond excited. It's a mere three weeks away.

IV

With the big day looming and no other alternative, we decide to rehearse in my room at 32 Cross Road so, one Monday afternoon when all students and toupee models are out, we lug in the gear and set up. We begin clandestinely, all acoustic and wire brush on snare, but within half an hour of plugging in we are at full tilt. Two hours later we are out the door and off to the Rifle. As we walk by, curtains twitch in neighboring houses.

And so it goes in the days and weeks leading up to the Marquee: full volume in a ten-foot-square bedroom. Ears constantly ring, but the band is getting tighter and better. So what's a little tinnitus?

One day there's a knock on the door. It is the distinguished-looking elderly gent in a cardigan from two doors down, imploring politely for tranquility to return to his leafy life. Can we please turn it down? Sure, will do, Pops. But in fact, can't do, Pops. It's the Marquee, you know? Sorry . . . ish.

More rehearsals, more neighbors knocking. Housewives in aprons, gents in tweed jackets, young mums, pensioners, all united under a banner of grievance toward this new malignance in their midst. Still we rehearse. No choice.

Next day, the knock is louder than usual. On the doorstep stand two policemen armed with billy clubs, stern expressions, and clipped tones: the full British arsenal. Even pencils. I say something, they write it down. This is unnerving. They ask my name. I tell them "Lou Sparks." The new Lou promises to keep it down in future. The policemen note this in their little books. They turn and slowly saunter off under the lamplight. One looks back over his shoulder. The new Lou waves.

The magical day draws nearer. All the girls from the Rifle say they will be in attendance at the Marquee. Brillo says he'll get his work's van and drive us. Sonja gives me a pair of her trousers to wear, white and skintight.

The rehearsal is our best yet. Lou plays like a demon and even Mal throws a pose or two into proceedings.

After this blisteringly sweaty workout we are heading to the Rifle, when a man in a three-piece suit with a two-piece mustache opens a briefcase, walks up to us, and thrusts some papers into my hands. Are we being served? Yes we are. A glance at the letter: the law firm of Quirk, Peevish, & Somesuch is accusing and warranting and foreswearing and generally demanding that Lou gets out of Dodge by sundown.

"How did they get my name?" asks Lou. I shrug my shoulders, crumple the papers into a ball, toss them in the gutter, and we continue to the pub.

Curtains no longer twitch; the neighbors stand openly at their windows, arms folded, faces dark and full of foreboding.

The day dawns—or at least it did twelve hours ago. This is the day that will change music history: September 30, 1972. We arrive at the hallowed Marquee at the appointed time, whipped up, nervous and excited. But we are ready to go, ready to burst onto a scene that won't know what hit it. We are rehearsed to the hilt. We can't get better than this. Ladies and gentlemen, direct from a one-month engagement in a bedroom in Bushey, a warm round of applause for the Queen. Thirty quid we get for this. Not bad.

We, the Queen, are the opening act, supporting some outfit with two singers, male and female. They operate under the sidesplittingly clever name of Mahatma Kane Jeeves. Their troglodyte roadies are irritable and stingy when it comes to giving us room to set up on stage. Roger and I get our verbals in front and center, stating our case. We get five minutes for a soundcheck. Things are frosty.

No fear. This is the launchpad. After tonight the world changes. Jack sends over a couple of rounds on the house. We hunker down in the closet-sized dressing room cunningly disguised as a stinkhole directly behind the stage, drinking our drinks, talking it up. Two slashes of red lipstick like a teacher marking a final exam, and I pull on and zip up Sonja's white strides with a top to match. Red velvet jacket, donned for the first couple of numbers at least. White silk scarf around the throat. Ready to roll.

Roger's in black leather, sporting my rock 'n' roll sweater underneath with black jeans and nasty boots. Stein looks fantastic, all heels and hair, green eye shadow, tight pink top. He's still got the damned blond 'tache, though. He looks like the Sundance Kid's nephew. When's he going to learn that the lip fringe doesn't jibe with the master plan?

Showtime nears. The lads peek through the curtain. The joint is filling up with the usual Marquee mob: the hippies, posers, tarts, and City boys. And musicians dotted throughout. Some, the exalted ones, with record deals, most without; some with bandmates, some with girls, some lone wolves. All of them hypercritical, feigning boredom, leaning on the bar or standing at the back of the room, here to be seen, here to watch. Here to sneer.

Sonja has brought along a haughty, icy, delectable coven of blonde-on-blonde au pairs. And the girls from the Rifle have made good on their threat. Some are almost unrecognizable in unfamiliar finery and kooky hair, and even though the night has barely begun, all appear to be well lubricated.

They're all out there waiting. It's a snake pit, really.

The crap, overwrought, "progressive" sludge pounding out of the club's speakers is at last switched off, and onstage somebody takes the mic. A cough, a scratch, a feedback squeal. The crowd rumbles expectantly. A voice, whose voice? Oily Jack? Don't know, but it begins to announce us.

"Ladies and gentlemen, welcome to the Marquee." The audience rumble goes up a notch.

Backstage, we stand up, shoulder to shoulder in the tiny, sweaty space. Are we ready? We'd better be. We shift around until Lou is first in the conga line and I'm last. That's the way. Drummers need to get there first, singers last. The voice at the microphone continues: "Tonight we welcome a new band, great boys, great name, irreverent name, please . . . hands together for . . . the Queen."

We're on, to enthusiastic applause—not to mention whoops, yelps, and squeals—from our stacked-deck portion of the audience. Lou, then Stein, then Roger, then Mal, and finally me, with enough seconds twixt me and them for Lou to get started with a rat-a-tat-tat and the lads to get plugged in. I walk onto the stage, as rehearsed a thousand times in the bedroom in Bushey, stare at the crowd for three beats, strike a shape, wrap my fingers around the microphone, press lips to Shure, and count the boys in: "One, two, three, four."

And what happens? What happens on this, the most important occasion in the history of our world? What happens at this crucial juncture, at this holy site, at this moment we have striven toward relentlessly through all the Snowy Whites, the biker chicks, the defections, the deprivations, the Yosemites, the countless hours of rehearsals spent honing the nastiest half hour of rock 'n' roll this world could ever witness?

What happens? I'll tell you what happens. The horrible happens. The worst, the most toe-curlingly embarrassing, crawl-into-a-hole-and-die hideous happens.

Nothing happens.

Well, not exactly nothing. Lou is in. Bashing away, cymbal crash on the count of five, full throttle. All the rest of us are dead. Dead microphone, dead guitars, dead bass, dead piano. Dodo dead. Doornail dead. Norwegian Blue dead. We've got a drummer thrashing and everyone else looking at each other wide-eyed, panicked, accusatory.

Roger, bless him, is the first to react. He dives to the Selmer amp on the floor, stage left, and in a blur unplugs this, replugs that, reaches up and plunks Stein's keyboard, looks over his shoulder and indicates to me that I should say something into the mic, which I do. "Hey," brilliantly, is all I can think of at the moment. But it works and booms through the Marquee over the top of Lou's drumbeat. Then Mal's Strat comes alive and we've got some weedy, tentative guitar and then, on his knees, Roger's bass is alive and well. He picks up the track.

Finally, agonizingly, we are all in and trying to revive any semblance of dignity, remnant of poise, or shred of the "dead cool" we thought was just naturally oozing from our pores. But "dead cool," like beauty, is in the eye of the beholder. And the beholders out there in the club know we've blown it. What an embarrassment. If I was standing on a vaudeville stage I would gladly pull the lever myself to open the trapdoor and send me plummeting down.

Musicians out there are laughing, actual bent-over-at-the-waist laughter. The song ends. Our supporters, those who haven't left the building or at least made a dash for the bar, clap fervently and smile grimly. We press on.

Halfway into the next song, the guitar amp blows up, complete with a blue flash and a spiral of smoke curling up to the ceiling. Piano, drums, and vocals forge on valiantly and, judging by the music police out front, to great comic effect. Twenty agonizing bars later, frantic replugging ends our brief career as a trio and Roger and Mal return, sharing the same amp. Mal, however, has no idea where we are in the song and appears to get more and more befuddled as it crawls to the edge of a cliff and throws itself off.

By the fourth song we are a bag of nerves, shaking like junkies in jail. By the fifth we come up with a brilliant idea for accelerating our career suicide and decide to do "Crying Time," a weepy, traditional country song in the middle of what is already the worst rock 'n' roll set in the history of music. But let's make it even worse, shall we?

There is a verse in the song that is spoken rather than sung, in true hokey country fashion, and in rehearsal we always let Stein do that bit because he does it in a hilarious unintelligible Norwegian/Nashville patois. The trouble is, we never actually got around to fixing that part, and here we are at the Marquee where the Music Gestapo are already sneering and shaking their heads, and then we reach that point in the song and away goes Stein with eight slow bars of Nordic gibberish.

We stagger to the end of our set like punch-drunk palookas: bleeding, legs gone, eyes swollen shut, hanging on to the ropes, and praying for the bell. Five minutes later, sitting in the dressing hole, dripping with sweat, utterly deflated, we decide not to discuss it.

Number 17 London Street the next afternoon. Stein and I are cracking cans of lager, *Exile on Main Street* is on the turntable. Two curs licking wounds. Stein telephones the Marquee at the prearranged time for the verdict. I can hear him in the hallway. Stein's not saying much, just listening. Finally, he hangs up and comes back to the room.

"What did he say?"

"He said we're not ready."

I go into a rage, ready to sack everybody, blow up the band, apply for a management-trainee course at Selfridges, knock over a betting shop, anything. I blame Oily Jack. Evidence showed that he had stepped on the plugs after introducing us, bending the inputs, cutting the power. I blame Oily Jack for his inability to spot glaringly obvious potential. I am plunged into a black, malevolent mood, sucking lager, cursing the fates.

But who am I kidding? Certainly not the long-haired Norwegian guy in the armchair. Truth is, we were fragile, unable to overcome the simple inevitability of an equipment malfunction. We were rookies, raw recruits. And we are nowhere near as brilliant as we thought we were.

And, personally speaking, I'd say the lead singer needed a bigger pair of swinging spheroids tucked inside Sonja's trousers.

V

Harrow Weald has a high street full of shop windows and I get a job washing them. The day begins at 7 a.m., which is insane and plays hell with my lack of circadian rhythm. Every day is foggy, gray, cheerless, and freezing; my hands are red and numb with cold. Every day I arrive late for work. Mercifully, at the end of two weeks I get the sack, while dodging the mannequins in Woolworths' windows.

I rise at two in the afternoon and I pull the blanket with me against the chill. No tea bags to be found in the kitchen. Maybe Angus, Ewen, and Dick take them into their rooms for safekeeping. I boil some water, pour it into a cup, and stir in two teaspoons of sugar. In the living room I plop *Something Else* on the turntable, sip my sugar water, and let the beautiful melancholy of "Waterloo Sunset" waft over me. Could be worse.

Could be like old Ivan Denisovich. I'm reading *one day in his life* by Aleksandr Solzhenitsyn. Ivan's trudging around his gulag with a shovel, in daft clothes and a funny hat, doing pointless jobs in wretched conditions. His personal hygiene is atrocious. His guards and overseers are, to a man, grunting, monosyllabic sadists. It's a dreadfully detailed account for such a slim book. Old Ivan eats better than me, though. What I'd give for a tin cup of potato-peel soup with a slice of sawdust bread.

The Marquee nightmare is still vivid and bumping around in my psyche, but an odd thing happened when I finally summoned the courage to go to the Rifle Volunteer again. The girls who came to the gig actually seemed to like it. At first I thought they were yanking one of my lower extremities, but no, they said they actually enjoyed the band and wanted to know where we would be playing next. A couple of them even seemed totally unaware of the various disasters that occurred during the set. But I'm under no illusions. We stunk out the joint. Still, it's a funny thing, an audience.

A funnier thing happens a few days later. I am alone at home swearing at some drivel on *Opportunity Knocks* when there is a knock on the door. I open it and there stands Lou, with a suitcase dangling from his arm. He moves in. Now two mouths to feed, but at least we're having a laugh.

Roger arrives at a bedroom rehearsal with news of a gig. Clambering back aboard the nag is just what we need. A certain Paul A. Quinton has heard of us, Christ knows how, and wants us to play the Greyhound, Redhill, on Saturday October 21. He has even sent along a one-page "agreement" between "Paul A. Quinton (Referred to as the Employer) and the Queen (Referred to as the Artist) for the said sum of 80 percent gate monies." We've never had an "agreement" before. And there it is, our name in print, "the Queen."

I am no longer enamored with the name of the band. The joke has worn thin and, anyway, I'd prefer a plural handle. The Something or Others. Lou and I like the Brats, but not just the Brats, the somewhere Brats. Lou suggests the Brixton Brats and even comes up with a pen-and-ink design for the bass drum head.

The only problem is that we've never been to Brixton, and we aren't planning a visit in the near future.

Back in Cross Road there is a stunted apple tree in the backyard with scabrous green apples dangling here and there. Lou picks a few and boils them up in a pot in the kitchen, adds sugar, and turns them into a lumpy applesauce. It's delicious and we eat nothing else for the next few days.

Afterward, in desperation, we turn to a life of petty crime. I discover that I have a knack for pilfering life-sustaining items. In a fake-fur coat with deep pockets I work quickly while Lou uses his charm and humor to distract the shopkeep. Tins of stew, salmon, and sardines, soap, toothpaste, rashers of bacon, bars of chocolate—all manner of necessities disappear in a blur into the inner confines of the faux fur.

It calls for sleight of hand, sangfroid, and steady nerve. At least we eat on a reasonably regular basis, brush our fangs, and wash our paws. Pangs of conscience and hunger, in a tug-of-war.

Cometh the hour, cometh the van. Brill drives us to Redhill, fighting through two hours of hellacious traffic until we find the Greyhound and pull into the car park shortly after 6 p.m. Within minutes it becomes frighteningly clear that this is yet another biker club. Everyone on the staff is in black leather, with bicycle chain necklaces on the girls and borstal tattoos on the guys. By 6:10 I'm petrified.

But it's a strange business, this rock 'n' roll thing. We were whipped dogs, tail-between-the-legs types when we slunk back to Bushey after the Marquee. I was a snarling, sulking, defeatist mess the day after at Stein's place. But this is now and this is here. And you know what? We do okay. We don't look anything like the audience. Lou, Stein, and I are in full makeup; I'm in Mr Fish and red velvet.

At first the crowd stares, cautious, caustic, and curious, then a few comments about how we look, some nasty and taunting, but from the first chord, from the first drumbeat, we've got 'em. These rockers want to rock.

They are strange, these Hells Angels types. I don't understand the breed with their filthy initiation rituals and fetishistic engine worship. One does, after all, hear strange rumors of pissed-upon jerkins and jerked-upon pistons.

All that aside, by the third song the place is a seething mass of black leather, chains, and stomping boots. We keep 'em bouncing off the walls for the whole night. The bikers love derogatory tales about coppers and sing along lustily to the chorus of "The Boys in Blue." Lou is on fire, Roger is in his element, Mal keeps up, and Stein and I just keep smiling at each other.

In the van on the way back we're yelling and laughing, and Roger waves a fistful of "80 percent of the gate monies." Lying in the dark, guitar case digging in my back, rolling along the A23, mental scalpel slicing away the jive, I know something is amiss in the guitar department and maybe in the rhythm section. It just isn't psychotic enough. And Stein's mustache has got to go down the drain.

Plus, we are running out of time. Stein is okay, he's eighteen, but Lou and I just turned nineteen. We're pushing it.

The students are out. Lou and I are on the couch mocking *Coronation Street* when there is a knock at the door. I open it to see an Australian with a duffel bag over his shoulder and a guitar case dangling from his arm. Mal moves in.

Now we've got three mouths to feed.

The three of us rise on freezing, teeth-chattering afternoons, wrap ourselves in blankets, and mope out to the kitchen to scavenge tea and scraps. We stand shivering like the Sioux waiting for government handouts in the days just before Sitting Bull was murdered. I point this out and we have a little laugh and dance in the kitchen as if around a campfire. Then Lou tells us he's actually a Micmac Indian. How about that?

One dark day Stein walks in with a look of classic Nordic depression on his face, like a woman about to launch into a bleak, self-centered soliloquy in an Ingmar Bergman film. Seems he has to join the Musicians' Union in order to work in the UK and he has slammed into a brick wall in his efforts to do so. He shows me a letter.

> *Dear Mr. Groven,*
>
> *I am in receipt of your passport and other documents but was expecting to receive a letter in support of your application.*
>
> *I should point out that we would normally not admit a foreign applicant who is without a permit to work as a musician in this country and would oppose the issue of a permit if we considered that there were British musicians available for the work.*
>
> *Perhaps, therefore, you would care to let me know what work you are hoping to do, giving full details if you have some specific employment in mind so that the Committee can take this into consideration when dealing with your application.*
>
> *Sincerely,*
> *Bernard Parris*
> *Secretary*
> *Central London Branch*
> *Musicians' Union*

Oh no. This is a disaster. I've just found the guy. He's all I've got. They can't send him away. The two of us spend the evening fretting, and Stein leaves under a dark cloud. Before he goes he asks if I will write a letter on his behalf. I will.

For two days and nights I work on the letter, writing and rewriting, trying to get the tone just right. Part pleading, part demanding, trying to get the point across that this man is irreplaceable to our band and that, despite many auditions, no British musicians wanted this job. Which is all too true, actually.

Eight pages I write, longhand, and I agonize over every sentence. Finally, at 11:45 of the second night, I fold the eight pages into an envelope, lick and seal the flap, lick and stick on the stamp. I walk to the postbox and, at midnight, after pausing one more time to consider yet another rewrite, I drop it in the slot.

Dick and his toupee decide to leave Cross Road. They get a new place somewhere on Aldenham Road, a few streets away. Lou and Mal sleep on the floor in my room. Angus and Ewen advertise for a new tenant. Life goes on. Food and music is all we think about.

We've discovered a band we quite like, and amazingly enough they're American. Alice Cooper is the name. They can rock but the music always seems to have a comedic sub-theme. Some of it is quite funny, actually. That's the problem. There's fakery afoot. There is a direct lineage from Screaming Lord Sutch and Arthur whatshisname, the god-of-hellfire bloke, not to mention that New Orleans guy who'll put a spell on you.

Alice Cooper try to pull off androgyny, but they've got muscles and underarm hair and never the twain should meet. They play in makeup but I bet they drive pickup trucks and shoot rattlesnakes. They drink Budweiser, for Christ's sake.

But they beat anything else I see around.

Bored out of our minds, ravenous and wide awake at 4 a.m., Lou, Mal, and I decide to go for a walk. Out into the dark, sleepy town we venture. We poke fingers into the slots of phone boxes and vending machines, digging for stray coins, but none are to be found. We are skittish jackals, jumping at sounds and shadows, sticking close together. No devilry or mischief in our bones, just wandering the wet deserted streets hoping to trip over a wallet. It will be dawn soon.

A few hundred yards down the street, a delivery van stops in front of a shop. Two men get out, take a white box out of the back, and carry it to the door of the shop where they leave it, get back in the van, and drive off. We make a beeline for the drop-off.

Turns out to be a fish 'n' chip shop. Turns out to be a box about eighteen inches square and seven inches deep, with tiny holes in the top and two plastic straps holding it all together. We're not daft—we know something fishy is going on here. Mal and I each grab a side and off we go down the road toward home, heads on swivels, eyes peeled for PC Plod.

The box is heavy, unwieldy, and something else. It appears to be moving.

"Was that you?" asks Mal, wheezing, breathless, and frantic.

"Was what me?"

"That movement, a lurch."

"Yeah, of course it was, keep moving." What's he on about? We stagger on down the road. More traffic now and the sky turning a lovely gray with orangey streaks. This is hard work, especially having to affect a nonchalant air as cars go by. We take a break.

"Your turn, Lou," I gasp.

We thump the box down on the ground and it sits still, but then—there's no denying it—the box gives a little heave.

"What the fuck is in there?"

"Fish. Fish is in there," I tell them. "Filets and chunks and it's just sloshing around in the ice or the whatsit, the brine. That's all. Let's go before a gang of fishmongers come charging after us."

We struggle off down the high street, taking turns holding the plastic straps.

Back at the ranch, the other cowpokes appear to have left the bunkhouse early. Or maybe they didn't come home last night. Whatever the case, we're alone as we clump the box down on the kitchen countertop. Fried fish for breakfast, a mouth-watering concept. We get a knife and slice open the edges of the box, lift the flaps, and . . . *Kapow!*

First the mass squirms, a disgusting, oily hydra-head, and then, like a cross between an erupting volcano and the jack-in-the-box from hell, out burst a dozen huge black slimy eels. We leap back, squealing like schoolgirls, as the eels slither lightning-quick across the stove, into the sink, drop with a squelch onto the floor, and eel off in all directions. Down the hall, under the fridge, behind the garbage can, and they're fast and ugly. They've obviously been planning this jailbreak all night, and now that they have their chance they do not intend to be taken alive.

They want to get back to the Thames and, believe me, we don't intend to stand in their way. That's why we are perched on chairs, shrieking at each other.

Eels are mean. They are nasty; they have rows of razor-sharp brown teeth. They look like dwarf anacondas in a bad mood. Finally, with no choice—we can't just let them slime around all over the house—we arm ourselves with a broom, a cricket bat, and a microphone stand. Tentatively at first, then with gusto, we beat some to death and the rest we herd out the back door and into the garden. The dead eels are flung out after them. Three hang from the branches of the apple tree.

We think we've rid ourselves of them all but we're not absolutely certain. Never again will we walk the house with impunity.

Or bare feet.

VI

Stein gets word to me, says it's an emergency. He used the word "crisis." What can it be? Is he being deported? Did Sonja wise up and hit the road? What can account for the sense of dread in his voice?

In his bedsit I sit myself down in the armchair. Silently, he hands me this week's *New Musical Express*, which I haven't had the opportunity to nick yet, open on a specific page. Oh no. There is an article, complete with a picture of a band from New York. Incredibly, they look just like us, and as I read a few paragraphs my stomach sinks into my boots. They seem to be doing exactly what we are doing. Not only that, but they are miles ahead of us, with gigs, a following, an impending record contract with Mercury Records, and, judging by this drivel I'm reading, great press. They are called the New York Dolls. I'm scared to hear what they sound like. Stein is right. This is a crisis. And the news keeps getting cheerier.

They're coming to England.

Lou and I are informed by Angus that there will be a party at the house this coming Saturday and lo, said prophecy comes to pass. The house is infested with the Rifle Volunteer mob as well as dozens of university students. The blather is unbelievable from the latter. Yakking away nonstop about disarmament, feeding the poor, good old Moscow, property being theft, have you heard the new Yes album, the Shining Path are basically good chaps, and all the rest. Puts a bit of a strain on the old gag-reflex.

The party staggers on till three in the morning, until finally it's just Lou and me slouched on the couch amid the overflowing ashtrays and debris, drinking beer and ruminating on the evening.

All is morgue silent, just the two of us drinking warm beer, quietly criticizing the world and everything in it. We're getting ready to call it a night, when there comes an unearthly wail from upstairs. We freeze, wide-eyed like a pair of amazed Louis Armstrongs. The wail, even louder, happens again, damsel-in-distress style. We've no choice. Up the stairs we must cautiously creep. Bravely, I indicate that Lou should precede me.

After searching the three bedrooms, Lou finds a woman in a closet, curled up in a fetal position and whimpering. It's a damsel, clearly in distress. We coax her out, helping her to her feet. It is a blonde girl whom we know casually from the Rifle. She is obviously plastered and cannot stand without our support. Her nose is drippy and she is blathering incoherently, with the exception of the repeated phrase "fucking prick."

We can't help but notice that she is wearing nothing but a black bra and panties.

"What shall we do with her?" Lou asks over her nodding head.

"We? You found her. What are *you* going to do with her?" I respond kindly, pushing her Lou's way.

"We can't just leave her."

"We again. There *is* no we."

"There is now," says Lou, shoving her back my way. The girl wraps her arms around my neck, looks up at me with glassy eyes, and slurs, "Fucking prick."

"Maybe she needs a hospital," says Lou.

"Oh yeah, right. So we'll wrap her up, walk her to the phone box, call 999, and wait till the bobbies come to pick up a half-naked tart in a blanket with two musicians at four in the morning. That sounds good."

The girl looks over her shoulder at Lou and, as if agreeing with my point, says, "Fucking prick."

"All right, let's put her on the couch. She can sleep it off."

With immense effort we drag her down the stairs, and a few fucking pricks later we have her stretched out on the couch. Lou goes upstairs and comes back with a pillow and two blankets from Ewen's room. He has also found the rest of her clothes, which he folds neatly and leaves on the armchair.

Like a couple of maiden aunties we get her tucked in and quietened down, then we turn the lights off and go into our room. We listen for trouble but, after a few minutes, all is quiet in the living room. Eventually we nod off. When we wake at two that afternoon she is, mercifully, gone.

VII

Stein discovered a club in Redcliffe Gardens, just off the Fulham Road, called the Café des Artistes. Now, we've never been to the sainted, venerated holy ground, the exalted Cavern in Liverpool, but this must be as close as it gets. The Café is a subterranean warren, a catacomb of brick caves with curved ceilings, looking like it once served as a dungeon for warehousing surplus fiends from the Tower.

We are told that right in front of the club is the spot where Tara Browne, the Guinness heir, crashed his car and died in 1966. You know Tara Browne. He blew his mind out in a car. He didn't notice that the lights had changed.

On any night of the week, when the Café is full of punters, the walls run wet with sweat and suds. Bodies heave and grind against one another in a timeless jungle boogie of suggestive smiles, snarls, snaking arms, and thrusting hips. And that's just to get to the bar. It is clammy, stifling, and thrillingly claustrophobic.

To venture down the steps from Redcliffe Gardens and enter the portals where the swarthy sweaty chap takes your rent money is to flirt with the edges of suicide, because if there is an emergency you can forget about ever eventually reemerging into a starry-skied Fulham night. There aren't any other exits. When you're in, you're in. You go through one brick cave and on into another until finally you arrive at the last one, jammed in by the hundreds of mad souls behind you. At the far end of this last room there is a stage eighteen inches above the dance floor. And when it rocks, which is never, it's the place to be. We're here to rock this joint.

On a late afternoon in early November, Stein and I plead and beg and coerce the owner to let us play. He looks at us from behind his desk and sticks a pencil, eraser end, into his ear and twirls it. Then he takes it out, sticks it in his mouth, and chews it for a second or two. He taps the wet pencil on his phone, then, using the eraser to flip the pages of the diary in front of him, purses his lips and sighs. The pages flip back and forth. Stretched out seconds of silence ensue, then for some reason he looks up, says yes, and offers £17 for us to play on the night of December 14, 1972.

The next day, Mal quits.

And as if that isn't bad enough . . . today brings with it the terrible, shocking news that the New York Dolls have beaten us to yet another milestone. Last night their drummer died of a drug overdose.

Stein has been telling me for weeks that what we really need is a death in the band. All the best bands have a death, he says. What is it with these Dolls? They always seem to be one step ahead of us. I'd lose Roger in a heartbeat for this kind of press.

Then again, I suppose it is dour news. Billy Murcia passed out at a party, which isn't unheard of. But then the clueless worst responders threw him in a bathtub and poured coffee down his throat until he drowned. Death by Nescafé. Poor guy.

It's sad when the cute die young.

But anyway, we've got our own problems. Back to the *Melody Maker* we go.

GUITARIST WANTED
Young, great looking
Drunk on scotch and Keith Richards
723-0759 after 5 pm

Call after call; all idiots. We're desperate and still nobody is close to fitting the bill. I'm just about to give up and go leap the Paddington turnstiles to Brit Rail it back to Bushey, when the phone rings one last time.

"Hello."

Pips.

"Ah, hello. I'm calling about the ad in the *Melody Maker*."

I can't believe it. I immediately recognize the voice.

"Are you that Irish guy, from Orange?"

"Are you that tall man?"

I quite seriously can't believe it. The guitarist I've had in the back of my brain all this time, the man from that daft Orange sale in Denmark Street all those moons ago, the Three Musketeers lad. It's him. I've often wondered what happened to him. The more I remembered him, the more perfect a guitarist he became, until he had attained Keith-like status in my imagination. I told Stein about him months ago and once, in a moment of desperation, we were going to stand outside Cricklewood station for a few hours, since that's where I remembered he had said he lived. He is given directions to Bushey.

The next night, I call Mal from the phone box. After much begging and wheedling I convince him to stay for the audition and play the gig at the Café des Artistes—but he has a price. That price, coincidentally, being the entire seventeen quid we are due to get from the gig. I seethe but through gritted teeth I agree.

The audition is in my bedroom, naturally. Duly Eunan arrives (yeah, that's his name; sounds like something a cow would say) and, strewth, it appears d'Artagnan has shaped up. Gone are the mustache and the chin spinach; the barnet is no longer parted in the middle like a bog-trotting Jesus, but is a layered fluffy affair of which even the great Keith himself would be proud.

Other than hello, I don't say a word.

We have a bash at "Down the Road Apiece." Eunan is not bad. But not exactly chicken fried in bacon grease. So much for the fantasy guitar boy I've had in the back of my brain all this time. We've got a tame pup here. This polite stuff makes me retch.

We do some more and it's okay. Just okay. He does look good, though.

Later, Stein and Eunan sit in silence on Brit Rail, traveling back to central London. A few stops down the line Eunan asks if he got the gig. Stein, looking out the window, answers encouragingly: "I don't know."

The next day, Lou and I leap a turnstile or two and meet up with Stein in London Street to discuss the Irish guy. Roger declines the invitation. Over cans of Long Life we debate the pros and cons of this guitarist. Con: he's got a weedy sound. Pro: he looks good. Con: he's got a tame personality. Pro: he looks good.

Ultimately, he gets three thumbs up. Hey, it's our world. And in our world, looks trump licks.

Eunan is a rabid Yardbirds fan with a serious crush on Jeff Beck. Biographical details I learned before I nodded off include the fact that he tore himself away from his mum's Catholic skirts and sailed to London in August 1968 aboard a tramp steamer, along with fifty or so other tramps. He scuffled around like we all do, *Melody Maker* in hand, and went to a hundred unsuccessful auditions per annum since. Finally, Lord be praised, he landed the coveted second guitarist spot with fast-fading popsters Love Affair. Yes, the same Love Affair that inflicted "Everlasting Love" on a suspecting public.

His shining moment with Love Affair was when they played a mid-afternoon show at Holloway Prison for Women. There's a photo of them traipsing in and smiling, huge stone walls behind them, with guitars in hand, wherein Eunan was instructed to avert his gaze and stare at the wall so as to fool their adoring public into thinking he was an original member. There it is, in the *Daily Express*: four grinning dorks, the other one staring at a wall. What a joke.*

And here we are, trying to turn him into a six-stringed storm trooper.

We rehearse the boy, shake him up, slap him into shape, put him through jackboot camp. Slowly, he begins to repay us for our lack of confidence. He works hard to get up to speed, which is good because the Café gig looms.

---

* Eunan Brady, London, 1994

"I met Andrew in Denmark Street, 1971. He was the first man I'd seen wearing makeup in broad daylight. We met again in late '72 when I answered an ad in the *Melody Maker* for a guitarist 'drunk on scotch and Keith Richards.'

Andrew had a mop of dark brown hair like a grown-out George Harrison cut atop a six-foot skinny frame, complete with a Hollywood profile . . . every guitarist's dream of a front man. But hey, he could be a fuckin' pain in the ass. This man had more front than Jayne Mansfield. They had a fully qualified geek on guitar and the bass department was dodgy. I was summoned to the palatial bedroom in Bushey for an audition. It was all a bit tense."

VIII

A Monday night in November, Lou and I are sprawled on the couch, Ewen is sunk into the armchair, and all six of our eyes are glued to *Colditz* on the Beeb. Robert Wagner, David McCallum, huge greatcoats and coarse wool scarves, furtive looks, scheming schemes, trying every week to thwart the dastardly Nazis and get out of this castle prison. The three of us are locked into the plot, hanging on every word, every meaningful glance, every nuance involved in the positioning and repositioning of the Kommandant's monocle.

A knock on the door intrudes upon our evening. And not just a knock, a loud knock. And not three knocks as per the polite norm, but five knocks of ever-increasing force and volume. I am closest and so reluctantly I uncoil myself from the couch and head for the door, never taking my eyes off the TV screen. Before I can traverse the twelve feet or so to the door, the knocking escalates to pounding and doesn't stop at five, but continues to an unheard of eight.

I open the door and a huge hand shoots out and grabs me by the throat, shoving me backward until my head smashes into the wall behind me. Half-a-dozen hulks of men burst through the door behind the hand that is crushing my throat, and following them are a dozen more. Some carry clubs and cricket bats, some have bottles and knives; all are yelling and swearing. They are baying for blood, and it turns out that the blood they are baying for courses through my veins. At least, that which isn't coursing down the wall behind me from the cut on my head.

All is a terrifying, painful blur. A hall lamp smashes to the floor. I am punched in the face and stomach. Thankfully, the foyer is a small, confined space, so the Neanderthals are prevented from getting at me all at once. Only the thugs at the front can effectively get their kicks and punches in. Through the white hurt and terror of the beating I can hear them screaming out things like "fucking bastard" and "fucking poofter" and "kill the fucker." This does not bode well for a peaceful outcome.

Existing, as I momentarily do, in the gouged eye of the storm, one thought occurs clearly. I'm about to be dead. I don't understand why. I don't know who these murderers are, but I bet some of them have tankards with their names on them.

I am choking, can't grab a breath, can't peel this ape's calloused mitt from around my throat, and punches are raining into my ribs. I am kicking out, trying to knee the brutes, but I'm a goner and I know it. And then a bugle sounds, and from a most unexpected source the cavalry arrives.

From nowhere, well, actually from the armchair, a denim dervish intervenes. Yelling and clawing his way into the fray, Ewen, of all the soya-sucking, ban-the-bomb, joss-stick-burning, love-beads-wearing tossers, fights until he has forced his way into this heart of darkness and stands, his back to my chest, between me and the bloodthirsty mob. But this is a Ewen nobody has seen before. He is forceful, dynamic, commanding, and insistent—as steely calm as Clint Eastwood and loud as Mussolini.

"Stop! Everybody, stop it! What's going on?"

The mob yells all at once. Ewen holds up his hands, palms outward. "Stop it. Just stop. What's going on here, in my home?"

Behind him I'm bleeding, gasping for air, and inwardly praying that Ewen stays right where he is for the rest of time. Somewhere in my peripheral, off to the right, I see Lou. He is no longer watching *Colditz*.

The thugs at the front snarl.

"He's a fucking bastard."

"Give us the cunt."

"Fucking poofter."

"Kill the bastard."

Despite the bad press, Ewen continues his inquiry. "What? What's going on? What did Andrew do?"

"He's fucking taken liberties with Julie, that's what he fucking did."

The rest of the choir sing backing vocals to the tune of, "Yeah, the fucking bastard."

"He did what? Andrew, what's going on?" Ewen turns to me and the mob closes in again. He turns right back around. "Get back. We're not going to do this. In fact, get out of this house." The mighty Ewen then pushes the first few of them in the chest and shoves them out through the door. But that's as far as they go. They stay on the front step, swearing and snarling. Ewen then turns his attentions to me. "Andrew, what's this all about? What's this stuff about Julie?"

"Who's Julie?" I splutter through a mouthful of blood.

This sets them off again, and in they surge with their poofters and bastards and knuckles. Ewen again holds them back. I yell, "I don't know who Julie is and I've never taken liberties with anybody in my life. What the hell does that mean, anyway?"

Julie, it turns out, is the leftover tart from the party. Seems that when she sobered up she started telling tales of drunkenness and cruelty, of being taken advantage of when she was smashed, and all these tales star me in a leading role. Me, of all people. Not even me and Lou—just me.

The lovely Julie took her damning testimony straight to that court of fairness and equanimity, where magna hates carta and where all accused are presumed guilty: the Rifle Volunteer. There, a jury of my peers sank a few beers and came looking to lynch.

Ewen listens to my protestations of innocence, and though I'm not sure he believes me he does turn around and order all the engraved mugs to bugger off. They finally do, but not before uttering loud vulgar threats and promises along the lines of, "We're going to fuckin' do you, mate." I believe them.

Ewen locks and bolts the door, sighs, shakes his head, and trudges upstairs with a look on his face that says, in future, considerably more care and attention will be paid when selecting a tenant.

Lou helps clean up the blood. We bandage my head like people inept at bandaging heads then sit around bug-eyed and terrified. That night we lie in bed wide awake, with the amps and PA columns stacked against the door for protection. The next day, Brill comes with the van. We toss our rags into our bags, load the gear, and scarper.

Homeless, nervous, and broke, Lou and I walk the streets of Watford and Bushey. Yonks ago, the highwayman Dick Turpin prowled these very roads, pistols primed and "stand and deliver" ready on his tongue. We are nowhere near as impressive but just as demanding. Come nightfall, we knock on doors and sleep on the floors of people we hardly know: Marquee girls, party girls, friends of friends. We borrow a quid here, a quid there. In shops we distract and pilfer. We stand outside Watford train station and sell our LPs to passersby. Lou is a natural, could have been a barrow boy or a carnival barker. He's got the gift of the gab, convincing commuters that they absolutely must shell out a mere two quid for this barely played *Gasoline Alley*, a paltry fifty pence for this mildly scratched *McCartney*. The only record I won't part with is *Something Else*.

We end up with nearly fifteen pounds. Food, pints, cigs for Lou, chocolates—we're on easy street for a day or so.

One inspired, desperate night, fast running out of quasi-acquaintances, we remember Dick and his toupee and we track them both down to 93 Aldenham Road. From street level, what a dump. The building is four stories high, plonked atop a boarded-up fish 'n' chip shop. Dick not only has a large room on the top floor, but he also has the pleasure of hearing his buzzer go at 10 p.m. one freezing, rainy night.

The unsuspecting man takes us in and we sleep on his floor for a few days, snoozing under blankets until the afternoon. Dick arises early and bustles quietly about, boiling water for tea and brushing his teeth while we toss and turn in our bed on the floor, muttering darkly into our pillows at the disturbance.

While he's away we eat his food, play his records (taking a couple of them for a walk to Watford station), enjoy his libation of choice, Newcastle Brown Ale, and lounge around watching his telly. Curiously, it's not long before Dick starts to get the same look on his face that Ewen had when he went up the stairs that night. Our fabulous new life goes on for five glorious days, until one evening Dick comes home and announces that he has found us a room on the second floor of the building and, in fact, has paid the first week's rent, £6.50. Well, ain't that swell.

We can't very well refuse. Refuse? We have to feign gratitude. I leave that to Lou, he's better at these things. But even Lou is having trouble with this one. The room in question is, frankly, disgusting. Twelve feet square, creeping mold on all four walls and the ceiling, small sink, hotplate, single bed, threadbare rug, garbage, papers, rancid foodstuffs and personal befoulments left by the previous tenants who, judging by this appalling level of squalor and stench, must have been junkies.

The bed is a stained divan with a slab of once-white, now-gray foam for a mattress. The hotplate is covered in a grime layer built up over years and baked-on brown stains. Long-dead insects, roaches prevalent and identifiable, lie encrusted and entombed in the grease like woolly mammoths in ancient tar sands.

Pinned by a red plastic dart to a small wardrobe is a yellowed newspaper clipping featuring a Page 3 girl, nipples accentuated with ballpoint pen. Inside the wardrobe is one bent hanger.

The sink is a putrid swamp, complete with algae and water running brown out of the tap, splashing over smashed dish shards and cigarette butts. The landlord's a fat greaseball.

We move in. Lou gets the divan and I get the gray foam slab. We sleep in an L-formation. The loo is right outside our door and serves the entire building. This proximity is pointed out by Dick as a positive. Think of the convenience. All too soon we can think of little else. Every time one of the other tenants visits the toilet we get to hear every intimate detail. And the more we get to know our fellow tenants, the easier it is to picture them and the worse this proximity becomes.

The day of the Café des Artistes gig. For the first time, there is no piano on site, but the ever-resourceful Stein has clocked this problem and come up with a solution. He has bought an upright piano and a can of red paint. The piano is a fearsome weight and collectively we have a strictly limited amount of muscle. He lives on the third floor. Have you ever lifted an upright piano? Of course you haven't.

Rog, Lou, Brill, and I show up at London Street, and next thing we know we are pressed into lugging this hulking stack of wood, wires, lead, and ivory, tacky with semidry red paint, down three flights of stairs. Thumping, cursing, down we go. Thumpety-thump, curse, times fifty, and repeat as necessary. By the time we arrive at street level we hate pianos and pianists.

Six o'clock at the Café des Artistes. Mal shows up, nervous and no eye contact, accompanied by two hulking Aussie mates. Bondi-Beach boys, preening and flexing, desperate for a Foster's. The three of them stand around in a fugue of bad clothes and worse vowels.

We set up the gear. There's no sign of Eunan. Seven o'clock comes and seven o'clock goes. Still no Irish guy. Eight o'clock, nothing, and we're on at nine for the first of four sets. The owner, the swarthy guy, hovers in the background, puffing a stogie, muttering, second thoughts ricocheting around inside his skull. Still no bog-trotting Strat-man.

Half past eight and the joint starts to fill up. We poke our noses through the curtain of our offstage lair and check 'em out. What's this crowd? What are these types? Never seen them before. The threads don't check out, the hairdos are off the scale, the makeup looks courtesy of a hand grenade tossed into the Max Factory. They're tourists: Americans, Japanese, all sorts. This could be interesting.

Five minutes to showtime and Eunan blasts through the curtain. Where's he been? He has been in jail. Well, of course he has. Just got released an hour ago. Nicked selling women's blouses, stolen of course, down the Portobello Road. Lovely chemise, madam, only a fiver.

Against all odds the gig goes all right. We get some stick from a few Yank louts but that's to be expected. Hardly Wildean wits, any of them, so they're easy to deal with. They get a bit stroppy, though. Not used to getting lip from a man in makeup. The dancers are leaping around six inches in front of my microphone and the place is stifling hot, not absolutely jammed but sweaty and stinking enough.

Then some drunken gyrating bird, undulating frenetically right in front of me, offers her hand, mid-song, as though I should kiss it like I'm some marquis in a French period drama. I'm game for a lark. I take her hand, lean over, and, instead of a peck on a knuckle, I give her fingers the merest lick. She squeals with delight. Well, who wouldn't?

The crowd quite likes it. However, her psycho body-builder boyfriend, whom I failed to notice, does not. He, in fact, takes umbrage, hauls her off, and punches me in the mouth. Curiously enough, that seems to settle the account as far as he's concerned. Lick my chick's hand, I'll sock you one. Then he keeps on dancing.

Okay then. Sounds fair. Fine by me, Mr. Atlas. May I call you Charles? I rub my yap and keep on singing. Something weird is going on, though. One of my front teeth is now sharp and jagged. Bloody hell, he's chipped my tooth.

Eunan turns out to be okay onstage, moving about a bit after I scream in his ear to shake it up baby, twist and pout. He is under-rehearsed and mimes some of the songs but the audience is none the wiser. During the second set he moves upstage to my right, cutting Mal out of the equation. After the first song I introduce the man from Dublin and tell the audience he just got out of jail. They eat it up. All in all, we pull it off.

Two sets later, it's early in the morn, they're escorting the stragglers to the door, and the owner hands over seventeen £1 notes. Better still, he invites us back for December 30, same money. We've never been invited back anywhere before.

Out in the street, we load the gear, including the bloody piano, into the van. The lads wedge themselves in among the equipment, wriggling and squirming like some eels I once knew. I turn around for Showdown at the Redcliffe Corral. Mal stands with his two blond beach bums behind him and sticks his trembling paw out for the seventeen quid. I counter with a short, sharp speech incorporating the words "extortion" and "ransom," and finishing up with a three-word Anglo-Saxon phrase beginning with "so" and ending with "off." I don't cough up one thin shilling.

There is absolute silence then some yapping and baboon-style posturing. I slowly back away and they don't follow, which is a relief because I'm bluffing. I've already been bopped once tonight and I don't need another. I climb in the van and Brillo guns it out toward Brompton Road. Through the window I see the three Aussies still standing in the middle of the street. The biggest kahuna gives me the finger. I just smile. Fair dinkum, buddy.

One day, on a bored wander, we find a huge wooden radio by the side of the road, lug it home, plug it in, and, surprise, it works, bringing in stations from all over Europe. Now we get Kid Jensen, some drip named John Peel, and the rest playing music up and down the luminous green dial. The trouble is, the music coming out of the speaker is insufferable, repetitive rubbish. It seems all we hear is "Superstition" by Stevie Wonder and "You're So Vain" by Carly Simon. We're sick to death of them.

We are always on the scrounge for shillings to put in the meter. If we don't have one we get plunged into the Middle Ages, with no cooker, no radio, and no one-bar electric fire. Every day is a miners' strike for us. We suffer a blackout every couple of hours.

On the morning of Christmas Eve, we awake, freezing and miserable, in coats and scarves. We saw a rat two days ago, big as an armadillo, bored and insolent, too. It sauntered away, didn't run like a normal rodent. Now I peer out the door, looking for the scuttling piece of pestilence. No sign.

Come nightfall, with enough money for one pint each, we walk to a nearby pub where all the denizens are giddy and flushed with Christmas cheer. Glasses around us are raised in toasts; not one is smashed into a face.

All too soon, pints nursed to death and sucking the froth of it all, we must head home. And when we do, when we arrive back at our scurvy slum, hope's lesser graveyard, there are two bags of groceries waiting at our door. And in those bags are Cadbury's chocolate bars, milk, cheddar cheese, bread, eggs, mushrooms, Jaffa Cakes, Tetley tea, instant coffee, Fairy Liquid, Smash, butter, sugar, bacon, mince pies, the lot.

And a note from Brillo, wishing us a very merry Christmas.

Makes you weep.

We play the Café on December 30. It's better than last time, wilder, more confident. The cast—Roger, me, Stein, Lou, and Eunan, in order of appearance—could just be the lineup we've been waiting for. After the last note of the last song of the night, we dive offstage into our dressing hole and hear a strange sound. We've never heard this before. It is the crowd yelling and whistling for an encore. This is a first. However, Stein and I decided the first week we met that the band would never do an encore. It was Stein's idea. He said, "Chuck Berry doesn't do encores." Ergo, neither will we.

It hasn't exactly been much of a problem until now. The other lads stare at us as though we're mad. But we just shake our heads and sit dripping sweat in our little cave behind the curtain, and let the audience yell.

It doesn't last all that long, actually.

I got excited in 1963 when I saw the
Beatles and maybe Helen Shapiro topped.
Later, in 1976 at the 100 Club, the Pistols
were a bit different. But in 1973 there was
nothing quite like the Hollywood Brats
at the Speakeasy.

Ken Mewis
Manager
Hollywood Brats

1973

I

Lou and I stroll the streets of Watford, Hertfordshire, England, United Kingdom, Nowheresville. We have chump change burning holes in our pockets. The window display at the Oxfam shop proves so alluring that we just have to pop in. We flick through the racks and the only thing that grabs our peepers is a couple of dresses. Mine is a silver lamé sheath and Lou's is a brown nylon affair, zip up the back with a modest ruffle around the hem. While we are trying them on and discussing their various merits, the elderly ladies behind the counter are flush-cheeked appalled, fanning themselves with newspapers and applying hankies to foreheads until Lou tells them we are in a band and then just generally swamps them in the warm, damp funk of his charm. Then the old dears are all smiles and helpful suggestions.

Two days later in London Street, a few doors down from Stein's, the band convenes for our first photo session. The photographer is an Italian guy, a hundred years old, with a mustache like a clichéd villain from any old wopera you care to name. He's even called Tony—pardon me, Antonio. Stein found him. So there we pose, late afternoon, cheap chairs, stark-white backdrop.

Roger's in leather, naturally, wearing my rock 'n' roll sweater, naturally. Stein's in white strides, tight top, bangles, fabulous hair. Eunan is in satin, both strides and top, with my red scarf, and a cigarette dangling from his lower lip. Lou and I wear, what else, our new frocks. Lou's brown nylon ensemble is complemented by beat-up jeans and plimsolls. Halfway through I switch to Mr Fish and black cords.

Oh yeah, Stein showed up sans mustache. Must have been his New Year's resolution. He has never looked lovelier.

We are desperate for a place to rehearse. Gone is the church hall, gone is the Railway Hotel club with the Pete Townshend ceiling hole, gone is Suicide University, gone is the Bushey bedroom. We must rehearse, at least semi-acoustically, one amp for guitar and bass, Stein on acoustic guitar, me crooning soft as Perry Como, Lou bashing away on whatever cardboard box is available. Eunan volunteers his place in Canfield Gardens, off the Finchley Road.

The band descends on his cramped bedsit on Monday night, January 8. And we are grateful to Eunan, the new chap, for coming up with this short-term solution to our rehearsal problems. We're so grateful that the first thing we say when we walk through the door—we can't help ourselves—is, "What a dump." First impressions can be so spot-on, don't you think? Always in life, always, judge a book by its cover. You'll never go wrong. Like now. What a tiny, squalid, effluence hole. This place makes our Aldenham Road slum seem positively hip.

After a warm lager we run through a few songs, and then comes a pounding on the door. Proceedings screech to a halt. Eunan cloppety-clops on his heels to the door and opens it. There stands an unkempt, hunched-over dead ringer for Ron Moody as Fagin in *Oliver!*, wearing a gray cardigan that moths apparently find delicious and slippers worn down at heel and perilously thin at toe. I mean perilously. There is imminent danger of a big toe that doesn't even know the word "pedicure" poking through this nasty, threadbare slipper, and that's a sight nobody wants to see. Not here, not now, not when, not then.

His hairy eyebrows stay as high up on his intriguingly bemoled brow as they can go, while he waggles his gnarled forefinger and demands that we keep it quiet or the pointy end of his right slipper will meet Eunan's Irish keister and, *kaboom*, out he'd go from these much-sought-after premises.

Eunan backs off, stammers, then blathers, and finally, his Catholic past reaching out and grabbing him by the raisins, almost genuflects in front of this still-raving twit.

I stand up and walk behind the open door. Lord Cardigan's spittle-flecked harangue shows no signs of abating so, with forefinger extended, I slowly close the door in the landlord's face. In the hall we hear one final snarling sentence then the sound of filthy, worn slippers plodding away over filthy, worn carpet. Then silence. I go nose to nose with Eunan. This is unacceptable. We can't let the world shove us around, elbow us to the sidelines. Come on, man. Rehearsal over.

Lou, Eunan, and I go to see *A Clockwork Orange* in Watford. What a film. And yet, throughout the screening there is a definite undercurrent of something untoward, p'raps a semblance of the old ultraviolence in the cinema itself? I do know this. People come out of the cinema after seeing that film and they're not talking about the subtexts of redemption, rehabilitation, social cohesion, alienation, or any of that malarkey. All they want to do, after seeing *A Clockwork Orange*, is to find somebody weak and vulnerable and beat them to death.

Afterward, the three of us sit in a coffee dive and Lou and I continue our quest to convince Eunan to rehearse the next day, which is a Saturday. Roger will no longer rehearse on weeknights. It probably has something to do with him holding down an actual job. But weekends are okay and so weekends are all we've got. And we have to rehearse. It's our lifeblood.

But Eunan's got some problem with tomorrow. Apparently other Saturdays are fine, but not tomorrow. He won't budge and he won't come up with a decent excuse, either. He mumbles and shrugs, goes all vague and evasive and murmurs into his drink, but he's adamant. I am not amused.

What the hell is he doing tomorrow that is so important?*

The photos are okay: stark, black-and-white. Everybody looks good all wrapped up in rouge.

Whatever the case, it's time to record a demo and get a record deal.

Eunan says he's found a guy with a home studio in Hackney Wick and we can record there for a tenner. We show up at the appointed time, Monday, January 15, with uncharacteristically chipper attitudes and characteristically tatty equipment. Roger pulls up to the curb in his Zephyr in a sour mood, due to the fact that he has had to miss a day's work. I can't ignore the fact that a

---

* Eunan Brady's Diary, January 13, 1973 (Saturday)

"At Praed St. clinic to have warts on my dick cauterized. Hurt like hell afterward. Must keep secret from my general public."

nagging, indefinable something is off-kilter in the Roger part of our equation, and it's been nagging for a bit now. Things are not as they were. I decide the best course of action is to be forthright and ignore it.

The studio is in a dark flat on the second floor of a large, rundown Victorian stack of bricks and timber-rot on a non-salubrious though leafy side street. It is pure hippy haven: general filth, of course; joss sticks and ashy bits of joss sticks everywhere; scarves with burn holes draped over lamps with red lightbulbs; huge four-cigarette-paper joints being smoked at 11 a.m.

There is also a hippy domestic scene going on, which, among other things, means two snotty little piglets in rancid, saggy nappies are crawling around the beanbags and milk crates like postapocalyptic floor creatures. The "studio" owner is Alvin and his "old lady" is Grizelda. Grizelda, whose twin-curtain hairdo is strapped to her skull with a tooled-leather headband, sports embroidered loon pants and a distastefully diaphanous flared-sleeve top. She welcomes us as though we are the living embodiment of polio.

So yeah, let's record our first music here. Very rock 'n' roll. Ta, Eunan.

Stein and I have written together every few days since the moment we met. We concoct ideas in our individual noggins, his while selling Union Jack paperweights in Paddington, mine while wrapped in a blanket on Aldenham Road, then we collide, when Sonja's out, at 17 London Street. Not one of our songs can we envisage ever being in the polluted, insipid charts or on the telly or anywhere else, for that matter. Still.

We haven't got the slightest clue what to do in a studio. We're at the mercy of Alvin, head hippy, engineer, and would-be producer. We cram into what must once have been a bedroom—purple walls, splintered wooden floor, egg cartons over the window. Lou sets up his drums, Stein has a wee electronic keyboard at his disposal, Roger and Eunan are cozy in a corner. Me? I'm in the kitchen, of course, hooked up with wires and headphones next to a greasy stove. I can't see the boys. What I can see is a sink full of crusty crockery, penicillin on every dish. I've never been apart from the lads before. What about my hand signals, my instructions, my general sniping and barking that they have come to so love and depend upon?

As it turns out, our initial stabs at recording in this manner are inept. Take after take we deem timid rubbish.

Stein, Lou, and I stop the world, we have to get off, get our bearings, get a Long Life. We have a chat. Against Alvin's "expert" advice we move me from the greasy stove into the tiny room with the rest of the band. Alvin bleats about microphone "bleed" and "leakage" and other stoned, "hey man" type problems, but we are adamant.

The difference is immediate. Yes, it's messy and noisy, but it sounds like what we want it to sound like. It is raw and exciting. This is bedroom rock and if there is one thing we know it's how to rock in a bedroom. We can do this blindfolded.

Alvin is going nuts, tugging and braiding his beard feverishly. He quite obviously hates what he hears, but he doesn't know what to do about it. Through his food-infested face hair he imparts ever-decreasing instruction. Grizelda, with her grim face, split ends, and massive-aggressive mutterings, infests the proceedings like an odoriferous vapor. Her *modus operandi* is to storm in, hiss in Alvin's lughole, and stomp off in a fury. Repeat as necessary. Can't she just stomp off for a long walk? Can't she stuff her smelly little kids in a sack and drag them along with her?

We lay down "Melinda Lee" and "Son of the Wizard."

Tuesday, and after a veritable athletics meeting of leaped turnstiles, coupled with Lou's charm with London Underground ticket takers, we are back in Le Studio Alvin. Roger is even less amused than yesterday. The way I see it, Boosey & Hawkes will just have to struggle on without him for another day. One fewer section of one fewer saxophone will roll down the assembly line because Roger Cooper is here in Hackney Wick, laying down the definitive bass track for "Southern Belles." So what?

Alvin doesn't look as though he has had the most relaxing sleep of his life.

We bash out "Southern Belles" in a couple of takes. Stein and I are taking over more and more, relegating a sulky Alvin to knob-twirler and tea-maker. I keep a wary eye on the tea process in case he decides to gob in mine. Grizelda is in an even fouler mood today. She opens the door in the middle of a take and sticks her nose in, the pint of patchouli oil she evidently poured down her knickers this morning barely overpowering the nostril assault of her personal body-funk.

Later, on the way to the loo, she traps me in the hallway and tells me, apropos of nothing, that I'm not half as good as I think I am. I refuse to be drawn in by this psycho, but as I squeeze by she adds that our music is, in her charming phrase, "fucking shit, man." She reminds me of a young, tie-dyed, and slightly less attractive Gertrude Stein.

Day three at Alvin's House of Horrors. We overdub some guitar on all three tracks. Alvin is baffled by the technology required to do this. He swears, he plugs and replugs, he rolls tape, rolls joints, swears some more, and rewires a mysterious black metal box. The original track and the new guitar track are miles out of sync. Take after take, Alvin adjusts and swears until the two tracks begin to sound less like an echo and get closer and closer to syncing up. Finally, he manages to bring the original recording and Eunan's overdubbed guitar within a split second of each other. He is about to make the last required sync adjustment when Stein and I, who have been staring at each other since the last playback, yell at him not to touch a thing.

That music, with its weird out-of-sync guitar track, sounds amazing. It sounds like that razor-chainsaw guitar concept we've had in our heads all these months but have been unable to throttle out of the guitar boys. Until now. This is the eureka moment. We get Eunan to lay down another track without hearing the first ones and, given his, shall we say, *unique* sense of timing, this one is ever so slightly out of sync with the previous two.

The effect is remarkable. It sounds like a raw, undisciplined guitar section.

Meanwhile, the lovely and enticing Grizelda can be heard in various other parts of the "studio" rattling pans and slamming doors. She is drunk on homemade nettle wine that she swigs from a succession of beer bottles. As we pack up she walks in to tell us to never, ever come to her house again, smashing a beer bottle into the wall behind us for an emphasis that is frankly unnecessary.

Eunan hands a ten-quid note to Alvin and the poor, stoned, bearded sod almost gets to pocket the dosh, but the missus snatches it and sticks it down the front of her stained purple smock, where it is completely safe.

Got the tape. We are out of there.

Down on the street, and out of the blue Eunan flips out about Stein and me taking the tapes. Seems he was under the impression he'd be waltzing off with the goods. He claims he paid the ten quid so the tapes should be his.

Lunacy. You daft sprite, sod off and sober up. Later that night he calls Stein and says he's quitting the band.

Next day, we all meet to talk to Eunan. I don't say much because I'm afraid I'll end up throttling the bastard.

Afterward, when everything is soft and cozy again, we join hands in a prayer circle then have a pajama party with hot chocolate and a pillow fight.

II

Chris Andrews wants to meet us.

Stein had seen an ad in, where else, the *Melody Maker*. The gist is that a new company, started by Chris Andrews, invites bands to send in tapes. We've now got a tape. So we did.

I hadn't the faintest who the guy was, but Stein educated me. He is, apparently, a sixties popster who had a couple of hits, the biggest of which was "Yesterday Man." I never heard any of that, but when Stein mentioned that the man also wrote "Girl Don't Come" by Sandie Shaw, I got the picture. I love that song.

We put the tape, one of Antonio's black-and-white photos, a paragraph or two by yours truly, and Stein's phone number into an envelope and stuffed it into a postbox in Paddington.

A few days later Stein tells me that Chris Andrews called, saying he wants to meet us. At an office near Oxford Circus we are introduced to the man himself and his sidekick Colin. Chris invites us to sit on the sofa while he settles back in his chair behind a kidney-shaped desk. He reaches into a small wooden box and takes out a cigar. For some reason, he holds it up to his ear, as though he feels the cigar wants to tell him something. That something turns out to be "please chop my end off." So Chris sticks the cigar into a miniature guillotine on his desktop, pulls a tiny lever, and down comes the blade—*thwock*. Chris then picks up a piece of marble the size of a curling stone that turns out to be a lighter. Three minutes of sucking, blowing, coughing, and lighter-clicking follow, until finally the thing is smoldering away nicely.

Chris coughs, looks at me, and says, "Cohiba."

I have no idea what this means so I reply, "Likewise."

Chris looks puzzled. "No, Cohiba. This is a Cohiba cigar."

"You don't say," I say.

"Yep, Cohiba. They're made exclusively for Castro. You can't buy them."

"No kidding." Jeez. Just what I need, a cigar tutorial.

"Yep. I get them in Geneva, from a diplomat."

Too bored to come up with a platitude, I let his sentence hang uncomfortably in the air.

Chris blows a cloud of smoke at the ceiling and leans forward.

"The point I'm making is that I recognize quality when I see it, or in this case smoke it. And I pounce. I want it, I get it. See that bin?"

He indicates a plastic rubbish bin filled to the brim with cassettes and reel-to-reel tapes.

"We've got two more just like it. And Colin here has had the dubious pleasure of listening to every one of those tapes. Right, Colin?"

Colin looks up, bleary-eyed, like a basset hound with the flu. "Right."

"And what did you think, Colin? What was your professional opinion about all those tapes?"

"That a rubbish bin is exactly where they belong."

Chuckles all around. Chris continues.

"There was, however, one exception to that verdict, and Colin immediately brought it to my attention. Your tape, lads, it was your tape. It is raw and, if you'll pardon my candor, terribly recorded, but I don't mind telling you it's the best sound we've heard in . . . what . . . years, Col?"

"Yeah, years."

"So, what I'd like to do is set up a rehearsal, have a look and a listen, then get you in a studio and lay down some tracks as soon as possible." He looks at me. "What do you say?"

I shrug and say, "Cohiba."

Within days we rehearse in an actual rehearsal studio on the King's Road, deep in the heart of Chelsea, courtesy of our new manager, Chris Andrews. This is a long way from a bedroom. We've got space, we've got volume, we've got carpet, and we've got a snack bar that sells cans of lager. Chris shows up to listen for a bit, leaning on a wall, hands deep in the pockets of an expensive-looking overcoat, head nodding. Then he hands us £30 and leaves. Coincidentally, seconds later, we wrap it up and take the thirty quid for a walk.

To the Chelsea Potter.

Days later, a telegram arrives at our slum with an urgent message: "Please contact Chris Andrews at 01-202-9601 immediately very urgent studio booked today."

Chris has us booked into Gooseberry Studios in Chinatown. Somehow, mostly thanks to a dedicated and insistent telegram guy, we make it almost on time. We show up excited, looking sharp and trying to act as though we are to the manner born. This place is so fab it's hard not to drool: beautiful carpets, huge speakers, boom mics and baffles, fabric on the walls and ceilings, mixing desk all the way from here to there. Shangri-la-la land.

Chris Andrews is the producer, the studio owner is the engineer. The first time I put on the headphones and move up close to the microphone—gadzooks!—my every breath, sigh, and swallow in echoing stereo all through my skull.

We record "Melinda Lee" and two new ones, "Nightmare" (lyrics finished on the train on the way in) and "Oh What a Show." Chris and the engineer keep trying to tame it down, eradicating squeaks and squeals, telling us it will be all right in the mix. All right is not what we're going for. The guitar sound is too clean and the vocals don't have enough attack. Throughout the afternoon we find ways to sabotage the saccharine, and by the evening the two rock tracks grind to a compromise conclusion. It's not what I'm going for, though, and I can see Stein feels the same. Take away our edge and we are dull boys.

"Oh What a Show" is a new song, acoustic, that I composed after reading a book on the French Revolution. This is also the first song we've written on which Stein has contributed some of the lyrics. The lad has come up with the chorus.

Oh what a show it's going to be
Oh what a show for you and me

I play a twelve-string acoustic I found in the corner of the studio, Stein is on the Steinway, Lou and Roger come in for the last chorus, and Eunan escorts us out on the fade with an ethereal guitar piece. Not bad. Bit of a departure, but interesting nonetheless. Chris likes all three tracks.

Next day, we're back for the mix and a photo shoot. Chris has lined up Clive McLean, the lensman famous for taking shots of naked babes for *Mayfair* magazine. So he's our hero. He's also famous for his *Mayfair* model wife, Stephanie, who isn't shy about getting her kit off. And for that we are extremely grateful as she comes equipped with quite an eye-popping set of headlights.

While we pose and preen in the studio, lipstick, mascara, and eyeliner slathered on, Chris handles the mix in the control room, tweaking this and adding a touch of reverb to that. Roger shows up with some sort of nasty virus that makes him look like an aggrieved bloodhound for the photo shoot. Not a terrible look. He bids us adieu right afterward.

The tape sounds good, competent, professional; it just doesn't sound like us, that's the problem. We like that three-guitar-track, slightly out-of-sync sound that we got at Alvin's. But what do we know? If this gets us a record contract we'll be driving around trying to find a parking spot on easy street. Chris must know what he's doing.

At the end of the session he says he's going to Germany in a couple of days to speak to Polydor, the record company he feels will be the best for us. As we head out into the frigid night he hands us £30. I wonder where he comes up with that figure.

It's great having a manager.

III

Once upon a time the ground floor of our non-beloved slum at 73 Aldenham Road in Bushey was a fish 'n' chip emporium, but now it is long defunct, closed to the public, filthy and cobwebbed. You peer in at street level through the plate-glass windows and see the counter, the chairs and tables, the deep fryer, and all the other fishy-soise covered in dust.

Sometime on Thursday morning the phone in the shop, never before heard, begins ringing and does not stop. It rings and rings, hour upon hour, the harsh *brranng* from the black British Telecom phone piercing the flimsy walls and driving us—all of us, as we come to find out—bonkers. It's tolerable in the daytime when you're busy making tea, toddling along, and listening to Little Jimmy Osmond or some such rot, on your roadkill radio, but at night, lying in bed, there it is, like Chinese water torture, drilling into your psyche, ring after ring. You wrap your noggin in a sweater, in a coat. Still the monumentally annoying ring gets through. We are on the second floor, but even Dick, when we see him, hurrying by so as not to be buttonholed for a loan of a quid or two, says that up on the third floor the incessant ring has him baggy-eyed and haggard when he rolls out of bed. That's a long way up for the sound of a phone to drive you nuts.

Saturday night, Lou and I put on coats, wrap up throats, and leave our doss house for the evening. Off to the pub with what remains of Chris Andrews's thirty nicker. Thirty divided by four (well, Roger went home, remember, so he disqualified himself) is not bad, so there are some pints to be had.

At the pub we meet a doe-eyed lass who is in possession of three tabs of LSD. Generally, I disapprove of lysergic acid diethylamide—not for any moral reason, but for its unsavory association with American hippies. No human being, and certainly no American, has ever been filmed dancing well or sexily while on acid. They all do that closed-eyes, flailing-arms, beatific-smile, snake-like body-heave, which makes you want to enjoy the laugh for a few minutes and then punch them in the mouth.

And I've never bought into that leaping-off-a-tall-building-while-thinking-you-can-fly rubbish. I'm all for those who do it, though. I heartily approve of culling the daft. Still, this pub bunny has these three tabs of acid. So down the hatch times three. It's a lark, and larks are in short supply in England these days.

Let me tell you, after half an hour the interior of an English pub is quite a sight when you're on hallucinogenics.

Lou and I arrive back home, happy as the Who's Jack, near midnight, and there in the hall stands the hippy mum from the ground-floor hovel, crying babe in arms, complaining that she hasn't slept in two days because of the phone. We've never met her before but we "aw, tut-tut," squeeze past her, and go up the stairs to our doss-hole.

Two hours later, brains truly stimulated and freakishly inspired, we decide to relieve our fellow slum-dweller's agony by breaking into the fish 'n' chip shop and disconnecting that damned phone. It is an excellent plan, well thought out, relying upon darkness of night, stealth, and Lou's undeniable talent for lock-picking.

Three o'clock on a deathly freezing night, under a bright streetlamp (there goes the "darkness of night"), I stand, laughing hysterically (there goes the "stealth"), while Lou works on his knees with a variety of specialized tools (a bit of wire, a fork, and the handle of a broken spoon) to pick the lock on the door of the fish 'n' chip shop. Inside we hear the relentless *brang, brang, brang* of the phone.

Lou succeeds, never a doubt, and the door swings open with a long, monster-movie-type creak, rapidly picking up speed and smashing into a metal display stand, which in turn topples over and crashes to the tiled floor with a sound like a particularly bad gong in a particularly bad Emerson, Lake & Palmer opus.

We dash in, closing the door behind us. What a caper. Went off without a hitch. We're master crims. Just at the moment, though, we are on our knees, busting a gut, cheeks puffed out trying to muffle the merriment, looking like imbeciles. Eventually, after a minute or so, this passes and we get to our feet. I walk to the ringing phone behind the counter and pick up the receiver. "Hello?" At the other end there is a click and then the dial tone. Then a blessed silence.

To us this is unbearably hilarious, and we fall back down on our knees on the dusty floor like Southern snake-handling Baptists with a sense of humor. Finally, in an orchestration of gasps, chokes, and mighty sighs, we stifle the chuckles, stand up, and head for the door. On the way, Lou spies an array of dust-covered bottles of Coca-Cola on the counter, and after inspection puts three of them in his pockets. We give a quick shifty peek outside for Dixon of Dock Green and then exit the grime scene. Lou locks up, and Robert's your mum's brother.

Back in our room, our upstairs progress unimpeded by weeping, grateful, back-slapping, flower-tossing tenants, we relax and laugh, safe in the knowledge that we've done our bit for our immediate fellow man. A couple of veritable Abou Ben Adhems. May our tribe increase.

The acid and pints of bitter, coupled with our cunning caper, take their inevitable toll and finally, near dawn and with no further option, we lay down our weary noggins. Lou and I bid each other bonsoir and succumb immediately to the lure of the land of Nod, where sleepy, not to mention heroic, musicians intend to remain comfy and comatose until the very late hours of the following afternoon. Peace and the silky darkness of deep slumber descend upon our squalid little world.

For twenty-two minutes.

The long arm of the law is sometimes replaced by the long leg, at the end of which is a big, shiny, black boot. And that is exactly what smashes through our door shortly after bedtime. Four coppers rouse us out of bed with maximum yelling, swearing, and kicking. We stand shivering in our underwear, bewildered, scared, and blasted out of our minds. (Note to all would-be psychedelic tripsters out there: I do not recommend you make this part of your trip, man.) They ask a dozen questions at once. Out of the corner of my mouth I tell Lou not to say anything, which earns me a hand around my throat and my head bashed into a wall. This is getting to be a habit.

We are told to dress and then we are marched out and down the hall. There stand three more boys in blue. We are haggard as Merle, half-dressed, shoelaces undone. Down the stairs, we are shoved into a police van then away through the night to the station, where we each get a cell to ourselves.

I sit there, wide-eyed and whacked, with a brand-new lump on the back of my head. Through the bars of my cell I spot myself in a metal mirror on the door of a locker across the room. "Woebegone" springs to mind. My eyes, ringed and streaked with two days' worth of smeared mascara, peer out from a cadaver-pale face. I am wearing black corduroy trousers, ballet slippers, and a black overcoat. It is cold and I am apprehensive, to say the least. Where's Spider Murphy when you need him? I jump every time I hear bangs and clangs, but otherwise I am left alone to read the graffiti scratched into the walls.

It's not very witty.

This lasts for almost an hour. A copper comes, and with some severe key jangling he unlocks the cell and orders me out and into another room, where another officer sits behind a desk with a pen and a form in front of him. He looks me up, down, and back up again, as though I am something steamy and earth-toned that he has just stepped in.

"What on earth do we have here, then?"

In a rush to state my case, I begin to answer, "I'm Andrew Mathe—" but he cuts me off.

"It was a rhetorical question, if you take my meaning." He clicks his ballpoint pen.

In a rush to state my familiarity with rhetoric, I begin to answer, "Yes, I know what rhetorical—" but he cuts me off again.

"Listen, sonny. It's late and I'm fed the fuck up so shut it. I am here to take a detailed list of such personal possessions as you may have on your person and then dispossess you of them. Once detailed on the piece of paper in front of me, you can rest assured that you may reclaim said items at the conclusion of this— which I suspect must be an extremely upsetting, though no doubt common, experience in your shabby little life. Is that clear, sunshine?"

I decide the word yes is my best recourse. "Yes."

"Right then, empty your pockets. Give me your wallet, your keys, the lot."

I reach into my overcoat pockets, fumble around, pull out the only items in there, and place them on the desk in front of the officer. He looks at them for more seconds than is strictly necessary and then looks up at me. "You cannot be fucking serious."

I nod and realize immediately that nodding is a mistake. He snaps to attention.

"What's that? Are you tired, my son? Are you nodding off? Are you falling asleep? I ask you a question and you fucking doze off. Is that it?"

I stammer a defense and an apology and an answer to the original question. "Sorry, sorry. Yes, I'm serious, that's all I've got in my pockets."

His chair scrapes, loud in the concrete room. He stands up.

"Do you have a nervous condition, a medical fucking malady that causes your head to bob up and down like a fucking bird? Do you?"

"No, no, no."

"Then why is your head bobbing up and down like a nancy boy in a cubicle in Piccafuckingdilly Circus? Eh?"

"I'm sorry. That's all I have in my pockets. Look." I pull out the pocket linings.

"Because if you like bobbing your head up and down in cubicles, I can arrange it so that you are handcuffed and locked in the most rancid cubicle in the British Isles. Would you like that, Sonny Jim?"

"No, no, I wouldn't. It's just that I was trying—" But he cuts me off again and comes around his desk to stand over me, hands behind his back, verbals on full blast.

"No, no, indeed. I concur. You would not like it and shall I tell you why you would not like it?" I wonder if this is rhetoric as well and so I just stare in terrified fashion at the wall. The question turns out not to be in the least bit rhetorical. He bellows, "I'll repeat myself, cloth ears. Shall I tell you why you would not like it?"

"Yeah. Yes, please." Yeah, officer, please tell me why I would not like being handcuffed in a police station toilet at five o'clock in the morning while smacked out on acid.

"I will tell you why. Because that is the cubicle assigned to two fucking Arabs we've got locked up here and they won't shit or piss in them. Why will they not shit or piss in them?"

I am beyond any answer. I try, "I don't know. Why won't they?"

"Because, according to them, their bum 'oles and willies would face Mecca if they did. So what do they do? What alternative do our Bedouin guests come up with, Sonny Jim?"

"I don't know? Hold it in?"

"Hold it in? Hold it fucking in? I'll tell you what they do, my curious friend. They turn around in that tiny cubicle and they do their filthy business anywhere but the toilet. Can you fucking believe that?"

Actually, I can't. And no, I do not want to be handcuffed in that cubicle for nodding my head. I make this known. The officer finally goes back and sits down at his desk. I am a bag of nerves, shivering and shaking. He reclicks his ballpoint pen. "So, I am led to believe that you only have on your person these two items. Is that correct?"

"Yes."

"I will describe the items out loud so that there can be no future dispute as to the descriptions thereof. Is that clear?"

"Yes."

"Right, then. First item: one coin of the realm, a two-pence piece. Correct?" He looks at me over glasses perched on the end of his nose. I concede to my current and foreseeable penury.

"Yes."

He examines the second item, reading the tiny words. In a voice dripping with disdain, he continues. "Second item: one tube lipstick, Cherry Blaze—Outdoor Girl. Correct?"

"Yes."

"You disgust me."

"Yes," is all I can think of.

The constabulary, in their zeal to maintain law and order for the citizenry of Hertfordshire, try to get Lou to turn, suggesting that I am the evil influence in our duo of criminality. To his credit he does not grass, does not even utter a discouraging word. Curiously, I am not offered a similar route out of our current troubles. They must truly think I am the criminal mastermind.

After our grilling we are charged with breaking and entering, and also with "permanently depriving" our slumlord of something or other. We are told that we will have our day in court. Then we are escorted to our cells by wisecracking coppers clearly enjoying this break from their regular Sunday-morning hose-down-the-drunks, mop-up-the-puke routine.

Though my brain is in the grip of acid, beer, and police-induced terror, the ridiculous thought occurs to me that I might actually have some rights, and with all the courage I can muster, which ain't much, I ask to make a phone call. Surprisingly, this works, and I am led into a room with a phone where the two officers step back while I dial the number. Carole answers and I ask to speak to Brillo. He is having a Sunday-morning lie-in after a long, hard week at the factory and is naturally thrilled to hear from me. I explain the situation, getting increasingly hysterical and babbling details incoherently, until one of the coppers steps up and, with the press of a thick forefinger, disconnects the phone.

In my cell I think about the past few hours. Somebody grassed, that's for sure. We got out of the chippy clean. The bobbies were there within a couple of hours. Ah, well. I wonder if the LSD, coursing through vein and brain, will let me get up to the roof of this building, jump off, and fly away.

Two hours later we are informed that Brillo is in the cop shop and has bailed us out. After I retrieve my two pence and lipstick, he takes us to Bradshaw Road, where Carole kindly forgets past grievances and feeds us a delicious Sunday roast with Yorkshire pudding.

Chris Andrews calls Stein and me into the office for a meeting. Stein reports a hint of excitement and a splash of pride in Chris's voice on the phone. Dare we dare to think positively? By the time we reach the office we are bubbling with optimism and have to get a grip on ourselves before we go in. We fight to maintain our cool as we go up the stairs.

Off to the side of the room we can see a small round table on which stands a dark green bottle of bubbly, cork unpopped, on ice, with a snowy-white cloth draped just so over the neck. The Norwegian and I sit on the couch. Sidekick Colin reclines in a leather chair, smoking a cigar. Chris leans back at his desk, hands clasped behind his head. His hair is an immaculate conception: part helmet, part Tony Blackburn wig, all natural.

He has a look wrapped around his mug like the cat that just ordered a canary sandwich. He says he's got good news. We're all ears.

Chris Andrews, "Yesterday Man" incarnate, tells us that on hearing our demo tape Polydor Records have offered us a deal: two singles and an LP, option for more, first single to be recorded immediately, album to follow. Cash advance of £2,000 in an envelope on Chris's desk as we speak.

Stein and I look at Chris. Then we look at each other. Then we look down at the mad swirls in the Persian rug on the floor. Silence reigns. A clock tick-tocks. Somewhere either a tap drips or a dog drools into a saucepan. The ice in the bucket holding the champagne shifts with a soft, wet crunch. The pause is pregnant. The delivery Caesarian.

Stein and I, by mutual unspoken consent, turn down the offer. Audible clops as jaws hit floor. Colin chokes on the stogie, splutters and coughs and coughs some more. Sentences follow, all high-pitched and beginning with the word "But."

"But I've got you a record deal."

"Yeah . . ."

"But it's with one of the biggest labels in the world."

"Um hmmn."

"But that's what you wanted, right?"

I stare at the ceiling. I've never noticed the ceiling before. The plaster is cracked—in three places. One crack must be twelve feet long, and I'm not a cartographer but it looks remarkably like the Amazon. Chris should do something about his ceiling. Instead, he spends time letting us know how aghast he is at our negative reaction to his German coup.

"You contacted me. You wanted a record deal. We recorded a demo. Two weeks later you've got a record deal. What could possibly be the problem?"

I yank my gaze from the ceiling. "Well, it's just . . ." I trail off, hoping for help from Stein, or God, or somebody.

"It's just what? Please tell me."

"It's just a little, well, on the chintzy side, isn't it? I mean, two grand?" I hold my palms out and shrug as though a fabulously wealthy potentate such as myself couldn't possibly entertain an offer as measly as this.

Chris splutters, there's no other word for it.

"But . . . but . . . but Polydor are committing. Committing to this record, committing to a serious marketing campaign. And we can record a single next week, or forget next week, three days from now. Say, 'Nightmare,' get some action on it, and then reshape the deal to anything we want. Renegotiate from strength."

I consider this "committing" business. "Yeah . . . but the fact is, we hate the demo. And if Polydor are expecting more along the same tame lines then they'll ultimately pull the plug anyway. Catch my drift?"

I stare back up at the Amazon, the longest ceiling crack in the world. Chris Andrews is drop-jawed and shaking his head in a parody of incomprehension. Finally, he croaks, "So go in the studio next week and cut what you want, and meanwhile take the £2,000 in that envelope right there. Colin, show them . . ."

Colin reaches across the desk, opens the envelope, half withdraws the notes, licks his thumb, and, with said damp opposable digit, fans the wad of bills in what I'm sure is meant to be an irresistible flutter of enticement.

Chris continues. "That is yours right now, to walk out of here and do with what you will. Call it a bonus, a perk—call it whatever you want."

I look at Stein, who says, finally, "Two grand? That's it?"

Chris opens and closes his mouth like a recently beached carp then says, "Didn't you tell me you live in a slum?"

We just don't like the offer. We think it's too cheap. We don't like the music, either. We want to rerecord. And who is on Polydor, anyway? Nobody we know. The ensuing discussion goes nowhere fast and soon after we are heading down the stairs.

The bubbly stays in the bucket. The envelope stuffed with the two grand stays on the desk.

There is no £30 pressed into our palms this time.

That night we play the Pied Bull in Islington. Not for the faint of heart. They don't like us; we don't like them. My ensemble includes a boa for the first time. It is not well received. Menace and threats all night long. We daren't go to the bar for a drink. They'd kill us. As it is, we barely get out of there with our teeth intact.

All this for a couple of quid each and a chance to shove a red piano up three flights of stairs.

Slade, it turns out, were on Polydor, and they turned out to be rubbish. After the promise of "Get Down and Get With It," the bovver boots and braces, the ersatz aggro, they've gone all safe and comedic. Now it's cheery pop with bad spelling, worse boots, mirrored capes, and bucktoothed smiles all around. A complete joke.

When Chris Andrews finally decides to speak to us again he says he will take our tape to the top record companies in London. When we finally decide to talk to him again we say great, get cracking.

On day one of his quest he calls Stein with the news that we have to change our name. There is already a band gamboling around town with the name of Queen. Not only that, but they have a record deal and are, in fact, in the studio recording their first album. Another band called Queen? I find this frankly astounding. It is a daft name, after all. And these guys aren't even using the definite article? They are simply "Queen"?

Well, this is no heartache for me. The name has long since lost whatever allure it once held. The joke just wore too thin. Perhaps not officially, but in my head, Lou's as well, we are the Brats. We just need to stick on a locale. I'm on the case. I'll figure it out.

A week later, with us on tenterhooks the entire time, Chris Andrews has presented our tape to everyone who is anyone in the London music biz. In the publishing and recording scenes he strides forth, bringing all his gold-plated connections to bear. His bum cheeks sunk into soft sofas, he meets with the movers and the shakers in plush offices and on the top floors of ornate buildings. These are the men with the power to make the decisions, flourish the fountain pens, and write the fat checks.

Every record company and every publishing company listen with their famous slavering greed to the forefront, their waxed ears cocked and eager to hear what gem their old chum has brought in. They listen, their smiles disappear within seconds, they shake their heads, they turn him down flat. Old colleagues question his sanity. He uses up favors owed. Secretaries who love him and think he's cute lower their eyes in embarrassment. In the hallways, tea ladies snicker as he slinks by. His reputation takes a bashing. Nothing compared to ours, of course.

But hey, what about that Polydor offer from ten days ago? Oh yeah, Polydor tell us to buzz off and never darken their porticos again.

Yet another postmortem meeting at Stein's place. The stench of failure hangs in the air—or maybe it's Lou's socks. There's no denying it, though:

everybody thinks we are rubbish. Record companies, publishers . . . every one of them, apparently. This is one sour night in London Street.

I'm in a dark, murderous mood, while Stein is thoughtful, working on the next move. Roger is disengaged, almost in a sulk. He was once the driving force but he has definitely moved away from the steering wheel. Lou and Eunan are larking about like a couple of chimps. The overriding question: What do we do now?

Stein and I find a quiet moment and put our heads together. We have both noticed that the gleam of excitement and interest has perceptibly dimmed in the eyes of Chris Andrews. He is certainly not doing a Brian Epstein and persevering against the cold indifference of an antiquated industry. He is not making a stand, making a point, dragging his saber across the sand. And he's certainly not doing what the best manager of all time, the great Andrew Loog Oldham, would do, which is something outrageous and unpredictable.

What's it been, anyway? A month? A month since Chris heard the tape we recorded at Alvin's hippy asylum? A tape, by the way, that I mightily prefer to the sanitized tripe we recorded at Gooseberry. But a mere month in, and the guy is in defeatist mode? Where's the commitment?

Where are the swinging balls?

We're fed up with the name the Queen but keep it a further month or two, purely because Chris Andrews says that it is annoying the four idiots who just recently signed a jealousy-inducing deal with EMI.

One night, Stein and I are leaning on the bar at the Marquee, drowning sorrows, drinking doubles, and sneering at the band onstage, when up walks a guy with hair like black straw and teeth like a particularly alluring camel. He fronts up. He starts yapping a mile a minute, waving his arms, exhorting us to relinquish the name Queen. Says his name is Freddie. "What, like Freddie and the Dreamers?" I ask. "You don't look like Freddie at all. Where are your specs? Do the Freddie and prove it."

Freddie drones on and sticks a finger in my chest once too often, which is once. Since I don't want Stein throwing a punch (we need those fingers for keyboards) my knuckles are designated to meet this twit's lethally protuberant gnashers at high velocity and full clench. *Kapow!*

He goes down like a sack of spuds, rolling around on the Marquee floor, dripping the red stuff and squealing like a stuck pig. Meanwhile, I'm holding my hand and trying not to say, "Yeeeowch!"

Oily Jack is not impressed.

We don't care. Keep the name Queen. You can have it. We've got our name teed up, and it's the Hollywood Brats. Hollywood. It came to me, the word we've been looking for to accompany Brats, as I was walking home from Watford singing "Celluloid Heroes" by the Kinks. When it got to the part "You can see all the stars as you walk along Hollywood Boulevard," that was it. The Hollywood Brats. It's got a dash of louche decadence to it. The rest of the lads approve.

IV

Is a cup of tea too much to ask for? Of course it is. Our remaining two tea bags were used and used again last evening. Then, after they lay tossed and discarded in the sink for six hours, Lou fished them out, eviscerated them, spread the damp leaves on a tin plate, and toasted them in the stove. Then he rolled them up in cigarette paper and smoked them.

He's a serious smoker, our Lou. He collects butts discarded on the street and on the floor of the Tube, brings the stash home, and painstakingly, on an LP cover, dissects them and creates his own blend. These are dispiriting times.

Sipping a cup of Tizer, I remember that I have arranged to call Stein at 2 p.m., and it's ten to. All clothes are rummaged through until 2p is located in Lou's jeans. I lean over him, pull the curtain aside, and peek out the window.

Rubble-strewn backyard, worn pitted brick walls, broken glass glistening in the gray drizzle. The fence, the crates of Tizer, a stained mattress only marginally grottier than the ones we sleep on, springs sprung, sprouted matting. A grim, freezing prospect, this walk up to the phone box.

I wrap myself up as warmly as possible and open the door with all necessary force to alert any loitering pestilence. No rat. I clump down the hall and stairs. Still no rat. Small mercies.

Out the door and through the debris-blighted yard, kicking a tin can in a beautiful arc. Small victories. I am so hungry. We must get something to eat today. Yesterday, all we had was a packet of stuffing. In the throes of cabin fever Lou had climbed on the sink to peek above the cupboard and there, among the filth, dust, and spiderwebs, he found a packet of instant stuffing. When opened it looked like sawdust with green specks and also bore a worrying resemblance to rodent poison. Hunger overrode the trepidation. We poured it in a pan, added water, boiled it, stirred it up, and ate the lot. It was like eating insulation, but nourishing, I suppose, in a Third World kind of way.

Sleet stings the eyes and infiltrates the scarf, chilling the throat, and, being the singer, I've got to be careful. We've always got colds, always sniffling and sneezing.

The phone box, red and cheery, not vandalized and mostly urine free. Quick prayer that Stein is there and pop in the coin.

Two rings, the pips, and then mercifully Mr. Groven. "Listen, we've been invited to dinner tonight," he says.

"Wow. Fantastic. By whom?" What am I saying? Who cares?

"Some guy who wants to manage us. Saw us at the Pied Bull."

"Jesus. We almost got lynched at the Pied Bull."

"Yeah, well, still."

"What's he like?"

"Dunno."

"Well, it would be great to eat."

"Yeah, and he might be good. But what do we do about Chris?"

Then the time runs out and we just barely manage to arrange to meet at London Street at seven o'clock.

Back at 73 Aldenham Road, through the backyard, glance up, curtain drawn so Lou's awake. Can't wait to tell him about dinner. Through the back door and out of the awful weather. I'm just about to go up the stairs when I see the thing halfway up, not a trace of hurry or scurry. It's huge, makes the skin crawl. *Rattus norvegicus*, I looked it up: Norwegian rat. Why Norwegian?

It glances back over its shoulder at me, and for one dreadful instant I think it's going to leap down the stairs and rip my throat out. But it just sneers, thumps up the rest of the stairs, and saunters off.

An eternity later I summon the nerve to go up as well, and what a fey spectacle I make of myself. Where did it go? My head's on a swivel, eyes wild, trying to locate the bastard. It would need a hole the size of a Volkswagen. I sprint down the hall and burst into our room, scaring the daylights out of Lou, who is wrapped in a blanket, smoking a tea bag.

I yell, "The rat's out there and we're going to dinner tonight."

* * *

Traveling from Bushey to Paddington on British Rail without a ticket is no mean feat. Leaping from moving trains, dashing from platform to platform, and ducking into toilets is not for the faint of heart. Slithering out of one railway car and into another at the approach of officialdom can be nerve-wracking. Hurdling barriers and darting about furtively is a dodgy enterprise at the best of times, but try doing it in a cocktail dress, platform soles, and full makeup while sporting the odd swastika. See how far you get.

Paddington station is notoriously tough, too. It's the Checkpoint Charlie of the London Underground. Stasi in pairs at the gate, palms filling up with travelers' tickets, eyes trained to spot the dodgers and reprobates. The prospect of the hundred-yard scarper always looms. But not a ticket taker do we spy. This can sometimes happen but it is a rare occurrence, and irritatingly enough it generally happens on those even rarer occasions when we have actually purchased a ticket.

But on this charmed night Lou and I amble through, sans tickets and unmolested, the picture of nonchalance. Down London Street and a kick on Stein's door.

Roger is perched on the edge of the bed, nightclub clothes ever so neatly pressed. He catches my eye and does a slight sneer and an eye-roll warning. What has he sussed? Eunan is stretched out on the floor, up on one elbow, dressed in tatty black satin.

In Stein's armchair sits the managerial candidate. First impressions are everything and this chump adds up to not much. He is a portly rumpledstiltskin in brown corduroy trousers and a saggy, musty jacket, tweedy as a Hebridean hedge. A broad cheerful face, ruddy as a butcher's, sporting three blood-clotted tissue bits congealed to the more effusive of his shaving nicks. Twin millipede eyebrows undulate over pale blue eyes that appear to have the chameleon-like ability to operate independently of one another. He seems to be looking at Roger over there and me over here at the same time. This is more than disconcerting. This is Slats Silverstein.

Stein handles the introductions. Slats raises himself with some effort and one grunt from the armchair and sticks a pallid, damp, freckled thing with assorted protruding sausage fingers out at me. Intuitively, I deduce that he wants me to shake it and politeness dictates that I must. It is like grasping a drowned ferret.

"Andrew, Andrew. Hello, Andrew. Pleased, I'm sure. Heard a lot about you. Loved the show, the gig—loved it."

"Slats?"

"Yeah. Window blinds. My office. Roscoe called me 'Slats' and it stuck." He withdraws the pallid, damp, freckled thing with assorted protruding sausage fingers, curls it into a tunnel shape, coughs into it, then offers it to Lou, a man with apparently no qualms about germy palms.

"And this must be . . . ?"

"Hi, I'm Lou, drums."

"Pleased. Pleased, I'm sure."

Nothing much happens for the next few seconds so I grab the reins.

"Well, let's blow this joint. I'm starving. Where are we going?"

Slats spreads his arms wide and says, "Yes, yes, we *could* go out. It's just that, well, I thought since we're all, well, here, ensconced like, cozy, I thought I'd take the liberty of . . ."

He gestures like a game-show floozie, two-handed, palms up, at the coffee table and the large paper bag sitting on top. Lou, not a shy lad, steps over and opens it up.

"Hamburgers," says Lou.

"Not just hamburgers," says Slats. "Wimpy burgers." He says it like they've just been rushed here from the Savoy Grill.

Wimpy burgers are to hamburgers what Lulu is to Brigitte Bardot, edible but not exactly mouthwatering. This is nothing like going out to dinner. This is a bag of burgers. Not even any chips in sight. I look at the lads. There is a lot of shoulder-shrugging and shoe-gazing. I scan the room for a like reaction but my incredulity meets only Roger's limitless supply of pragmatism. He sighs.

"Yeah, well, I'm bloody starving. Let's just eat."

Slats holds out another bag. "I've brought beers, lads." His saving grace.

We get stuck in, eating like a pack of wolves. We don't talk. The only sounds we make are guttural, primal noises, probably identical to those made around peat-and-dung fires in caves a few thousand years ago.

Then we lean back and get to work on the tubes of lager. Slats Silverstein clears his throat, sucks wetly at an unlucky piece of gristle stuck somewhere in his mouth, and shrugs off the tweed jacket. Draping it over the back of the armchair, he announces, "Before we get down to, quote, biz, unquote, I think I'll just go and point wee Percy at the porcelain. Heh, heh."

As soon as he's out the door Eunan, ever the artless dodger, reaches over and methodically goes through all the pockets of the tweed, coming up with nothing but a damp crumpled tissue and a few balls of lower-working-class lint.

Presently, Slats returns minus blood-clotted tissue bits and plonks himself down in the armchair. He sticks a hand into his right trouser pocket, rummages around a bit, and pulls forth a pipe, black of stem and gnarled of burl. Clamping it between his teeth, he proceeds to suck and blow like a mechanical Popeye getting up a head of steam. Then his eyes cross as he examines the bowl for shine. Plucking the pipe from his chompers, he begins to rub and buff it on his inner thigh, close to a zone generally regarded in more comely individuals as erogenous. He examines the bowl, decides it is still too dull, and so strokes it, with a lack of self-consciousness that is, frankly, repulsive, along the sides of his nose, which evidently produces the desired sheen.

He admires it briefly then tucks it, unsmoked, back into his pocket, where it remains for the duration of our meeting. Stein, being Stein, gets to business.

"So, tell the boys what you were telling me."

Slats crosses his legs then uncrosses them. He pinches the material of his trousers at the knee and squeezes an inch-long crease into existence. One "ahem" is followed by another, neatly spaced. He begins.

"Yes, well, you boys, you lads are . . . interesting, I must say. Unrefined, of course, but oh, yes, interesting. Caught your act, your gig, quite by chance, yes, hmm. Something there, something there, no denying it so why try? It's rough, of course, angry you might say, needs manipulating, needs kneading, needs a bit of . . ."

"Needs needing?" I ask, confused.

"What? Yes. Yes, exactly, precisely. Needs kneading."

"Needing?"

"You got it. Kneading, like dough. You're like dough."

"Needs needing?" I persist.

"No, no, no," says Slats, exasperated. "Kneading . . . kneading. It's a . . . comparison, a . . . metawhatsit . . . adage, whatever. *Kneading* . . . you know . . . ?"

Here, he sticks his hands out and wiggles his fingers in the manner of a chap playing a concertina or strangling a chorus girl. "Kneading. Like you boys are dough, you know? A big lump of dough."

He notices the way we are looking at him.

"Great dough, mind you. I mean, dough like this doesn't come along every day. Know what I mean? But dough, nonetheless. No, no, no. I see your faces. Don't get me wrong here. You can have the best dough, made from the best ingredients, you know? Best flour, an egg, fucking *marvelous* yeast, whatever the fuck else. Best dough." He lowers his voice, conspiratorial like, and wags a forefinger.

"But dough, even the best five-star dough, needs a fucking good knead before you can stick it in the oven and fry it up. Get my point?" He doesn't wait for an answer.

"You've got that definite summink, that indefinable *je ne sais* whatsit. It's raw, mind you. Fucking raw, if you ask me, but it's different. A cut above. It's what separates the dicks from the cunts, is what I'm saying. Know what I mean?"

What language is this chump speaking? We don't say a word. Encouraged by the stunned silence, he rattles on.

"It's the audience, see? The reaction of the punters is paramount. I stand back, clocking the reaction of Jack 'n' Jill Normal, right? It's my way, my modus whatsit. Standin' back, clockin' it."

He taps a forefinger on the side of his recently degreased nose.

"And the audience, all them punters, were in a state of . . . how should I put this? . . . Transported into a state of utter . . . utter . . ."

"Revulsion?" I suggest, remembering all too well. The lads chortle and nod but Slats decides to say "no" five times.

"No, no, no, no. No. Far from it. They were in a state of . . . ah . . . what's the fucking word? A state of . . . of . . . *agog*. That's it. A state of agog is what they were in. Well, didn't know what to make of it, did they? Never seen anything like it, 'ad they? Lads in lipstick? Fucking boas? Trousers? Do what? Tight? *Tight?* Heh, heh. I mean, come on. No Hebrews in this band, right? Am I right?

Heh, heh. No offense, mind you. I'm of that persuasion myself. Silverstein, know what I mean?"

He pauses to let us fully drink all this in, using the time to examine the soil content of his fingernails. Then comes the pitch.

"But . . ." he intones dramatically, "you need that summink . . . extra. You need to take it to the next stage, the next level, the next . . . stage. Now, modesty prevents me from extolling my virtues, talents, business savvy, whatever, but . . . let me just say that, after due consideration, I may—*may,* mind you—be open to adding you lads to my roster, my stable, if you will, of artistes, exclusive management-wise."

He stops and leans back in the armchair. What a performance. It demands a response. Roger beats me to it.

"And who are you, anyway?" he asks. Slats seems taken aback. His eyes shift one after the other to look at Roger. Sort of.

"Well, I'm . . . I'm actually quite well known, regarded that is, in certain Northern circles."

"Any horse we know in this stable of yours?" I inquire, politely enough, considering.

"Well, deary me." He starts counting on his hand. "There's . . . well, there's DJ Jammin' Roscoe Barnes and his Sounds of the Islands Cavalcade; Didgeridoo and his Aussie Revue, currently packin' 'em in at Pommies in Doncaster; Freddie Paunch, don't get his humor myself but the old dears in Margate love him; fabulous mime troupe, well, mime and juggling really, Marcel and the Marceaus. Who else have we got? There's James du Maurier . . ."

We can stand it no more. Hands shoot up to staunch the verbiage. "Whoa, whoa. Who are all these specimens?"

Slats looks at us, affronted and incredulous.

"Come now, lads. I mean, I can understand p'raps Didgeri and Roscoe, certainly Roscoe, what with the work permits and the police and all. Not quite household names, those two. Not yet, anyway, I hasten to add. But I mean, how about James?" Heads shake. Roger rolls his eyes for the umpteenth time. Slats is at an astounded loss.

"I can't believe it. James du Maurier, the dancer?" No reaction. "Matinee idol looks, cross between a young Olivier and Bruce Forsyth?"

This guy's off his nut. But he's not letting that stop him. "Christ, just last week, two weeks ago at the most, he was backing up Lionel Blair on ITV. Fuckin' extravaganza, Cilla, Engelbert, the works. You *do* know Lionel Blair, right?"

"Can you get us a record deal?" Guess who? Stein, of course.

"Ah, yes . . . no . . . not as such, not right away, like. But I do have some quite tasty connections in . . ."

The time has come to interject. I stand up. "Yeah, yeah. I'm sure, but listen, here's the story. Yes, we are looking for a manager, that's true, but not just any lower primate that drops out of the palm tree. No offense."

"None taken."

"We want a manager with a certain image. We need someone who'll get us a record deal and look good doing it. Someone prepared, no, *programmed* to go for the jugular on our behalf. What we want, actually, is the next Andrew Loog Oldham. All style, balls, and bottle. Wearing a sharp suit, tooling around town in a sports car. Wimpy burgers, island DJs, and a vanful of mimes? What is this, a circus? No offense."

"None taken."

"All I'm saying is, I'm not sure we'd fit in your . . . what did you call it?"

"Stable of artistes?"

"Yeah, that."

I sit down. An awkward silence descends. Around me bums shift, throats are cleared. Eunan giggles quietly. A beer is opened with a soft crack and a softer fizz. Slats, ruddy cheeks ruddier than ever, fidgets and glances surreptitiously at his wrist, where there is no watch. Seconds crawl by on broken legs.

Outside in the night a steady rain falls, gently soaking the Derelict of London Street on his piece of sodden cardboard outside Ladbrokes. He sips Brut aftershave for comfort and, like Blanche DuBois, relies on the kindness of strangers. Unlike the rest of him, his breath smells lovely.

Inside Stein's flat the silence has reached squirm-inducing proportions. Something must be said. Something. Anything. Something apt. Ease the tension. Strangely, it is Slats that says it.

"Listen, lads, I was just wondering. How would you like to attend the premiere of Cliff Richard's new film next Tuesday?"

Well, what were Ladbrokes' odds on that being the silence breaker? We are struck monosyllabic. All we can come up with as a response is "What?" and "Huh?" and the like.

"Yeah, it's just that Cliff's new film premieres Tuesday night next, gala event, 'course, and, ah, I just thought you might like to be my guests for the evening. Cocktails afterward, nibbles I'm sure, chance to meet the director and Cliff, naturally. Cliff'll be there. Mayfair, actually, or is it Holland Park? Well, Leicester Square for the film and then off elsewhere for the reception, I should imagine. Should be a lark. Meet Cliff, have a drink, have a nosh. What say?"

Well, you could knock us over with a feather boa. We can't say yes quickly or grovelingly enough.

"Fine, excellent. That's good, then. Yeah. I'll send a motor for you that evening. Shall we say sixish? Right, then. See you, lads. Ta-ta."

He's in the tweed and he's out the door. Just like that.

V

The next thing you know, the Hollywood Brats are splayed in the back of a big, black limousine driven by a big, white driver named Edgerton. And let me tell you, this is the life.

Outside, through the smoky-glass windows of the Roller, the pavement is teeming with Londoners, faces gray, grim, heading home, *Evening Standard* under their arms, looking forward to *Nationwide*, fish fingers, and Smash. I usually live in barely suppressed, green-raged envy of these Tetley Tea Folk, but not tonight.

We're done up to the nines and beyond, dolloped, feathered and frilled, jangling with junk jewelry. It's not every day you go to a film premiere.

I don't really know much about Cliff, England's answer to a question nobody asked. Polite quiff, government-approved sneer, riding a double-decker with the Shadows in *Summer Holiday*, doing things they always wanted to. Bachelor boy, favorite of the Queen Mum and Eurovision, been around forever, has a hit every eight months or so. Actually, now that I think about it, my Bushey housemate Ewen had an old LP in his collection with Cliff doing a thing called "Move It." His first single, I think. I played it a couple of times and it wasn't bad. But that's about it, sum total of my knowledge of Cliff.

Eunan prods the upholstery, trying to find the hidden bar. As is his bewildering wont, he often turns out to have an almost encyclopedic knowledge when it comes to a variety of oddball subjects. One of these subjects turns out to be Cliff. We find out, for instance, that his real name is Harry Webb. This information is seconded by Roger. "Yeah, Harry Webb," says Eunan. "But forget *Summer Holiday*; his best film, his absolute classic, man, is *Expresso Bongo*."

This announcement brings out the heckler in all of us.

"No, really. It's brilliant, man. Brilliant. Cliff plays this working guy, Bongo Herbert, who occasionally sings and plays bongos at this club called Expresso Bongo. He drives the chicks wild and gets discovered by this manager played by Laurence Harvey, who's brilliant, man. 'I'm gonna make your boy a star' brilliant: bent fedora, shrugging shoulders, really lays on the Hebrew. Great flick."

"Yeah, I remember," says Roger. "Topless dancing girls in kilts, right?"

"Right, right. It's brilliant, man. If this film's half as good as *Expresso Bongo* it'll be a gas."

Around Piccadilly we go. Eros, Aphrodite's kid, winged god of something or other, gazes down on the traffic, tourists, heroin addicts, and cubicle chancers. Past the shop I Was Lord Kitchener's Valet, outside of which one night a couple of months ago Stein and I were loitering without the slightest intent, when all of a sudden Piccadilly went pitch-black. Miners on strike and refusing to hack out the black stuff and here's your consequence. Chaos. Screaming, cursing, squeals of delight, outrage, fear. But I finally got Stein to calm down.

I remember cars and taxis slamming on the anchors, pranging into one another, police whistles blaring, a thousand voices, a dozen languages, everybody yelling and yapping. Two double-deckers, both traveling the same route and both naturally traveling bumper to bumper in tardy tandem, ground to a halt in the jam, passengers' faces pressed up to the windows, peering out.

It was a surreal sight to witness but I witnessed it mainly without Stein. He was nowhere to be felt. Twenty minutes later, the lights came back on, some jobsworth at Battersea Power Station having located a spare bag of coal and stuffed it in the boiler. Stein wandered back, cool and calm, having dashed into Lord Kitchener's under the cloak of darkness for a spot of opportunistic thievery. Great. Just what we need. Three Big Ben paperweights, a London Underground tea towel, and a handful of Beefeater key chains.

Tonight, though, it's the film premiere. Searchlights, red carpet, toff liggers no doubt, the odd politician, a threadbare royal or two, Pinewood starlets. Drive on, Edgerton.

Anyway, back to Leicester Square. But this isn't Leicester Square. We've turned right and right again, I think. What street is this? Shop windows full of dangling, glistening, plastic-looking dead ducks. We've slowed to a crawl. As far as I can tell it's so we don't run over any of the many Chinese people milling about. They're everywhere. Barrows and stalls overflowing with sandals, vegetables, Mao couture, jars full of gelatinous things, and hanging dried skins of recently living things clog the pavements. Crushed tomatoes and melons splatter the gutters, through which our black expensive tires squelch. Little kids in beanies take potshots at us with peashooters, spit-drenched peas dinging off the windows.

Around another corner we come to a halt in front of a less-than-distinguished gray building. There are about twenty people out front but it doesn't look remotely like a film premiere. At least, not the ones I've seen on telly. Maybe we've got a flat tire. Maybe we ran over a cat. What am I saying? Everyone knows there are no cats in Chinatown. Maybe we're picking somebody up.

A ruddy-complexioned wide mug, complete with oscillating eyeballs and yellow smile, bumps into the window. We all flinch away in fright. It is an obvious lunatic and he's gesturing, beckoning for us to get out. But where are we? Can this really be it? Can this be the film premiere equivalent of a bag of Wimpy burgers? Yes, it can. We disembark into the waiting fussiness of not a lunatic, as such, but impresario extraordinaire Slats Silverstein.

"Hello lads, good evening, you made it. Everything all right, then? How was the motor? Yeah? Yeah? Yeah, I know. Thank you, Edgy . . . Edgerton, my good man. Come this way, lads. You look smashing. No other word for it. On my life."

"Is this it?" I ask him.

"Yeah, great, innit? Hello, Cynthia," he says to a woman's rapidly departing back. In we go. There is no red carpet, no pomp or circumstance. "I've got your seats saved, Andrew. Reserved, as it were. Smell that excitement?" I smell damp, musty old cinema.

In with the straggling strays of the crowd we go. Some crowd. They're aggressively, stridently bohemian, mums and dads, dog-collared clergy, heavy-knit sweaters, fish pendants everywhere. Slats seats us in the back row. No sign of Cliff. The lights dim, chatter is hushed, the air expectant; the red velvet curtain rises.

Lou belches. We laugh.

The screen comes to life with a wide shot of Trafalgar Square at dawn. Nothing but pigeons, statues, bronze lions, and the ubiquitous American tourist clad head to toe in patched denim with the usual headband, backpack, unkempt hair, and mustache. Her boyfriend stands nearby. Otherwise, the square is gray and deserted.

Lord Nelson stands atop his column, looking off down the Mall. Thanks to some foreign swine's cannonball the right sleeve of his naval tunic hangs empty. There's no arm in that.

Timpani start low and build to a pounding thunder. Large red letters appear across the screen.

JAMES SWACKHAMMER PRESENTS

Jack Swackhammer? Now there's a handle and a half. Sounds like a railroad boss driving that ribbon of steel through the Rocky Mountains for the Union Pacific in the 1800s. Mopping his brow with a red bandanna, laying those ties, hands blackened with creosote, pounding in them spikes, drinking whiskey, standing on a hillock reading blueprints, chopping the pigtail off a quivering flunky for some minor infraction.

More timpani.

A JAMES SWACKHAMMER FILM

Trumpets join the timps. Then the title appears.

WHY SHOULD THE DEVIL HAVE ALL THE GOOD MUSIC?

Oh no. It can't be. Oh yes it can. For the next eighty minutes we are subjected to an experience so excruciatingly dull as to make tedium an attractive option. The film captures a day-long free (big surprise) concert in Trafalgar Square, featuring bands and singers mewing into microphones about Christ, forgiveness, second comings, hallelujahs, and other yawningly boring things. This is no *Summer Holiday*. The production seems intentionally designed to be as cheesy as humanly possible. The handheld camerawork is jerky in both senses of the word. It's enough to make you see-sick.

Interviews with the performers reach heretofore unplumbed dark depths of vapidity. Interviewees praise Jesus in fervent automaton cliché then bound onto the stage to play some of the worst music these ears have ever endured. In the back row we laugh, razz, and catcall. Lou is particularly hilarious, but our ecumenical jive is shouted down by other patrons. We even hear a couple of "Repent, sinners!" I mean, seriously. Beware the wrath of the publicly righteous. They're very touchy.

The film plods inexorably toward a frenzied moment: the entrance of Cliff. Here he comes, folks—bouncing, buoyant, teeth and flares pearly white. He runs onto the stage flashing peace signs, and the band lurches into a clapped-out version of "Put Your Hand in the Hand." The audience on the screen and in the cinema goes wild. The camera pans to the crowd and they are rapt and joyous, many of them sporting the thousand-mile stare indicative of mass psychosis. It's as though everyone knows a mere glance from Cliff can turn wine into water.

And they adore him for it.

An overhead shot reveals that the crowd in Trafalgar Square has swollen to capacity. A polite riot looms. Shoving, swaying, jostling for position—the better to see the man in white—the crowd gets slightly out of hand. Police link arms to push and contain the besotted. In a touching echo of bygone times, Christians are thrown to the bronze lions.

Next, a slow song breaks out like a four-minute itchy rash, causing much gazing at the sky, hands on hearts during the chorus, and some serious shoe-considering during the instrumental. Cliff emotes, mums swoon, grown men mist up and run their fingers morosely through their sideburns.

Flowers dot the stage and have been landing like God's grenades since Cliff's arrival. When the song stumbles to a halt he bows from the waist, and while he's down there he flicks a rose petal off the toe of his white platform shoe.

Cliff says one more number and then he has to go. Cue the cheers from the back row of the cinema. It's a singalong and everybody else is on their feet, swaying and baying. Afterward, Cliff exits, blowing kisses, touching outstretched fingers and gratefully accepting bouquets.

Are there Christian groupies? I wonder. Tarty little Mary Magdalenes with kneepads and a backstage pass?

Roll credits. Time-lapse long shot of dispersing crowd. We don't need no stinkin' time-lapse long shot, we're out of here. In the lobby we stand, an island unto ourselves, Christians eddying around us. We snicker and shake our skulls. Then along comes Slats, full of chat, millipede eyebrows jumping on his forehead.

"So, what did you think, lads? Cliff? Still got it, right? Palm of his hands and all that? Eating out of it, they were. I heard you, lads—naughty comments. Never mind that, though. Let's get moving." He herds us through the believers, out the door and into the night.

Our limo is parked beside a newsagent. In we climb and Slats presses a button to lower the glass partition that separates us from the driver. "All right, Edgy . . . Edgerton? Good, lovely. Onward, squire."

"Righty-ho," says the driver. "Don't forget, you've got the eleven o'clock run to Gatwick. I'm off at ten and . . ." but feverish button pressing raises the partition and cuts the driver off mid-gaffe.

The car zooms off, and we are just about to start criticizing the film when Slats pokes a finger into the upholstery and—presto!—out pops a bar. As Fluff Freeman would say, "Way-hey, not 'arf." First round gets served and disappears down our respective hatches. Two whiskeys, a gin, and a couple of cognacs. Big ones. Second round, and we're helping ourselves.

Slats Silverstein is nervous, twitchy. "Steady, lads, steady. Plenty of evening left. Best behavior, mind. Powerful people you'll meet. Best not to say much. Leave it to me, yeah?"

Alcohol doesn't waste time going straight to your cerebral cortex when you haven't eaten a crumb. I've no idea where we are or where we're going. There goes Lancaster Gate, Bayswater, but I'm not sure. Before I can ask for my third drink we are delivered to an address in what appears to be Holland Park. A chap wearing white gloves disturbs the peace by opening our door and, by gesturing ludicrously like an escaped mime, indicates that we should exit. Reluctantly, we do, tumbling out, drinks in hand.

Once inside, whew, what a joint. Whopping great rooms, ceilings way up there, chandeliers dripping with sparkling crystal, gleaming wooden floors dotted here and there with expensive-looking Arab ruggery. Dark wood, knobbly-kneed tables, chairs, desks, Art Deco lamps, huge oil paintings of humorously unattractive people—this world bears no relation to our existence in the boondocks of Bushey.

But the main attraction for us is a long table piled high with glorious food in tureens, bowls, on trays, platters, and gilt-edged plates. Naturally, we head straight for it. Where to start?

Frogified squares of pâté on cross sections of baguette, cheeses, smoked salmon, oysters, leg of lamb, Cornish game hens, roast beef and tons of it. We pounce on the feast and eat, and eat some more, until we are sated. Maybe. This is light years removed from a box of eels or a packet of stuffing.

Waiters keep showing up and forcing glasses of champagne into our hands. We are far too well-mannered to decline. The bubbly goes down nicely and sits well on top of the three large cognacs I guzzled in the limo.

Down the other end of this aircraft carrier of a table is the dessert section, featuring treats as varied and succulent as the victuals up this end: cakes, tarts, tortes, trifle, custard, cream, pastries, puddings, and more.

An extremely wide woman, wearing a black spangled pup tent suspended about her girth by spaghetti straps so sunk into her blubbery shoulders as to appear to be emerging straight from her flesh, pushes a cream-filled éclair into her gaping mouth. While chewing, she licks the fingernails of one hand while the other gropes for more. She's like a five-car collision. I just can't look away.

Annoyingly, Slats shows up. "All right, lads? Nice food? Leave some for others. I want you to meet some people. Best behavior. And mind the language, for fuck's sake."

I take in the rest of the crowd. Same bunch as back at the cinema, bolstered by a couple of dozen upmarket liggers. A bit short on the Pinewood starlets, though. I spy a bow tie here, a floor-length gown there, a monocle, which I covet, by the way.

A few men of the cloth are in evidence, local vicar types, recognizable not only by the white collars and puff-pastry pallor, but also by the lascivious looks on their faces as they stare down the fronts of ladies' dresses or, alternately, gaze longingly at the departing bums of the waiters.

There are knots of people here and there. Perhaps Cliff is in the midst of one, surrounded by a coterie of fawning sycophants. We are led to one such gathering, in the center of which stands a large man with a black coat draped theatrically over his shoulders. Underneath, he is wearing a beige safari suit. A shock of unruly white hair flops forward into his eyes, only to be flicked back with a jerk of his head at thirty-second intervals. His face is very animated, especially the mouth part, out of which comes . . .

"And so I say, 'At least Larry didn't desert the stage the minute Louis B. snapped his fingers,' and Liz shrieks—she'd had a snootful—'Richard did not desert the stage, you . . .' and then she called me a ten-letter word beginning with 'C.'"

The ladies surrounding him do the arithmetic and the spelling, and giggle on cue. Slats elbows through the throng. "Jack, Jack. How are you, Jack? Loved the film, the movie." The man looks at Slats Silverstein, impresario extraordinaire, as though he can't quite place him but nonetheless finds him distasteful. Undeterred, Slats presses on. "I'd like you to meet these chaps. Jack, I give you the Hollywood Brats."

Jack turns his attention our way, looks us up and down, and says with a plummy voice, "Lovely plumage. Is this your manager?"

Slats blurts in. "Ah yes, well, in negotiations, many a slip twixt and all that. We're toing, we're froing—feeling each other . . . out, you know. Boys, this is Jack Swackhammer."

Jack Swack sticks out a hand and proceeds to crush all of ours. "Hey, boys, pleased to meet you. Hollywood, huh? Wild stuff, wild stuff. I see you've been enjoying the hospitality." He gestures at the front of Eunan's black velvet jacket, covered in pastry crumbs. "Were you at the premiere?"

We nod. At this point it strikes me that I am actually quite drunk. The room has gone a bit dream-sequence, as in a psychedelic film—*The Trip*, for instance. Jack continues, "So, tell me, from your perspective, as musicians, what did you think of our little celluloid adventure?"

Little celluloid adventure? Where does he get this stuff? I grab another glass of champers from a passing waiter. It occurs to me that the other lads are waiting for me to answer the man's question. Drat. I drain half the glass and give it a go. "Well, sorry but we don't think your little celluloid adventure was all that good, actually."

There is a collective gasp.

"Indeed," says Jack, flicking his hair back with a vengeance.

"Well, yeah. If anything, it did suggest that the devil does indeed have the best jukebox." Jack goes pink and does another hair flick.

"Oh, it did, did it? Is that what it proved?" He looks back at his retinue and gives them a slight shake of the head.

As I drain my glass of champagne I can't help reflecting that, according to the biography I recently read, Napoleon is reputed to have designed the champagne glass to perfectly fit the dimensions of the Empress Josephine's breast. Must have had a bit of time on his hands that week, saucy tyrant. Though it must be said, on this evidence the girl had modest jugs. I continue, "Yeah, well, I mean in terms of Cliff's career it's no *Expresso Bongo* now, is it?"

Aside from general unrest and sputtering from the Swackman, things go all awkward and quiet. Silence is not as golden as the Tremeloes would have us believe. Right here, right now, it's just the tiniest bit leaden and uncomfortable. Slats looks like he wants to disappear, immediately after murdering me.

All is decidedly not well. I don't want us to be turfed from this Aladdin's cave at such an early juncture. I snatch another glass of champagne as it tries to sneak by unnoticed on a tray. I'm lost, adrift—can't think of a mollifying something to murmur.

From over my right shoulder a voice comes to my rescue. "I think I can answer that."

The impact of these words on the people surrounding me is immediate and galvanizing. They gasp, they fawn, they go all leg-before-wicket, for the speaker is none other than the great Bongo Herbert himself. The man whose very name invites you to run to the edge and throw yourself off: Cliff.

He sticks out his hand and shakes mine. He stretches his lips over his incisors, the better to display his two-story pearly smile. He is tanned, coiffed, and resplendent in appalling garb. He says, no he really does, "I applaud the opinions of this young man, refreshingly candid, I say. And to answer . . . hello, Jack . . . to address the point, what was it, *Expresso Bongo*? Cheeky. You remember that one? I participated in Jack's film for the simple reason that I believe in the cause."

The people in the room applaud. A scrum ensues. We are engulfed by

Christians, and Cliff and I are parted by the throng. That was wild. I am feeling a bit queasy. P'raps one last glass of champagne to settle things down.

I must have a slash. In fact, it's beyond that. I'm bursting. I just noticed. This is desperate. Off in search of a loo. Waiter points down that way. Down that way I go, and within thirty seconds I'm lost in a leafy hallway with ferns and other jungle greenery. Half expect to see a chimp come swinging along. In the bladder department this is getting perilously close to the point of no return. Try this door, no, a cloakroom. Try this one. No. And another. No. I'm unashamedly holding my knob through my trousers now, throttling the bastard. Squeezing it round the throat. Don't you dare, mate.

Try yet another door: locked, but with watery sounds within. Two hands on Percy, choking him to death. Bouncing up and down, cross-legged, bending at the waist, pogoing back and forth in the hall, squealing quietly. Tears in my eyes. Niagara Falls at the end of my penis, held back only by a two-fisted tourniquet. I can't do it. I just can't hold out.

Whip elegant vase off small table, look around, coast is clear, yank forth engorged penis, point it in, and let it go. Ahhh . . . blessed, blessed relief. The vase is deep and beautiful, white with blue Oriental nonsense all over it. There I stand, slightly bent at the knee, prick deep in the thing, staring at the ceiling, urinating like a racehorse, when the toilet door opens and out steps the fat lady in the black spangled pup tent.

Her hand flies up to her mouth, her eyes widen, she staggers back. Has she never been taught that it is impolite to stare? Despite her lapse in manners I can't help but feel I am the one at a social disadvantage. I summon a degree of dignity.

"Good evening, madam." Remarkably, I am still urinating. She, meanwhile, seems to have lost the ability to form coherent phrases.

"Well . . . I never . . . I should . . . oh, Lord."

"Run along now, madam. As you can see, since you are not averting your gaze, all is well in hand."

She backs, then waddles, off, thighs rubbing together like wet inner tubes. I have some privacy at last and, though perilously close to the brim, I finish with a one-spurt flourish and a quarter of an inch to spare. Ah, the relief of it all, indignities aside. I carefully place the vase back on the table, and while I am reholstering the love pistol and zipping up, another woman enters the loo, locking the door behind her.

Heading unsteadily back to the party zone, I am about to ambush a mime carrying a trayful when I feel a tug at the sleeve. Gadzooks, it's Bongo himself.

"Excuse me. I was quite interested in what you were saying earlier. Your turn of phrase. Would you care for a cognac in the library?"

Cognac in the library? I've been waiting for invitations of this ilk my entire life, and now here it is. And with Bongo Herbert, no less. Lead on.

Back down the hall with the ferny foliage and the incriminating vase now steaming slightly in the cool air. Through this door and, wow, an actual library. Completely and utterly Basil Rathbone, with leather-bound volumes shelved to the ceiling, beautiful desk, fireplace with elbow-high mantel perfect for leaning, pipe in mouth, smoking jacket . . . Be still, my beating aspirations.

On one side there is an oxblood leather sofa, where I sit on its circular furry cushion, which turns out, yelpingly, to be an elderly dachshund.

"Oh sorry, sorry. Excuse me, I didn't . . ."

"Not to worry, not to worry. I don't think he's supposed to be on the furniture anyway. Let's just get a splash, eh?"

Bongo canters over to the liquor cabinet. He pours himself a small frothy green drink then tilts a crystal decanter and pours me three fingers' worth of cognac into a snifter the size of a goldfish bowl. I am collapsed, spread-legged on the now-dachshundless sofa, with the room spinning before my eyes. I sit up straight and try to focus on Bongo as he approaches across the mile or so of floor space and hands me the fishbowl. This will straighten me out. Wow, it's big. I could almost stick my whole head in.

Bongo chats away and I must concentrate. I walk that well-trodden line between not appearing overly chummy and yet still having my drink replenished at regular intervals. He asks about religion; I mention Ray Davies. He tilts his head back and laughs. Truth be told, even through the bleariest of double-visioned eyes, Bongo *does* appear to be in exceptional nick. Maybe he's got an oil painting of George Sanders up in the attic.

He's a conversational marvel, zipping here and there, offering opinions, asking questions, while at the same time remaining ever-attentive to my rapidly drained goldfish bowl. He really does have lovely teeth. And my front one broken and chipped at a time like this. Inquiries take a personal turn. I drain another fish tank while he asks me about my home life. All right, Bongo. You want it? You got it.

I describe our slum and I do not skimp on the adjectives. I chat about mice and lice, brackish tap water, raw sewage, *Rattus norvegicus*, and more. Then through the alcoholic haze I begin to consider that there may be the possibility of an outlay of Christian charity, and I begin to lay it on thicker. No food, no medicine, coppers at the door, Fairy Liquid shampoo . . . Lou would be better at this, but I forge ahead.

Bugs in the rugs, rickets, frozen feces, anything I can think of. Persecuting landlord, no toothpaste . . . this is worthy of a UNICEF campaign. I couldn't have done better had I been a teary young black child covered in flies.

Bongo backs away, turns reflective, contemplative. He strokes his chin and drums his fingers on his knee. He comes up with something.

"I'm thinking. Would you boys like to get away from it all? I've got a place in the country. You guys could come and stay, relax, recharge the old batteries. How about it? You could rehearse, even. Bring your gear. Loads of room. Do you good. What do you say?"

I can't believe my lugholes. What did he say?

"Bishop's Stortford in Hertfordshire. Not far. Fair-sized place. Rehearse, relax—do you the world of good."

Bloody hell. I'm drunk but my ears do not deceive. Moments later I follow Bongo back toward the main room. The floor is uneven. Didn't notice it before but it definitely slants this way and that. Makes it difficult to affect any semblance of a nonchalant stroll. In the hallway a small, old sausage mutt scratches his claws on the spindly leg of a table, sniffing at the vase on top.

In the main room, over by a pair of big, fat red lips fashioned by some recent escapee from an institute for the psychotically hilarious into a two-seater sofa, stands Stein with Chathammer. The other three lads lounge nearby and I head toward them. It is not easy to walk. Some strange geophysical force is making me veer to starboard. I lean my torso to port in a counterbalancing maneuver and bump into a couple of idiots who can't seem to stay out of the way. I lurch up to the boys like Quasimodo. "Hey, lads. Guess what? We're going to spend next weekend at Cliff's joint in the country."

They look back at me with uncomprehending, strange, twisted faces. Somewhere far off there is a crash of porcelain, a strangled bark.

And a scream.

VI

Twentieth of February dawns slate gray and bollocks freezing as usual. Another day in Bushey. Frost covers everything. This is court day. Lou and I get up early and dress as conservatively as possible. I dress in black: black trousers and shoes, black turtleneck, black overcoat, black scarf. If I had a top hat I'd look like a Victorian undertaker. We set out on the walk, teeth chattering and nervous all the way to Watford.

At Watford Magistrates' Court on Clarendon Road we are treated like diseased sheep, herded and prodded into a small wood-paneled room to stand for an hour. Then we are summoned and escorted by two coppers and Watford's answer to Ichabod Crane along corridors and upstairs to emerge in the dock. All heads turn to view the scumbag criminals.

It's all showbiz really, so I smile and give a slight wave. There is tittering among the assembled. But in the words of the odd yet funny Frankie Howerd, titter ye not. Three policemen in the dock crowd around me and let me know that there will be no more of that.

Minutes fly by and then a dulcet voice intones, "All rise." We aren't sitting so it doesn't make much difference to us. In walks the judge. He does not look like a barrel of laughs.

The judge sits at the bench arranging his robes like the train on the wedding dress of a Versailles bride, then, and only then, surveys the court, eventually turning his withering gaze on Lou and me. Without so much as a pretense of impartiality, he twists his thin dry lips into a sneer and slowly shakes his wig in undisguised disgust. He then consults the papers in front of him, containing, as they must, the details of our dastardly deeds.

The rest is a blur of evidence and witnesses. I can't stop giggling. I can't believe the overkill at work here. I look at Lou and he is equally astounded. The arresting officer says his piece. Our slumlord says his. It's the first time we've actually clapped eyes on him, and what a nasty piece of work he seems to be; waving his arms and pointing at Lou (who, in fact, is the actual tenant, M'lud), he resembles a bloated Eydie Gormé.

The grass remains anonymous, doesn't testify. I lean toward our trio of coppers and ask, "Hey, why don't we have a lawyer?" The biggest, nastiest one turns around and says, quietly but pleasantly, "Shut your fucking cakehole."

Cakehole shut, M'lud.

It ends with us being found guilty, what a shock, and sentenced to a fine of £25 each or, as an attractive alternative, a month in jail. We don't have 25p between us, never mind £25, and our prospects for acquiring it don't exactly inspire confidence. Yes, M'lud, fine, M'lud, three bags full, M'lud. We will undertake to pay said fine for our crime.

And exactly what crime might that be, you ask? Breaking and entering? Malicious damage? Trespass? Vandalism? No, the crime committed by Lou Sparks and Andrew Matheson on that fateful night and for which they are duly convicted and sentenced is thus: "Theft of three bottles of Coca-Cola," entertainingly if ominously expressed as, and I quote, "Permanently depriving the landlord of three bottles of Coca-Cola."

They got us on the "entering" but not the "breaking." Lou picked the lock so cleanly they couldn't prove anyone actually broke in.

In addition to the sentence imposed, Lou is required by the court to attend counseling sessions once a week. Why Lou and not me? Am I considered beyond redemption?

We, and when I say "we" I mean Lou, weasel our way out of having to ante up the twenty-five nicker on the spot and negotiate a £2.50 per week payment scheme each. The word "scheme" figured prominently in our thinking. Thanks to our charming drummer, the authorities set us free once again to menace the streets of Watford.

Breath in white hissing puffs as Lou and I trudge back to our slum, stopping only for a spot of thievery on the way: tin of beans, tin of salmon, bar of soap in my coat pockets; packet of bacon tucked down my trouser front. Shuffling along Aldenham Road, Lou hits the jackpot when he finds a couple of very long cigarette butts.

So yeah, that's our morning. How was yours?

The next day, walking aimlessly, bored out of our skulls and convinced that life can't possibly get any worse, we pass a newsagent and stop dead in our tracks. There, on the front page of the newspaper in inch-high letters, it says "Costly Coke." Underneath the inflammatory headline the article tells in detail the hilarious story of two idiots who broke into a defunct fish 'n' chip shop in the dead of night for the sole purpose of stealing three bottles of Coca-Cola.

Then it names the two idiots.

The only bright spot is that today Stein turns nineteen. Good. Now he knows how it feels to get old.

Winter wheedles its way into March, and the band is off to Cliff's for a swinging weekend. We've hired a cheap Ford Transit van plus a cheaper roadie for the gear, and Roger is taking all personnel in his car. He's dark and snarling, even more than usual, muttering about the paltry amount we kick in for petrol, the tuppence, the 50p's, the palmful of shillings. He's got a point but what can we do? Each of us has a stash of cash tucked away in our trousers for future lubrication. Can't waste it on petrol, can we?

When the van stops at Eunan's joint we see he's got a Vox 100 in tow, cost him fifty-three quid. Stein was with him in the shop when he put it on hire purchase, and he whispers the story to me. Eunan had to give his age and Stein was shocked to hear that the man is twenty-three. Keeping that on the quiet is the boy. If we'd known he was that old we'd never have let him in the band.

Eunan works at a ladies' wig factory. Just found that out. I don't blame him for keeping that quiet, either. I picture him there, shampooing and moisturizing donkey manes and the shorn locks of desperate lower-caste Indian babes, putting curlers in synthetic tresses for grannies and trannies. But twenty-three? This won't do.

Stein and I bragged to Chris Andrews about where we're going, acting like this sort of invitation happens to us all the time. Good for us, he said, and told us to pop by his digs in Hertfordshire on the way to Cliff's to pick up some spare gear he's got stored in a garage. He won't be there but we are to help ourselves. Something we're good at.

Hence, after a lengthy search along the labyrinthine hedgerowed country lanes around the ritzier side of Chorleywood, the van and the Zephyr pull up to a garage beside a huge house in Quickley Lane, and in we go. I look at the fabulously big and luxurious house in awe. The man has had two hits as far as I am aware—"Yesterday Man" and "Girl Don't Come"—and look at this place. I mean, nobody's heard of Chris Andrews in America but check out his house. There's coin to be coined in this business.

We root around in the garage, and it turns out to be an Aladdin's grave of old equipment. We nab microphone stands, two PA speakers, various plug boards, and a Vox electric organ. The organ is red with chrome, like an Italian motorcycle fitted with eight sets of false teeth.

Two lager-sodden hours later, the Zephyr and the Transit van pull up a long crunchy gravel drive and stop at the front door of Bongo's massive Tudor mansion, just outside Bishop's Stortford. I don't know anything about the Tudor era except that they were obviously big on dark oak beams and white plaster, and this joint has both in eye-popping abundance. It's three stories high and as long as a football pitch, set in beautifully sculptured grounds with topiary, shrubberies, and gigantic ancient trees, under which Druids no doubt once frolicked.

A large curved wooden door swings open on ornate hinges and we are greeted by a woman who is the spitting image of a clean-shaven Jesus. She's got the center-parted hair and even stands in that iconic "I give up" pose, with the arms slightly held out at the sides, palms up. (You know, that pose Jesus is always depicted in when he's made of plaster and painted in garish colors and sold in Portugal or Peru?) The woman holds that pose as though she's saying, "Welcome, and you are?" But it turns out she has been expecting us and leads us inside.

Wow. What a pad. The cavernous entry hall leads into a vast reception room eight times the size of most clubs we've played. It is furnished with antique carpets, brass and pewter bric-a-brac, lace frothery, oil paintings, and uncomfortable-looking ancient chairs and sofas. Horned beasts, boars and stags mostly, poke their heads out of the paneled walls disturbingly, glass eyes ever-watchful, calculating, plotting revenge. Heraldry abounds: tapestries, flags, and banners dangle above.

"Cliff's not here," we are informed. "We don't care," we keep to ourselves. After we unload the gear we are fed a fab feast of roast pork, potatoes, Brussels sprouts, applesauce, and some vegetable we can't identify and never want to see again. This is followed by cake, ice cream, and coffee.

Then we are shown to our rooms by the staff, all of whom hover about like hippy automatons, helpful enough but with mirthless half-smiles perpetually smeared across their faces. Up the stairs we go.

My room is huge, with beamed ceilings and leaded bay windows, deep pile carpet, a bed straight out of a *Penthouse* photo shoot, and a fireplace that someone has been kind enough to equip with a roaring fire. On the bed is something I've never seen before. It's like a fluffy stuffed sheet. And there are no blankets to go along with it.

I sit on the velvet seat that wraps around one of the bay windows and look out at the beautiful grounds and the lovely rolling landscape beyond. This is perfect and clean and Christmas-card picturesque. It does one's noggin the world of good. I could sit here, undisturbed, for hours. Of course, there's an immediate knock on the door. It is Stein with a grin, two beers, and a guitar in tow to play me this song idea he's been telling me about. It's always business with this guy.

First, we yap it up about this fantastic planet we've landed on. When I show him my weird bedding he explains that it's a duvet and that until he came to England he'd never slept in a bed without one. He and Sonja walked into the London Street bedsit and found only folded sheets and blankets. They stood baffled, not knowing what to do with them. "Duvet" sounds French. It is fluffy and inviting, like Sacha Distel. The continentals may not be able to rock, but they sure can make a bed.

Stein plays his idea for me, strumming his usual oddball chords in his usual unpredictable key and singing his nonsensical words. The song is pretty good, though. It's got something. A tad slow, perhaps, but it seems to me that it will fit with this idea I have for a song about a girl who inherits some cash.

We mess around with the chords for twenty minutes or so, debating this and that, taping it for me to work on later, then we go and round up the troops for a night out in beautiful downtown Bishop's Stortford.

Into Roger's Zephyr and off we go to investigate all that this burg has to offer. It's a wee postcard village with three pubs at the most. The first one we come to does nicely, and there we stay, pouring liquid down our throats and spouting the word "Cliff" at every possible opportunity until closing time. Three barmaids take the bait, so it's into the Zephyr and off to the house on the hill.

Back at Cliff's, the tartlets—Giggle, Wiggle, and Jiggle—squeal with delight as we smuggle them through the curved wooden doors and smack their bums on the way up the stairs to our rooms. Wine is guzzled. Hashish is smoked. Shenanigans ensue.

Two hours later and, alas, it turns out the glass slipper fits none, so it is time for the ladies to go home. Giggle and Wiggle stubbornly refuse to leave, and Jiggle, the cuter but nastier one, is running from room to room in naughty underwear (as though she were naturally anticipating a saucy encounter at the end of her shift), opening and slamming doors like she's in one of Peter Sellers's dopier films, screaming, "Where is that bastard?"

Cheerful Roger is dispatched to quell the uproar and chauffeur the ladies back to wherever it is they live. Such fun were the lasses having in our company that they have to be wrestled into the car, or so I am later informed. Finally, the Zephyr sets off down the driveway, with the ladies safely inside yelling loud, vulgar sentiments out the open windows into the pastoral silence of the Hertfordshire night.

I join the other three in Lou's room, where there is a bottle of cognac Cliff had inadvertently left in a locked liquor cabinet and a massive plate of snacks from the fridge.

The four of us laugh it up for an hour or so, drinking, eating, inhaling hashish glowing orange on a pin, and throwing newspapers into the fireplace for the sheer conflagration of it all.

Occasionally we think, Where the fuck's Roger? Then we drink, sniff, and laugh for another hour or so before—out of the blue—there comes a loud, ominous, bring-out-your-dead thump, thump on the door.

The fun, fun, fun slams to a halt as though Daddy just took the T-Bird away. The other three turn and look at me. I say, "Relax." I think it's probably Hairy Magdalene from downstairs, complete with a mild reprimand and a tray of cocoa, so I unwind myself from the floor and answer the door. I'm ready for some Christian approbation served with warm milk, but instead there stands our man Roger. And not just the common-or-garden Fender Jazz Roger we all know and love, but a darker, somehow more sinister Roger.

He's still got his wounded, maltreated, vicious-basset-hound look, but now it comes complete with strange black streaks like commando camouflage scraped across his cheeks, a throbbing soon-to-be-black eye, assorted scratches, and a general sartorial dishevelment. His formerly fabulous tablecloth-check jacket is askew, hanging ripped off his right shoulder, and the left lapel dangles, torn from the collar, like a dead dog's tongue—a fashionably wide, yellow-and-black check tongue with a buttonhole, but nonetheless.

Even better, Roger has a steering wheel—the steering wheel from the fabulous nausea-green Zephyr—in his hand, down by his side like a suitcase. He looks as though things have gone slightly awry.

I react in a welcoming, kindly manner: "Hey, pal, this ain't a fancy dress party," and slam the door in his face.

The lads convulse in laughter at this brilliant witticism, rolling around on the floor until the door swings open and in walks Roger, face glowering, oblivious to the hilarity.

Turns out the drive was a bit of an ordeal, what with the girls swearing, crying, and yelling, and the one directly behind in the backseat swatting his head with her handbag at regular intervals. Also, as geography would have it, the girls lived at various locales nowhere near each other, which meant that, while the volume decreased as each disembarked, there were still many miles to drive around unfamiliar winding lanes before he was finally rid of the lot of them.

Roger, by now frazzled and of course teeth-grindingly resentful, put his foot down to get back to Funville as soon as possible and, screeching around the umpteenth unlit country corner, the Zephyr shot off the road through a hedge, glanced off a tree, and came to rest in a field of potatoes.

Through the smoke and oil and steam, and the incongruous aroma of roast spuds, Roger tried to maneuver the car back onto the road, but the steering wheel felt strangely slack and unresponsive. His befuddled brain finally deduced that it was because it wasn't attached to anything.

So there he sat, cursing our existence and plotting dark, bass-player-type revenge until a friendly local drove up and offered assistance. His car was towed to a garage, closed, of course, and he and his steering wheel got a taxi back to Bongo's.

This all puts something of a dampener on our little party so, soon enough, after a few poorly received commiserations, we all head off to our snug duvets.

Goodnight, all.

Next morning, at breakfast, with four throbbing skulls, one fingernail-ravaged back, and one puffy black eye between us, we are forced to listen to a lecture on morality. The peeved and pious stand arms folded, with faces wearing stern but pleading expressions, as they admonish us about the bacchanal they apparently overheard the previous evening and can recall in the most minute detail.

We sit silently, trying not to laugh, mindful that we don't want to get kicked out and give up our duvets and fine food just yet.

The lead inquisitor walks up and down before us, droning on about Christian behavior being generally incompatible with girls screaming, running in hallways, and refrigerator looting, as I try to indicate to him, with meaningful sideways eye movement, that I think Lou is the main culprit.

The guy gets the message and directs the remainder of his lecture at Lou. Afterward, Lou, on a smarm-and-charm offensive, pledges that we have seen the error of our ways, we are truly repentant, and that the outrage will not be repeated. Amen.

On that cheery note we are off to a full day's rehearsal, to be interrupted, presumably, only by a delicious lunch. Roger comes into the main room having delivered the steering wheel to the garage and finding out that, along with the various dents and scrapes, the car's track rod is kaput. From the look of him, that same diagnosis could apply to Roger.

Sullenly, he plugs in his bass and begins to tune. His mood is dark and comes complete with a cartoon cloud hanging menacingly over his head. In his mind all the aggravation of the last few weeks—forget that, the last few months—has come to a head. He's had it. His demeanor says eloquently: life just can't get any worse.

This, of course, would be the precise moment Eunan picks to walk backward in high heels, trip over a coil of wires, and crash his scrawny Irish body into a speaker cabinet. The cabinet flies backward, sending airborne the heavy Hiwatt amp that was perched on top, which flies for only a millisecond before it plummets downward and lands like an intercontinental ballistic missile in a splintery, twanging crunch on Roger's acoustic guitar. Even to the eye of a non-musician, the guitar is obviously, completely, not to say comically, destroyed. The guitar Roger loves and has owned for years is now a V-shaped, Picasso tangle of broken wood and snapped strings.

The rest of us freeze, unable to look at one another, desperately trying not to giggle, trying to think of the most unfunny things known to man, like Labrador retriever puppies run over by trucks or children with dreadful afflictions or Benny Hill. Anything, just so we can save the raucous laughter for later. Roger slowly turns around and surveys the scene with his one working eye. Calmly, eerily so, he takes off his bass guitar, puts it carefully down, and walks over to the crime scene.

He sighs, bends down, and lifts the Hiwatt amp out of the middle of the mess and places it to one side. Then, shaking his head, he picks up his crushed, mangled guitar—basically two sections of exotic firewood with wires attached—holds it in his hands, and stares at it in dead, reverent silence. Nobody makes a sound. No words seem appropriate.

Then Lou says, "Hey, Rog, can you give me an E?"

The day goes from mad to worse. We sound terrible. Maybe it's the hangovers. Maybe it is because we are not used to rehearsing in such a large space, in such luxury with such full bellies, but something is definitely wrong. The music sounds thin, Eunan is at his tame, timid worst, and Stein's new Chris Andrews Italian organ sounds like it should be the comic accompaniment to a clown convention.

We force it for an hour then take a break to wander off and sulk separately. We try again and argue our way to lunch. Roger is just going through the motions. He acts as though he'd rather be anywhere else, back at Boosey & Hawkes, perhaps, polishing his umpteenth spit valve.

I bark at Eunan to try to get him going. He snarls back and plays the remainder of the song with his back to us, facing his amp, like Stuart Sutcliffe in Hamburg, his bony rear end defiantly static. If only the music was half as angry as the band. Then Roger tells us he's not crazy about the new songs Stein and I are writing, which begins a shouting session that soon erupts into shoving and swearing.

You can go from peacemaker to antagonist in two seconds with this mob. One guy holds another guy back, saying "Calm down, calm down," then it's "You fucking calm down, cunt," then those two are going at it. Then another guy tries to break them up but catches a clip in the mouth, and soon it's a three-for-all. Within ten seconds we're all punching and swearing and knocking over cymbal stands; microphones are flying and feedback is screaming.

Into the room run five or six peaceniks, waving their arms and yelping shrill orders like "Don't touch the tapestries." One particularly demented-looking specimen actually clangs a large gong he's carrying.

It is this gong that cuts through our bloodlust. So ludicrous does it look and sound that we turn, hands still gripped around throats or clutching lapels, to stare at the mad gonger.

This guy could be a star on the prog-rock circuit. With his beard, filthy hair, and sandals he'd be a cert for, say, Blodwyn Pig or Uriah Heep or any other unkempt herd of posers.

So we endure our second lecture of the day, this one even more religious than the last. They even phone the great Bongo himself to double-check that he actually invited these maniacs into his home. I get on the phone and blab away about misunderstandings, miscommunication; I apologize a bit and lie a bit more.

"Hey, c'mon, Cliff, you and the Shads must have had a few wild nights and maybe even the odd slap-fest." His mood improves by degrees and all seems fine; Cliff's a complete gentleman about it all. I put Scary Magdalene back on the phone and join the boys picking through the wreckage.

Luckily, we didn't break any of the room's precious chattels, though our crap equipment took a few shots and the amps are buzzing and popping even more than usual. We take a break for a beer. This helps matters enough to put grudges aside and get through the rest of the rehearsal without killing each other.

Roger gets his car back from the garage. It cost a bomb but at least the steering wheel is back where it belongs and the potatoes have been hosed off the undercarriage. After dinner we climb in and head off to the pub. Well, not *the* pub, of course, but another one, and this time, except when pouring drinks down, we keep our traps shut. Like a good Christian lad, I'm back under my cloud-like duvet by midnight.

Next day, Sunday, we suffer half an hour of hymns at breakfast sung by a motley assembly of troubadours in the room next door. They go by the name Agape and have a hand-painted sign to prove it. We sit there scoffing scrambled eggs and rolling our eyes, mocking and giggling. Lou sings along to "Rock of Ages." Then we get to work in the main room.

Today, the music is better, tighter, more fun to play. Roger even smiles once. Sort of. Late in the afternoon, we pack up, say good-bye to the sect, and head back to Bushey, Hatch End, Finchley Gardens, and London Street. Before we leave, Lou visits Cliff's liquor cabinet with a hairpin and a fork and liberates a souvenir bottle of whiskey.

The hippies stand in a cluster at the door with distinctly un-Christian expressions of relief on their hairy mugs. One of them half flashes a peace sign then thinks better of it and scratches his ear instead.

On the long drive through Hertfordshire my thoughts go back and forth between two things.

This is nowhere near the sound Stein and I are looking for.

And I will really miss that duvet.

VII

Chris Andrews (unaware of Slats, of course) has us booked to play a gig at an Air Force base in West Wittering, wherever that is. Well, that sounds promising. We are the support act to a bunch of no-hopers he signed a few months ago. They have a whiny little pop number, a simpering plea to a babe called Ivy, which has taken up a sure-to-be-fleeting residence in the upper 90s of the Top 100.

West Wittering is a million miles away and, despite Brillo's psychotic rally driving, we arrive late enough to induce some straight-arrow type in a gray uniform with egg-yellow stripes on the arms and really shiny buttons to go absolutely berserk.

The base is a world unto itself. Straight Arrow passes us on to two bullet-headed, no-neck freaks that look at us as though we're Martians. They show us to the dressing room. Chris's band is in there: permed hair, drinking orange juice, wearing denim. They freeze when we walk in. Freeze they may. We've got an even bigger chill in store for them.

We don't say a word. We act like they don't exist. We occupy 90 percent of the dressing room. Slap on the war paint, wrap the boa, strap on the belts and all the armor. Away we go. No soundcheck.

Shock news! The air force hate us. The sea of drunken stubble-heads and their country-bumpkin girls hate us the second we tread the stage. They bay and whistle and hoot and yell out their thick invective, howling afterward at their wit like moronic post-kill wolves. Before we play a note, before we plug in, before Lou shifts the snare between his legs just the way he likes it, they hate us.

I'm adjusting the microphone, twisting it up to lip height, when the first splash of beer hits my shoes. The bleary-eyed fly-boy who did the splashing is standing front and center, waving an empty glass, arm around his council-estate slattern. His sandpaper skull is at a perfect football height and I pull my leg back like I'm going to volley his head into a goal twenty-eight yards away. He flinches and ducks behind his tart. Then he gestures that I should come down and stand in front of him where we could, I don't know, fight, I guess. Eejit.

The first two crashing chords of "Melinda Lee" shuts 'em up, or at least drowns 'em out. For three minutes and five seconds. Then the baying boys are back. They're crowding in on the stage, pointing their fingers, throwing things, spitting. Look at these specimens. The sons of the Few. They are a disgrace to the Royal Air Force.

If they think they are going to intimidate us, they are wrong. Drunken provincial twits.

The four lads behind me, bless 'em, rise to the occasion. Gone are the divisions and rifts of the weekend at Bongo's. They play a blinder. We rock this shiny-buttoned-uniform joint under a constant barrage of garbage, beer, and lout-speak.

We end the set on our terms: crashing, feedback-drenched chords to shake up their tight little auditorium. After the last ear-assaulting hog-howl of Eunan's guitar dies, I give the fly-boys a Nazi salute and a "Sieg heil" as a final attempt to win their hearts.

Then we exit stage left, like Snagglepuss would have wanted it, to an absolute screeching cacophony of drunken RAF derision. They want to kill us. Well, scramble your fighter planes, boys.

Back in the dressing room, Chris's headlining act are mouths-open in shock and perms quivering, having heard the reception their "warm-up" act garnered. As we walk past the little popsters, with their song at number 94 in the charts, Stein looks at them and out of the side of his mouth sneers, "Follow that, pussies."

Two days later Roger quits. It is not a shock. It had been coming. The gulf between him and the rest of us had been widening. He's got a real life; he lives in a house; he's got a car, a job, an ironing board. He doesn't like the direction Stein and I are taking this thing. He won't wear makeup—don't ask him. He wants to play the blues and he's not used to being constantly booed onstage. Perhaps he's been feeling increasingly marginalized.

It is a watershed moment for me. He is the last of the old guard. The last original member of the band for which I auditioned way back when. He joins the list of former members who either couldn't take the heat or were elbowed out the kitchen door: Tim, Martin, Yosemite, and Mal.

So now it's back to, where else, the *Melody Maker*. On April 7 we place an ad.

WANTED
Young bass player
Wymanesque
For outrageous band
Essential: Pretty face (No beards)
Slender build
Look, act, think like a star
We offer fame & fortune
Phone 723-0759 after 5 pm

Brian is tall, slim, good-looking, nineteen years old, with black Japanese-straight shoulder-length hair parted in the middle, King's Road clobber, Fender Precision. There's only one problem.

He's American.

There's a letter nailed to our door, addressed to Mr. Spark Matheson—an eviction notice from the law firm of Claude Barker and Partners. This is the second home in a row for Lou and me and the second eviction notice, third if you count Dick giving us the heave-ho. How dare he attempt this legal ploy. How can he reasonably expect us to come up with rent every single Monday without fail? We are musicians, for Christ's sake.

This life is brimful of tedious irritants, and it's beginning to get on my nerves. Booed, threatened, arrested, evicted, convicted, spat upon, named as a nincompoop in the newspaper, starving, pissing out of windows, reduced to common thievery for sustenance, scrounging shillings to feed the meter. This life has sunk to the most low and demeaning level possible.

Lou chooses this moment to announce that he has a boil on his arse.

A frost-covered Wednesday evening. Famished, gaunt, forsaken, and for-

lorn, the two of us sit in our slum, on the brink of eviction and with nary a
shilling to our name. Lou sits sort of sideways on his bed.

So dark is it that we can barely see each other, not that we particularly want
to. We're wrapped in blankets and coats, and one of us, I'm not saying who, has
a tea-towel hat. Make that a boil on his arse and a tea-towel hat.

Apparently, this boil has been developing for a while now and, coincidentally,
Lou has been forging a reputation as something of a gentleman for the numerous
times he has given up his seat on the bus for a lady.

This morning he summoned the nerve not only to tell me about it, but also
to ask me to lance it.

"What? Are you out of your mind?"

"Come on, it'll take five seconds and it's killing me."

"You're serious? Are you crazy?"

"Yes, I'm serious. I can't sit down. Help me out."

"Even if I knew the first thing about lancing boils, what makes you think
I'd lance a fucking boil on your arse?"

"It's easy. You stick a needle through it and drain it."

"Oh Christ, spare me the visuals. And if it's so easy, you do it."

"It's on my arse. I can't reach it. I had to look in a mirror to even see the
bastard."

"Forget it. You've lost your mind, mate. I'm a singer, not a boil lancer."

"But you're my friend."

"To hell with that. Friendship has its limits. And believe you me, arse-boil
lancing is the fucking limit."

"But . . ."

"Take it to the girl in Clapham."

Lou's got a girl in Clapham. Rule number five broken again.

Now it's nighttime and we don't have one shilling for electricity. Wrapped
in blankets, with freezing fingers we play endless games of Crazy Eights until it
gets too dark. For a forlorn hour neither of us has mumbled a syllable. Misery,
thy name is Lou and Andrew.

Then Lou is struck by an idea so brilliant that at first we just continue
sitting, stunned by the sheer genius of it. Next, we are kneeling on the floor,

tea-towel hat flying into a corner, me striking match after match, all the better to illuminate the electric meter as Lou, working with a pin and fork, attempts to pick the lock of the attached coin box. It is difficult and the obstacles include an imprinted lead seal, the breaking of which is meant to alert the authorities to malfeasance.

As we have by now learned, no lock can withstand Louis John Sparks armed with a fork. This meter is no exception. With a metallic pop the lead stamp falls apart, the back of the meter swings open, and a cascade of shillings spews out onto the floor.

We yell and laugh and celebrate and count them. Over ten quid. Ten quid! It's after midnight. All the stores are closed and shuttered; all the streets are dark and bare.

Then Lou is struck by a second idea almost equally brilliant as the first, and we are out the door in seconds, pockets swaying and clinking with the weight of our—possibly, arguably—ill-gotten gains. He has remembered a vending machine just down Aldenham Road, and there we go to load up on twenty or so chocolate bars. Back in our sty, we scoff chocolate and swig Tizer until we are bloated, groaning, and sick.

For the next few days we keep the back of the meter open and use the same shilling over and over again to power our new luxury lifestyle. Meanwhile, we stock up on cigs, cheese, bread, eggs, and a couple of pints. What a caper.

Four days later Lou patches up the meter and melds the lead seal back together. Eunan says he's found a squat in West Hampstead. A squat. Charming.

We've got another gig coming up in April at the Café des Artistes. Rehearsals with American Brian are going okay. He can play all four strings and he's reasonably fast on the uptake. Not to mention he's got an amp that works and doesn't buzz or hiss or burst into flames at regular intervals.

And he is a jolt, an adrenaline shot—a new bass player after all this time with Roger. He's got energy aplenty but he doesn't understand our look or philosophy or attitude. He wears stars-and-stripes trousers, for Christ's sake. He says "far out" at annoying intervals until I take him aside and tell him to knock it off. Take a break down the boozer and all he talks about is the Doobie Brothers.

That's it. Rule number six in my rock 'n' roll template: No Americans. They can't dress, can't shave, can't rock. No Americans. I wanted a band of Englishmen and what have I got? An American, a Norwegian, an Irishman, and a Micmac.

How'd that happen?

In the days before the gig, Stein and Eunan (I've completely lost patience with that name; it is about as non–rock 'n' roll as it is possible to get—must come up with something) go to Kingston, upon Thames I'll have you know, to a music shop called Bargain Basement.

They "part exchange" some of the junk from Chris Andrews's garage—one 50-watt Bendix PA amp, two 4 x 10 columns, one El Pico microphone—for a Hi Sound speaker cabinet and a small but deadly piano that doesn't require five guys to lug it up and down the stairs at London Street. Total cost of transaction: £83.60. Cost to the lads: £0.00. Thanks, Chris.

Café des Artistes, April 21, 1973: Eunan, now living in a squat in West Hampstead, gives us heart palpitations by showing up, yet again, five minutes before showtime. Incredibly, he'd been arrested earlier in the day for selling, guess what, stolen women's blouses on Portobello Road. They just let him out of jail an hour ago. It appears we've got an elderly, none-too-bright, petty-criminal wide boy on guitar. Anyway, we're back, and from the first note we take no prisoners. Down in the catacombs of the Café, the joint is jammed at 8 p.m. and by midnight you can barely breathe. We mainly play our own songs, debuting one called "Running Wild."

We can hardly take a break between sets as the crowd is so raucous, demanding we continue. I'm not so sure that they're in love with us; they're just drunk and don't want the music to stop. Or maybe they really don't want the between-set disco. Maybe they do indeed want us. They go mad when we come back onstage, and for the third set we just play what we did in the first.

American Brian, with blue streaks on his cheeks like a glam Comanche, blue stack heels, white strides, and a shimmery blue T-shirt, has definitely added another dimension to the sound. And we're glad to be back in London.

West Wittering was an absolute delight, but this is our kind of town.

After paying expenses, the van, and the man, we don't end up with much. They want us back next week, though, and they can't have missed the effect we had on the punters. Afterward, Eunan and I spend the night at Brian's place in Marble Arch. He lives with his dad, who appears to be some sort of mid-level diplomat, with the accompanying belly over belt and polyester leisure suits. They've got an American flag in the foyer. Either that or it's Brian's trousers draped over the banister. Great pad. Eunan and I share a large bed, with a glass dome way above our heads. Rain beats down on the dome. The dome leaks. The leak drips on the pillow between our heads. We spend the night far apart, clinging to the outer edges of our respective sides of the bed. This is more than fine by me.

Before we nod off I tell Eunan he's got to do something about his name.

A knock on the door. We hate knocks on the door. Come to think of it, when, in the history of the world, has a knock on the door ever meant anything good? Naturally, we freeze and look at each other with fear and dread in our eyes. Naturally, we don't move a muscle. The knock comes again, louder this time. We still don't so much as bat a mascara-encrusted eyelash. A key rattles in the lock and in walk two Pakistanis. They seem as shocked as we are and start chattering away between themselves in a language we don't understand, but which we enjoy as a brief comedic interlude. Turns out they are here to empty the electric meter. Well, of course they are.

The two of them rattle some keys and fall to their knees in front of the meter. Lou and I look at each other and shrug our shoulders. One of them fingers the lead seal, eyes it suspiciously, and babbles something to his buddy, who looks at us. I say, "What's the prob?" They stick the key in the lock to release the seal, and another to open the back of the meter. Takes them two whole minutes before it swings open. Amateurs. Lou did it in seconds with a fork.

The two of them stare inside. They look at each other and then start yammering a mile a minute. One of them reaches inside and takes out the lone shilling that is in there. Lou and I look at each other, wondering how we missed that one. The meter hasn't been emptied, officially, since we've lived here, and I get the impression that these two were expecting considerably more shillings. They were so optimistic that they even carry a canvas bag to put them all in.

The two of them spring to their feet, bolt out the door and down the stairs. The one word in their babble we were able to make out is "police."

The next few minutes are a whirlwind of activity. No discussion is required. We whip all the clothes into two suitcases, toss them out the window along with the frying pan, shoes, books, and the records that have escaped Lou's bargain-record emporium at Watford station. Next, Lou goes downstairs and stands under the window. I drop our wooden radio into his arms. Good catch. I tear off down the stairs. We gather it all up in our arms and hump it all, glamorous-ragged-refugee style, down Aldenham Road. Two pence in a phone box and we are rescued for the umpteenth time by Brillo.

Fifteen minutes later, we're off to a new life in a West Hampstead squat.

VIII

In West Hampstead (the ugly sister of the other three Hampsteads), at the end of a narrow, winding thoroughfare officially named Railway Walk but known locally, with good reason, as Dog Shit Lane, in a boarded-up, condemned, two-story shell of a Victorian house, Eunan has found us a squat. Squat we must, so squat we will.

On the doorstep to greet us when we get there, what else but a dead rat? What's with the rats? Why are there rats everywhere? Why are they a constant, a motif, a theme in our lives? It is baffling and disgusting. Lou finds a stick and pokes it aside. One knock and Eunan clumps down the stairs and opens the door.

Inside, we spy bare, splintery, rotting wood floors. Blue, flowery, peeling wallpaper, featuring stinking fungi from floor to ceiling. An all-pervading smell of domestic grease, dust, mildew, and grime assaults the nostrils. First door on the left, over Eunan's shoulder, out pops a sweet little ancient lady—gray hair in an unruly bun, cardigan buttoned wrong, dusty burgundy housecoat over top, once-pink slippers—who says, "Kettle's just boiled, boys. Would you like a cup?" We decline, but what a lovely creature.

Suitcases in hand, shrinking from contact with the walls, we go up the creaking, rotting stairs. Up to a hallway and on to the kitchen. Whatever secrets this kitchen had to tell, whatever memories of familial feasts and warmth the room once held, are long, long gone. It is impossible to conceive of anyone actually having the nerve to bring food into such a disgusting place.

All that remains to identify this space as a kitchen is a grease-encrusted stove, gas-fired and miraculously still working but all knobs and dials smashed or missing, and a gray sink filled to overflowing with filthy cracked dishes, chipped cups, and mismatched pots without handles, the lot of them covered in an oleaginous mossy-green scum.

A three-legged table leans drunkenly against a far wall, a garage for the rusted guts of an old Norton motorcycle piled up underneath. Eunan says the electricity and gas are, incredibly, still working. His guitar and amp poke out from under an old blanket in a corner. He says he's had them cranked up at all hours and the old dear downstairs can't hear a thing.

The loo is behind a one-hinged door off the hallway, a nasty, reeking little nook with brown porcelain and overhead chain dangling from a green cistern balanced on a wobbly lead pipe, which is detached from the wall. There is nothing resembling a bathtub.

A small bedroom at the front overlooks the entrance door and Mill Lane. A large bedroom, again at the front but with a locked door, is apparently occupied by a large hippy who, according to Eunan, goes by the handle of Zlatan the Mysterious. Fair enough. Another big room with a defunct fireplace and a small window overlooking the backyard is up for grabs. Eunan and I nab the big room, Lou wants the small one up front, the better to occasionally shag the girl from Clapham.

Done deal. We move in.

Two good things happen. The guy at the Café wants to upgrade us to Saturday nights (about time), effective *tout de suite*, and also we've got a gig coming up, in Mayfair of all places, on May 5. Apparently, some chap in the audience at the Café tried to speak to me but I fobbed him off on Stein. I can't remember. Turns out he signed us up for something called a "debutante ball"— some weird rite for members of the uppertocracy, I gather.

The evening of the Mayfair gig, we show up to a huge flash pad with a big ballroom full of horsey babes in a selection of what look like pastel bridal gowns. The men are a penguin parade, all tuxedos and protruding teeth. I'm not sure what this "deb" scene is all about. I think it's like an auction; the women parade their goods and the men pick which one's bank account they'd most like to annex. Something like that.

We set up, doll up, and let 'er rip. The place goes instantly barmy. Punch

Backstage pre-Southend biker gig. Mal—ashen, terrified, beneath unforgiveable haystack hair. Me—lager-lubed and ready for action. A bit Rita Hayworth but what the hell.

Outside the Rifle Volunteer pub, Bushey. Back: Roger Cooper, yours toothily, and Casino with his favorite mustache. Front: Lou Sparks and Mal.

First photo session, January 1973. From the left: Roger Cooper in a biker jacket he earned the hard way, Casino, me (in the Oxfam cocktail dress), Lou, and Brady.

Mill Lane slum, summer 1973. Me, Lou, and a fab Brats poster from the disastrous gig. Mere days before the Speakeasy.

Ken Mewis. A scoundrel, a rogue, and the greatest manager in history. He's to blame for all of this.

Lou leans out the loo window at 11 Mill Lane and, for the benefit of future tourists, points out the Phlegm Wall.

Lou and Brady, the day after the attack at the Black Lion. Brady's eyes puffy from punches but Long Life lager held high and furry tongue stuck out defiantly.

Christmas 1973, Fulham Broadway. Lou cooks turkey with all the trimmings, in stark contrast to the tear-jerking, Dickensian deprivation of last year. Turkey carcass blown to smithereens with fireworks shortly thereafter.

Gered's studio, 41 Great Windmill Street. Freezing to death, up the stairs to the floors above. Home to whores, pigeons, and Brats.

En route to Plymouth. Stopped for petrol. Drunk as daft lords. Left to right: Lou Sparks, Derek, me (armed with a crocodile water pistol), Brady (crotch soaked courtesy of crocodile water pistol), Casino Steel brandishing near-empty bottle of Old Grand-Dad. Nine hours to showtime.

Plymouth Tech, 1974. Pink satin chop-frock and Mr. Fish chemise. Brady playing an upside-down Les Paul and Lou looking for the quickest way out of town.

Yeovil (wherever that is), in the dressing room prior to blowing the fragile and increasingly whiny "Stray" off the stage. Quick swipe of Cherry Blaze–Outdoor Girl lipstick across the yap and let's go.

Stray. Back: Buffo, Mildew, Stringy, and S'tunned, some chap, and Ken Mewis. Front: many impressive gold records surrounding the handsome and dangerous Wilf Pine.

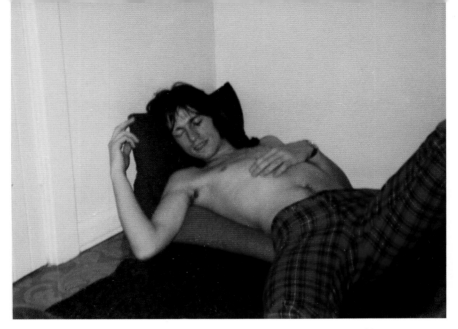

Conked out in a house overlooking Richmond Park, owned by a German woman who kidnapped me after a gig at the Speakeasy. I expect she thought I'd be rather more fun than this.

Sailing HMS *Brats* across the North Sea to Leighton Buzzard. Derek holding Wehrmacht helmet and me in Royal Navy Whites. HMS *Brats* sign courtesy of Lou Sparks.

Flaneur, strolling the streets of Fulham, summer 1974.

The Brats are dead. Just me and Cas left. What could we do? This apparently. Shot in Rupert Court, Soho. Chosen for its undeniable charm.

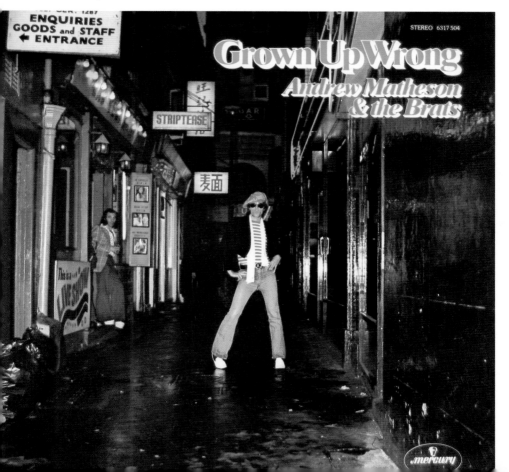

The Hollywood Brats. We will never see their like again.
And thank God for that.

bowls are sucked dry and it appears these gals and their chinless wonders want to shake it all over. We blast them for an hour without coming up for air. We break for ten minutes and are immediately surrounded by debs, to the obvious chagrin of the tooth boys. The air is full of "I say, I say" and "Would you mind awfully playing a song by the Rolling Stones?" Yeah, don't worry, sister; we can play any song awfully.

Just as the next set starts, hundreds of bottles of champagne are lugged in by liveried servants, and within seconds a barrage of corks are blasting off all over the place like antiaircraft guns. Some kind, deluded soul sends a few to us, and I shake one up and spray the dancers in front.

It is a mad scene and we are thoroughly cranked up, rocking the ball, when through the huge doors stride ten coppers who proceed to walk straight to the stage and make gestures like we should stop playing. No dice, officer. We almost make it to the end of the song, but one enterprising bobby rooting around at the side of the stage finds and yanks the plug. One second of silence then the air is full of braying debs and their consorts making with the "I say, I say" bit and the "What on earth do you think you are doing?" and "Do you know who I am?"

Turns out there have been a dozen or so complaints about noise from the more sedate elements in the neighborhood. Bit of overkill, though, sending an entire plod platoon. A few of the head penguins sort it out with the coppers, promises are made, and finally they shove off. As soon as they are out of the street we start it up again, louder than before. We rock until half past midnight, with only one more visit from the cops.

Toward the end of the engagement I wander upstairs in search of a loo. I try door after door to no effect, and then I try a door that opens onto a tableau I have heretofore not encountered in my nineteen years. It is a large room, unlit save for the glow from a fading fire, and there, in the soft light of the dying embers, is a chap splayed, chicken-skin nude (save for black socks and a bowler hat), belly down over a coffee table. This of course, to me, is rather astounding in and of itself, but the truly fascinating aspect, and the one that really grabs my attention, is that he is being mounted and shagged robustly by a Great Dane in striped oven mitts. And when I say a Great Dane I'm not talking Hans

Christian Andersen in kitchen couture here. When I say a Great Dane I'm talking a huge, gray, slobbering mutt with oven mitts over his paws, ramming his canine cock into the arse of a toff I am soon to know as Rupert.

Two other future parliamentarians stand near, fully dressed, sipping champers and commenting on the form, shouting encouragement like "Come on, Rupert, old chap" and "I say, well taken, Rupe." The dog is commenting too, in between thrusts and while drooling on Rupert's back. According to him, Rupert likes it "ruff."

I don't linger.

Back at the squat, we've got a new routine. We rehearse in the kitchen for hours every day. Consequently, we are getting tighter and tighter. Apparently, the girl in Clapham lanced the boil on Lou's arse last week. I'll take his word for it. The last thing I need is visual evidence. That must have been quite the romantic evening. He's playing better, though.

I finish the lyrics for the song we started at Cliff's place. It is called "Chez Maximes" and it is already one of our favorites. We'll unleash it on the Café crowd on Saturday.

American Brian is going nowhere. He's not getting better. He peaked a long time ago, and this Doobie Brothers fixation is pushing me over the edge.

We've got a gig at Flicka, which, according to Stein, is a club at the bottom of Regent Street on an alley off Piccadilly. They put up a fantastic poster calling us a "Great Five-piece Band." It's a glitter-ball disco palace with an older crowd and all they want is nonstop American crap funk junk. What are we doing here?

There is an audible gasp from these cadavers as we hit the stage and an inaudible cry of disbelief when we hit 'em between the ears with the first two chords of "Melinda Lee." No sooner does the song end to desultory applause and a tidal wave of boos than the manager runs up and tells us to turn it down. "Sorry, pal, can't do that. One, two, three, four . . ." and away we go again.

This time a few people get up on the dance floor and begin gyrating, including, to humorous effect, American Brian's old man. Eunan plays like rubbish, Brian's worse. The manager and a few heavies force the issue and bring the show to a premature close. Then they stiff us for the money. Lovely night. So much for the "Great Five-piece Band" they gloated about on the poster.

Day after day in Squatville, the three of us have nothing but rice to eat. Twice a day we eat a bowl of rice. Some days are better than others; the days when I manage to nick a tin of beans or something else to throw in the pan. If I get out of here alive I'll never eat rice again.

I come up with a great idea to remedy the Eunan name situation. It hits me as Lou and I walk down Dog Shit Lane. I run it by Lou and he likes it. We bring the idea to Eunan and he goes for it. Simple solution, just use his last name. That's it, that's all. From this day forth he's known as Brady.

IX

There is only one club in London we now want to play: the Speakeasy. Everybody who is anybody in the music biz goes to the Speak. If we can play there we'll get a record deal. Simple as that. We just know it. Same way we know David Cassidy is four feet eight inches tall. We just know it.

On May 26 Stein and I climb the stairs above the Speakeasy on Margaret Street, intent on meeting Laurie O'Leary. He's the boss of the Speak and, as far as we can gather, Mr. O'Leary is well connected in general. Maybe he'll manage us. We just want to get going, slip our machine, currently idling in neutral, into gear.

We arrive unannounced, as is our custom, having learned that attempting to arrange meetings or appointments never works. Nobody ever wants to see us. Nobody ever says, "Yeah, come on in and see us, boys. What can we do for you?" No, we always have to ambush them, and so far even that is not working.

Up the creaking wooden stairs we go, until we arrive at a small, cluttered outer office manned by a pretty blondish secretary. She heard us coming for a while, squeaking up the stairs. She is ready. What she thinks of us, who knows? We are in über Hollywood Brats regalia: full makeup and Fourth Reich foppery.

She goes into gatekeeper mode, but we mix a gallon of insistence with a thimbleful of charm and soon there comes a barked command from the inner office to enter. Enter we do, to find an obviously busy but accommodating man who stands up, shakes our paws, and tells his secretary to hold all calls. We start yapping a mile a minute while he sits back and listens intently. This is highly unusual for us. The guy is really listening and at various points asking pertinent questions. Such as, do we have a tape? Nope, we don't.

Finally, he interrupts our torrent of self-praise and says he isn't interested in managing anybody, since he has just signed something called the Heavy Metal Kids, but if we tell him where we're playing next, he'll have someone pop down to see us. If we pass muster we get to play the Speak. Wow. We're playing the Café on Saturday so we tell O'Leary the where and the when, and two minutes later we're clattering back down the stairs.

Reaching street level, we try to be cool, contain ourselves, but we are bursting inside and just barely make it around the corner before we start grabbing each other by the lapels, yelling and whooping. This is it and we know it. This is the biggest connection so far. We know a turning point when we see one, a pivotal moment after which all is changed. All we have to do is slay whoever the mystery man is on Saturday night at the Café des Artistes.

We have just enough coin for coffee so we head to a little place not far from Oxford Circus. It is a basement café, and whenever Stein and I are out scuffling and scratching for the Brats we usually wash up here to lick our wounds or celebrate our minuscule victories. We sit for an hour or so nursing one cup and a refill each, honing the set list for Saturday night.

We split up soon after. Mercifully, no drama encountered slinking onto the Tube at Oxford Circus or jumping the turnstiles at West Hampstead. A short run through traffic and on to the relative calm of Dog Shit Lane, head north on Sumatra, pop into Delhi Convenient to buy some Rolos and swipe a tin of salmon, then on to 11 Mill Lane.

Up the stairs, and I catch a rare glimpse of Zlatan the Mysterious: tall, skinny, hunched over, with hair way down his back and all over his face, under his nose and whatnot. He lives in the large front room with the bay windows he has completely covered with taped-on pages from *Time Out*. He's a furtive sort, with a permanently unfocused look in his eye. He doesn't have much truck with us, nor we with him, which suits both parties to a T. We never see him about the place and generally forget that he even exists. He never complains about us rehearsing in the kitchen at all hours, not that it would do him much good, but still, it's nice.

Zlatan invites us into his room one night and, bored stiff as usual, we accept and traipse in. The streetlight outside shines through the yellowed *Time Out* pages, giving a jaundiced light to a room completely hung with ornamental

Eastern carpets and swaths of that cheesy Indian fabric with shiny bits sewn on the ends. Sequins, you know? Whatever.

The floor is covered in even more dusty ruggery. Joss sticks are stuck everywhere, jossing away like mad, making the room cloudy with that nauseatingly sweet fug that hippies can't seem to breathe without. The ghastly, tinny ricochet of sitar music bleats from two big speakers. Zlatan is dressed in a mauve kaftan. There's a theme here.

He has recently returned from Nepal or Afghanistan or some other utterly repellent outpost and has with him a souvenir slab of hashish. Said slab, he tells us, has been smuggled across various borders taped to his inner thigh. I suppose in the frazzled recesses of his hippy brain he thinks this intensely unsavory detail will render the drugs even more enticing. It doesn't.

He finally asks, would we like to buy some? Tree, wrong, barking, mate. Zlatan's hospitality evaporates.

Soon after, back in our room, we concoct a plan. Not much of a plan, really. It goes like this: Zlatan the Mysterious leaves premises, Lou picks lock, we locate stash and break off chunk he's bound not to notice, Lou locks place back up. We smoke stash. Flawless.

We drink tea and wait, listening intently for the sound of Zlatan buggering off. At midnight Brady, having to work the next morning in the wig factory, peels off his reeking socks and climbs into bed. Lou and I wait until three in the morning and then we also conk out.

Next day, noonish, Lou creeps along the creaking hallway and places lughole to door. He reports sitar, tablas, and shuffling about. So we wait some more. We drink tea and play Crazy Eights throughout the afternoon and into the evening. Brady arrives home from his wig gig and joins the vigil. Lou boils up a pan of rice and stirs in a delicious tin of recently swiped cocktail wieners.

Finally, mid-evening, we hear Zlatan's door open and shut, followed by the rattle of skeleton key in lock. Then the sound of sandals shuffling past our door, down the stairs, and out into the London night. We dash to Lou's wee room at the front of the house and twitch the blanket he has nailed over the window. There goes Zlatan the Mysterious, trekking off past the streetlamps, loon pants flapping like pavement sails around the masts of his bare bony shins.

We spring into action. First step, run downstairs and prop a chair under the doorknob to stall the Mysterious one, should he unexpectedly return mid-heist. Next, Brady is stationed at Lou's window to watch out for same. Then I scan the outline of Zlatan's door for taped-on hairs or any other low trickery meant to discern uninvited entry. Lou gets out his tool kit of bent wire, hairpins, a nail, and a knife.

Lou drops to his knees and applies gentle, experienced fingers to Zlatan's knob. For a safecracker of his expertise the lock proves no challenge whatsoever, and within thirty seconds we're in.

If the lock provided no test whatsoever, we could have sent Ray Charles in to search for the stash. No Sherlockian sleuthing required, no ransacking. There it is in the middle of the muddle on a small table, sitting unwrapped on a Santana album. *Oye como va.*

Lou decides that, rather than breaking off a chunk, which will stand out like a bite in a sandwich, we should take off a few nibbles from around the outside. He's right. The slab looks unmolested. So we take some more. Then, just to be sure, a little nibble more. Then there is a voice right behind us. "You found it."

We jump out of our skins. It is Brady.

"Christ! You're supposed to be on lookout. Get back to the window."

"Hey, it's no problem. He won't be back for hours."

"Just get back to your post and stop bloody scaring us to death."

Brady returns, muttering Gaelic oaths, to the front bedroom but immediately begins yelling in a non-manly octave. "He's coming back! He's coming back, quick, quick!"

We drop the block of hashish back on Santana's *Abraxas* and tear out of the room. I dash off down the hall, cupping the dark brown crumbles in my hands with Brady hot on my heels. Lou feverishly works with his paraphernalia to change break and enter to lock and scarper. Then Brady remembers the chair blocking the entry door and leaps off down the stairs to yank it out of the way in the nick of. He makes it back to the top and dives into our room, just as Zlatan's key begins scratching and poking around the outside lock.

With a final, desperate twist of the bent wire Lou hears the blessed sound of dead bolt clicking into strike plate, scoops up his tools, and runs on tiptoes along the hall and into our room. He palms the light switch down and we stand in darkness, barely breathing, listening to the scratchy plod of Jesus boots ascending the stairs and passing our door.

At his door Zlatan pauses, no key jingling, no doorknob turning. We stand in the dark of our lair not making a sound, terrified that the robbery has been discovered and soon a hairy, emaciated, hippy-swami, drug-smuggling maniac will be pounding at our door for revenge and retribution. But the first hurdle is hurdled. He opens his door and closes it behind him.

We await the discovery of the benibbled slab. Perhaps he has scales and weighs it at regular intervals. What am I talking about, perhaps? Of course he does. He's a purveyor, after all. But nothing untoward happens. Just a bit of muffled shuffling about, then silence, then Ravi Shankar. I'm saying it's Ravi Shankar but I don't really know. It's sitar so who else could it be?

The plan worked, the larceny went undiscovered. We stuff sweaters and assorted T-shirts into the cracks at the bottom and top of our door, turn on the light, and examine our loot.

Not a bad caper.

X

Saturday night at the Café des Artistes. Outside, for the first time, there is a huge blowup picture of the Hollywood Brats and a lineup fifty feet down the street. It is eight o'clock and inside the Café, well, the place is sardine-can jammed. This must be against every fire regulation in existence. Other than the front door I've never seen an exit, nor have any of the lads. If the IRA decide— on a whim, you know, the way they do—to bomb this joint we're doomed. Nobody can move down here. The kids just sway or lean en masse to the bad pop hits pounding out of the speakers. The brick tunnels and warrens glisten with moisture and smell of cigarettes, perfume, beer, and tourists.

The five of us sit in the anteroom, just off the stage. We've been here for hours with no food, just cans of lager. We did a soundcheck earlier that is utterly pointless now that there is a seething, baying mob in the place. Through the frayed, red velveteen curtain we can hear them yelling for us, but we're not moving until nine o'clock.

Lager, sweat, noise, and adrenaline; Lou keeps it light but we're on edge, nervous yet itching to get out there and kill whomever Mr. O'Leary has sent to suss us out. American Brian looks like, any second now, he's going to puke all over his brand-new Kenny Market stars-and-stripes booties. (What's with Americans and their flag, anyway? They're always either burning it or wearing it or staring at it, mumbling, with their hands over their hearts.)

Nine o'clock, and the DJ kills the vinyl. Now the crowd really goes at it, yelling and stomping their feet, chanting, "Hollywood Brats, Hollywood Brats." Unbelievable. We've never heard that before. We're standing up but we make them wait just a little more. Finally, at ten past, we can't delay any longer, it's getting stupid out there. Lou leads the way, entering stage right, followed by Stein, American Brian, Brady, then me. The joint goes psycho.

The stage is barely a foot off the floor, so standing at the microphone it all erupts right there in front of me. We don't waste time, we don't chitchat, we don't introduce ourselves. We've got this congregation's salvation and we hit 'em with it right where it hurts—and we do it quick. All it takes is those first two chords of "Melinda Lee" and we've got them in the palms of our hands. Look at them go, bouncing up and down. And I can't believe it, but I'm starting to recognize some of these characters out front. Some of these boys I saw last week, and the week before that. Now they are wearing makeup. Well, I declare.

We usually slow it down for the third song, giving them Little Walter's "Confessin' the Blues," but tonight there is no chance. They want what we do best and that's fast and loud, and we do not disappoint. The crowd is pushing in waves from the back and idiots are crushing in on us, Japanese girls pushed onto the stage.

Halfway through the set, some wild pharmaceutical boy in slap 'n' slash makeup does a stage plunge and shoves the microphone into my face, right in my kisser. It must be painful but I don't feel a thing, until we're back in the dressing alcove soaked in sweat.

If Mr. O'Leary's man is out there then he'll see that we have done the business. He can't have failed to notice that we deliver the goods, and if we can kill 'em here we can kill 'em down the road on Margaret Street at the exalted Speakeasy. We keep expecting the guy to stick his head in and say something but nobody shows.

Half past ten, next set, and more of the same mayhem. Wait a minute. What did I say? Same mayhem? Nah. This is worse. Much worse. The crush of bodies pushed right up to the stage is insane. Are they just ramming them in out there at street level? There is no security, no management, no control, no nothing. And down here at the business end, things are getting downright dangerous.

We kick it off with Chuck's "Little Queenie": Brady alone on stage setting the rhythm, snarling chords, teetering on guy-heels, playing the crowd. We let him roll for a full thirty seconds before Lou walks onstage, sits down at his kit, yawns, and then joins him, adding the thick thud of the kick drum to the potion. Then we introduce Yankee B's walking bass lines, me at the mic, standing, staring, then Stein strides to the keys, sticks out a thumb, and executes a tumbling, descending, four-beat glissando. Lou picks it up on the three with a snare roll, and on the cymbal crash we're all in.

And after that? Well, after that it is pure insanity.

And if Little Queenie's too cute to be a minute over seventeen, what about these four Japanese chicks squashed up in a line right in front of my microphone stand? One has definitely pissed herself. American Brian notices—well, it's obvious—and he's laughing and pointing it out to me. Her orange stockings are soaked, her high heels are splashing in a pool of used Chablis but, to her credit, she doesn't seem bothered in the slightest. Well, she couldn't exactly go to the loo and come back, could she? She's got her priorities smack on. Grab some floor space, defend it, and watch the Hollywood Brats. My kind of gal.

But it's one of her friends that has my attention. She is quite simply the most beautiful girl I've ever seen in my life and she's not taking her eyes off me. She is gorgeous. Who is the most stunningly beautiful Oriental babe you've ever seen in a film? Well, whoever it is, she's nothing compared to this pouting, yowza package not twelve inches away from my drooling lips here in the Café des Artistes this night, this fated night.

The midnight hour comes and goes down here in the rancid, sweaty warren of the Café, and the Hollywood Brats wrap up proceedings with "Nightmare" followed by Bobby Troup's "Route 66," which we peel off for five or six minutes, Brady and Stein trading solos. Stein's doing Jerry Lee; Brady's careening back and forth between Keith and Jeff.

Crescendo. And that's it. We wave good-bye, I tip the top hat, slip through the velveteen, and collapse on the wooden benches. Sweat is dripping. The barkeep sends in a tray of Carlsberg. Must have needed armed guards to get it here. We're exhausted but wound up tight at the same time. The crowd is screeching for a little more, more, more attention, more noise, but that's not our style. We did what we came to do.

We drink and lark about and talk to the brave souls who seek us out in our sweaty little cave. Visitors arrive, visitors depart, but none seem like they could be an emissary from the exalted realm of the Speakeasy.

The DJ is back, earning his coin. T. Rex, Stevie Wonder still very superstitious, O'Jays riding the "Love Train." People are dancing. Japanese tourists come into our little cave to say hello. One of them is my gorgeous little geisha. Her name is Markido and she asks me to autograph her pink plastic handbag.

I nab my share of the £25, take hold of Markido's delicate, blood-red-fingernailed hand, and suggest we exit into a London night crammed with promise and intrigue. Her English is minimal and cute beyond repair, and she relies a lot on the words "sexy" and "yes," which I assure her will do perfectly for me.

But first, as Markido indicates via sumptuous silent-film eye movements, I have to deal with a hatchet-faced crone of a chaperone I hadn't noticed before. However, as luck would have it, said crone is more than distracted by the other three, especially the one who had the rather damp front-of-stage moment, so Markido and I make our escape through the sweating cave warren of the Café and the outstretched hands of drunken well-wishers into a warm Fulham night. You know, the night. The one I mentioned earlier, full of promise and intrigue and whatnot.

Markido knows the way back to where she's staying and there we head, holding hands and looking up at the night sky, where a beautiful, glowing full moon bursting with romance and portent would be if only there was a god of romance taking care of such matters. As it is, we can't even see one paltry star.

Who cares? Every fifty yards or so, we duck into cobbled alleys and down white basement steps for wet kisses, caresses, fumbles, and garment inspection. Finally, we arrive at the beautiful Georgian mansion where she is staying.

We can't go in, of course. There would be outrage, an international incident at best, reputations left in tatters. But she's not letting me go that easily, either. She grabs a handful of Mr Fish chemise and pulls me into a sheltered courtyard, beneath the discreet canopy of a swaying weeping willow. We kiss deeply, softly, then ravenously, lit by the willow-diffused light of a distant streetlamp.

Markido whispers "sexy" and "yes" at all the right intervals, and then, panting, she tears herself from our clinch, reaches out, strokes me through my velvet trousers, and says something I interpret to mean, "Get it out, big boy."

Madam, your wish is my command. I undo the button, slowly slide down the zipper, reach inside, and release my rearing, straining manhood into the air. There is the usual sharp intake of breath, the gasp of surprise at the length and girth, the murmur of astonishment and approval.

And Markido liked it, too.

XI

Days of nervous drudgery follow. We sleep until 3 p.m. then get up for tea and
a bowl of rice. I'm sick to death of rice. At least in those countries where rice is
a staple they throw in a few bits of dog or snake now and then to liven it up.
We've got nothing unless I swipe it.

It is boiling hot outside and yet I go to the shop dressed in a gray faux-fur
coat. Sweating rivers while Lou distracts the shopkeeper, I stuff what I can into
the deep pockets. What I nab depends on which aisle I'm in when Lou creates
the diversion. Today, it's soap, toothpaste, and a tin of beans.

No call from Mr. O'Leary. Stein hovers around his phone every day, waiting
for him to ring. So far, so what? Maybe he didn't send anyone to see us.

Brady gets home, has some rice, and soon after, American Brian and Stein
show up. We rehearse for a couple of hours.

We're working on a new song, called "Courtesan," which we want to sound
like a Panzer tank cruising across the Polish countryside. American Brian is
having difficulty grasping this concept.

He's seriously getting on my wick. Lou and he don't seem to be gelling and,
worse, he's wearing a T-shirt with a peace sign on the front. He's got to go.

Days drag by and still no call from Mr. O'Leary. Stein and I argue about
the merits of calling him at his office. It's tempting but we hold out. Lou goes
to see the girl in Clapham. It's that bad.

Brady breaks out some cunningly hidden wig dosh, and we have a few too
many lagers and then venture out to the Marquee for the first time since I
popped Freddie from Queen. As a career move, I mention to Oily Jack that he's
got bad judgment and that we're going to be playing the Speakeasy, and ha, ha,

ha, and so on, something brilliant along those lines. Three baboons escort us to the door.

On the way back to West Hampstead, nursing a new grievance and complaining for the hundredth time about American Brian, Brady comes up with an idea. Seems he used to hang around with a bass player, go to auditions with him and such—says he looks okay and plays okay. He says the guy's in a band but he's been sniffing around, asking about a gig, so why don't we go talk to him.

The four of us get done up and travel to meet the bass player. His name is Derek and he lives in Swiss Cottage. We go in and I'm immediately wary. He's got a girlfriend, two Siamese cats, and a white shag carpet. Three bad signs. He's in some band with a name like Piledriver or Steamroller, and he shows us a publicity photo.

They look like every band in the world: the jeans, the hair, the mustaches. You'd have to be a saint not to sneer. He looks half-decent, though, and with the usual overhaul we might be able to slap him into shape. So we talk, Brady taking the lead, for about an hour, then Derek says, "No, thanks." Bright boy. What a waste of breath. We give Brady some serious grief on the way home.

Later in the week Lou, who has been in Clapham for days, gets back and he's walking even funnier than usual. He tells us a black guy shot him in the arse. He drops drawers and shows us the bandage. Fifty-two stitches on three levels and a deep, pointy probe rooting around in his right bum cheek to dig out the slug. Yeeowch. His arse has been through some drama lately.

On the operating table—facedown, arse up, white and bleeding under the lights, recently lanced boil the least of his worries—Lou gave the police a description of his assailants. There were two black guys. One was wearing a trilby and the other looked like Johnny Nash, the "I Can See Clearly" guy.

Clapham police are on the case.

Jesus. Shot in the arse. Not quite the death in the band that Stein craves but not bad. Not bad at all.

From the debutante ball gig we get another booking in Mayfair, this time at a club called Samantha's, £25 for two sets. I'm a bit concerned, sussing the crowd, checking the decor because of the Flicka fiasco, but we go down a storm. We have fun all night long, and the nastier we play the more this Mayfair crowd likes it. I spy a few lads in the audience that were at the Café last week. Done up to the nines they are, too, with makeup and all sorts of nonsense. American Brian's old man is also there again, and dancing again. He's a chubby dervish in a three-piece suit with love beads and rapidly disappearing inhibitions. He's like a polyester-clad Alley Oop. Look at that caveman go.

At the end of the last song of the second set Stein stands up and pushes his piano off the stage, then he kicks his amp over. It starts buzzing, popping, and screaming feedback. The audience goes crazy. Charlie George, Arsenal ace, is clapping and laughing.

Next day, we give American Brian the boot.

Day after that, the blondish babe from O'Leary's office calls and says we're booked into Regent Sounds Studio on July 13.

Another ad in the *Melody Maker*, another dickhead avalanche. Another night in the squat but, thanks to Samantha's, we're drinking beer and eating rice with sausages. Bit of Zlatan's hash, then it's off to bed. Lou goes to his little room at the front and we turn the lights out and nod off to a deep, dreamy sleep born of sausages, hashish, lager, and laughs. The sleep of the just.

Two hours later, in the dead of night, there is a mighty smash as the front door is kicked in. Dogs are barking, many dogs, big dogs, Baskervilles size by the sound of it, and "barking" doesn't even begin to describe it. They are howling for blood. We're bolt upright in our beds, blankets to our chins, eyes wide and terrified in the classic karate defensive stance.

A thunder of boots up the stairs behind the dogs, malevolent voices screaming, swearing. In seconds, they are at our door, which comes smashing inwards, followed by three snarling, barking, salivating Doberman pinschers choking at chains barely holding them back. Hey, Robert Johnson, hellhounds might have been on your trail, mate, but they're on my bed, two feet from my scrotum.

You think you got the blues?

The men behind the dogs are all huge, hairy, dressed in black, and carrying clubs and cricket bats and crowbars. They speak just like you'd imagine they would.

"Get the fuck out of this fucking house. We want you gone, fucking gone, or even your fucking mothers won't recognize you. We'll kick your fucking brains in."

At this point, for quite unnecessary emphasis, he takes his club and smashes our radio to bits with one blow. Despite this, the pile of electronics, wires, knobs, and splintered mahogany somehow turns itself on, and the odious Sweet are suddenly in the room singing "Blockbuster," just to add to the Fellini-esque ambience. A kick in the dial stifles Brian Connolly's squawk.

The terror doesn't let up, and down the hall we can hear Lou and Zlatan getting the same treatment. The dogs are positively throttling themselves in their attempt to get at me and rip my throat out. Brady starts blathering about attempting to pay rent but the lead ogre cuts him off.

"Shut the fuck up or I'll let the canines tear your face off for dinner. We don't want your fucking rent, we want you to fucking fuck off fucking quick. You got that, you fucking mick cunt? Fuck off back to fucking paddy land, you IRA shite, or I'll have my dogs on your bollocks."

I am standing on my bed, squeezed into the corner beside the window and a heartbeat away from jumping two floors down into the alley stark naked while not under the influence of LSD. One dog is up on my bed, snout drawn back from glistening rows of three-inch-long teeth snapping at the exact height of my crotch. Two other thugs step in and start smashing things at random. Thankfully, we haven't got much so it's over quickly.

Thug number one then yells something and the dogs immediately shut up and back off, gasping for breath, whining with disappointment and begging for another chance. He walks to the side of my bed, leans over me with beery breath, and snarls, "You got it, Nancy?"

Nancy replies, "Yes." And then they're gone. Thumping down the stairs and out past the front door hanging off its hinges, down the step and off into the night. It couldn't have lasted more than five minutes.

Lou is as shaken up as we are, but Zlatan comes strolling down the hall, dirty feet poking out from underneath tie-dyed jelabba, composed, cucumber cool, rolling a joint with one hand. He sees our terrified faces.

"Be cool, be cool. I'll get it sorted in the morning. I'll have a word. All will be cool."

"You'll have a word? With who?"

"With the man. Who else? I'll have a word with the man and all will be . . ." He pauses to lick his spliff.

"Cool?"

"Precisely." What that means, we haven't a clue. With a final "Be cool," Zlatan wafts away back down the hall and into his room.

Next day, with a rock we hammer two screws through the bent hinge to get the front door working, then we hang around, terrified, for the rest of the day. Lou, sitting on the floor, fiddles with the wires dangling from the smashed radio. He twists a few together and turns the knob to "On." The pile of junk sputters then, miraculously, comes to life. The Osmonds are singing "Crazy Horses."

My cheapo acoustic guitar, permanently borrowed from Brillo, survived the attack because it was under the bed. It's a pathetic old thing, but we've been through a lot together and I've written some good music with it, so I'm glad it's okay.

Our busted-up room is shocking and depressing; it mirrors the rest of our existence. That night, to relieve the tension, we go out and get half-ripped. At the end of the evening we lug home more booze and complete the job. I pull my acoustic guitar from under the bed where it had been hidden, tuning pegs trembling with fear, during the recent assault. I look at it lovingly, strum a sad A minor, then smash it to bits on the fireplace.

We are all going slightly mad.

Days pass, and nothing violent or kneecap-threatening happens. Nights of fitful, nerve-wracked sleep pass without further dog attacks. Shakespeare says a coward dies a thousand deaths; we must be at least in the two hundreds by now. The old dear downstairs, shuffling blissfully around, doesn't seem to have noticed a thing. Perhaps she's deaf. That would be a blessing.

And it would account for her not complaining about the endless stream of bass players we audition. One of them is a lump from Sheffield. I hate Sheffield. He shows up in a brown corduroy jacket, carrying a Rickenbacker bass, the first one I've seen up close. He also has a seriously great name, Warwick Rose. On the downside, he is unforgivably portly and, final nail, has a wobbly thicket of curly hair bouncing around on his head. Standing on our recently de-ratted front doorstep, he looks around and marvels, "You must see a lot of stars in this neighborhood."

Yeah, mate.

I'm sick. I have a permanent cold and a cough that just won't quit. This is bad news for a singer. Lou and Brady convince me to go to a doctor. I find the nearest one, just down Mill Lane in a ratty little office. The doc is old and trodden down, stooped and surly. He looks enough like Josef Mengele to make me wonder, Is this where he's hiding out? Or, if he's British, what's he doing in this armpit?

When he was young, popping and dispensing forbidden pills and nailing nurses by the dozen, did he think this is where he'd end up? Doubt it, but here he is, holding my tongue down with a popsicle stick and peering down my throat. He shakes his head, sighs, and plucks a bottle of light brown muck out of a cabinet. One teaspoon twice a day, starting now. It pours slowly, a thick sludge, and it tastes awful, like turpentine pudding. Says I've got bronchitis. This is bad news for a singer, worse news for a singer with a recording session coming up.

Days of rice, bass players, frustration, Crazy Eights, horrible-tasting medicine, and, our new pastime, competitive spitting. The window near my bed faces out onto the back wall, just below the loo window. Due to my condition I have to spit a lot, so spit I do, right out the window, with gusto and an ever-increasing level of aim and aplomb. When the lads need a quick gob they do too. The brick wall under the loo window begins to look, frankly, revolting. We christen it our Phlegm Wall.

We are aware that this is disgusting.

Thirtieth of June, in the year of your Lord 1973. Thirteen days to go before the Regent Sounds session and we haven't got a bass player. Regent Sounds on Denmark Street is holy ground to us. Why? Easy. That's where the Rolling Stones recorded their first album. "England's Newest Hit Makers," the album cover screamed. And we do feel like the natural spawn, the progeny, the bastard boys not mentioned in the will. We are truly excited about this but the bass-player situation is getting desperate. Don't want to let Mr. O'Leary down. Don't want to blow our first break, like we have all our other first breaks.

We browbeat Brady and finally pry some of that wig factory cash he's been hoarding out of his strongbox, and the three of us go out to the Swiss Cottage pub. Brady's noticeably tight with the pound notes and, come to think of it, this is the first time I've seen him buy a second round. Nonetheless, pints are downed, lies are told, laughs are laughed.

On this night I'm debuting a beautiful new pair of strides Sonja made for me, bless her heart. She's great at this wardrobe business. The clothes she comes up with are better than anything you can find on the King's Road or in Kensington Market or anywhere. And I am exactly her size, which is a blessing as I get her hand-me-downs. These particular trousers are a fab shade of green, tight where they need to be and loose where it counts least. I intend to wear them at our next gig.

A dark-haired girl sporting pink lipstick and a white dress takes a bit of a shine to me. She hears me yapping about the Kinks and tells me she used to go out with Dave Davies. You don't say? You really got me. Brady's talking to some girl who's trying to be blonde and trying even harder to stand up.

More drinks are poured down throats, closing time approaches, and Brady, obviously traumatized by shelling out for a few rounds, takes his tottering tart and leaves, hoping to escape buying one for the road.

Soon enough, Lou and I and the young Kinkette leave the pub. It's a picture-perfect night, it is: warm, stars probably shining somewhere up there, traffic roaring by as we make our way slowly along Finchley Road. The girl takes my arm and the three of us stroll along, chatting. Lou is the first one hit, a blow to the back of his head sending him to his knees.

The girl screams. Something lashes across my back. Out of the corner of my eye I see three of them jump on Lou, putting the boot in. I turn to face a dozen dodgy droogs straight out of *A Clockwork Orange*, white jumpsuits, bowlers, codpieces, and all. I am lashed again across my chest and instinctively grab whatever the weapon is. I then, just as instinctively, let it go. It is a modified bicycle chain with small spikes, and the palm of my right hand is smeared with black grease and blood.

I duck the swing of a cane aimed at my head, and three of them force me out into the traffic of Finchley Road. Cars swerving, screeching brakes, honking horns, the girl's screaming, a van narrowly missing me, its mirror banging into my back.

The droog with the chain keeps swinging it back and forth, and I'm hit twice across the thighs, which tears my trousers to shreds and draws blood. Only because of the traffic do they back off. I see Lou on his hands and knees, trying to protect his head, getting a kicking from at least four of them.

Some cars have stopped, others are braking hard and squealing to a stop behind them, drivers cursing. With one final kick at Lou, the Woolworth droogs run away, laughing and whooping. Like a sleepwalker at Brands Hatch I come to my senses and realize I'm standing in the middle of racing traffic. I make my way unsteadily to the pavement, acting as a matador to the cars. The girl is crying and begging passersby for help. Lou is lying on his side, holding his face and moaning.

His face is kicked in, one eye almost closed and his mouth bleeding— maybe he's lost a tooth. I slowly help him get to his feet. We stand there, holding on, checking each other out. The traffic quickly resumes its frantic Friday pace. Nobody stops to ask if we're okay; nobody calls the police.

The girl does not live far from here. She wants us to come in so she can patch us up. She wants to call the police or an ambulance. We decline. We just want to get home. Bye, bye. We must do this again sometime. An hour later—after a staggering, fearful walk, leaning on each other, spitting blood—we are back at 11 Mill Lane. We wash our wounds at the kitchen sink. Of course, we have no bandages, medicine, antiseptic, or even an aspirin. We don't even have Dettol. Which you have to dilute, by the way. One part Dettol, ten parts water. But we make do.

Seems Lou has lost a tooth, but not a crucial one. His eye is closed and he has bruises everywhere. He managed to successfully protect his man bits but his Achilles' arse, of course, got a thorough kicking.

My back, legs, and palm are bloody and greasy, and I do my best to clean the wounds with dish detergent. I wash my back wound. The soap hurts like mad. Then we make a cup of tea. Not bad, really. No bones broken, no stitches required. Lou's mouth hurts.

Shame about my trousers.

We've tried out twenty-three bass players. It's July 10, three days before the session at Regent Sounds. Most of the time they hate us as much as we hate them. And that's fine by me. It's not the music; it's personal.

Late afternoon of a bad day. Lou says he saw a fiver on the pavement but somebody nabbed it just before he could pounce. This is a tragedy. Two o'clock in the aft, Stein walks through the splintered door at Mill Lane and up the stairs with yet another four-string wonder.

Out of the case comes a white Fender Jazz. Not bad. We plug in, turn the dials up, and away we go. This time, though, everything is different. This guy is seriously good, immediately making the entire band sound better. He and Lou get locked in sync right from the first bar, giving us a rock-solid rhythm section perhaps for the first time ever. This is a different sound, a different world, and we like it.

This is the Hollywood Brats sound we've been starving for.

XII

Regent Sounds Studio on Denmark Street and, ladies and gentlemen, behold, a newly minted five-piece. Me, Stein, Lou, Brady, and now, Mick Groome. At high noon on July 13, 1973, we walk in like tourists on a pilgrimage, gaping around awestruck, imagining the great Brian Jones falling off a stool here, Charlie bored stiff there.

For about thirty seconds. In truth, there's not a great deal of gaping around to do. It's a medium-sized rectangular place with the control room at the far end. Despite this, the Stones were here and now we are here. That's good enough for us.

Two engineer types help get us set up and, from the outset, it's clear that they are not exactly giddy with excitement about the session and are even less impressed with our gear. Join the club, mate. Our gear is holding on by its fingernails at this point. Every amp we've got is working only because of solder, gaffer's tape, and threat.

We're doing two numbers, "Melinda Lee" and "Nightmare." We are perfectly rehearsed and itching to go. Mick might have joined just seventy-two hours ago but it feels like he's been in forever. And this is the Brats' second studio experience, third if you count Hackney Wick's patchouli boy and his harridan hippy harpy. So we feel ramped up and ready to rock 'n' roll tape.

Tune up, get the sound, mic the drums, sort out the levels, one, two, three, four, and, riding a combo of lager and adrenaline, away we go. Two bars into the first take of "Melinda Lee," the Laney blows up with a muffled but loud *phut* and a concussive bang. A three-foot-wide Nagasaki mushroom cloud forms above the amp, flames and sparks shooting out the back, scorching the fabric on the wall behind.

Engineer number one runs in and tries to smother the flames with a bunched-up *News of the World* that promptly catches fire and burns his hand. His reflex action is to shriek like a girl and throw the newspaper away. It lands at the bottom of floor-to-ceiling curtains that must be made of polyester or nylon or gunpowder, because they instantly burst into flames. Engineer number two rushes in, brandishing a big red fire extinguisher, and sprays white foam over everything, saving the day.

After various blood pressures descend and hearts go from expresso bongo to bass drum, we are encouraged to go to the pub while the place is mopped up, aired out, and returned to whatever normal was at Regent Sounds on Denmark Street before the Hollywood Brats walked in.

When we return from downing a couple of calming jars at the pub our popularity has not noticeably increased, and the engineers' enthusiasm for the project seems, if anything, to have diminished a tad. Still, a replacement amp has been found and we are instructed to press on.

Four hours later the session is finished. On playback we hate every note. The sound is watered down, insipid, and tame. My vocals, turpentine-pudding Mengele medicine notwithstanding, are rubbish. No matter how we try to manipulate some action into the tracks, the engineers have found ways to smooth out our jagged edges and make it milquetoast. We are bereft. Those jagged edges are what make the Hollywood Brats.

Engineer number one says that they have orders to get the tapes to Laurie O'Leary right away. The way he says it leads us to believe that orders from Mr. O'Leary are to be obeyed right away. *Schnell, schnell.*

"Don't worry," says engineer number one. "Sounds great," says engineer number one.

But engineer number one is the same guy that tried to put out a fire with the *News of the World.*

We troop out of Regent Studios downtrodden, snarling, seeking revenge, disappointed with the results as usual, and dragging our smoldering equipment behind. We have to figure out a way to record things the way we want them recorded. It's just not rough enough, not exciting enough. We want that Slum Kitchen sound. We want control.

In the ensuing days in the doldrums *tempus* does not *fugit*. *Tempus* drags its arse. No calls from Mr. O'Leary's office. We've blown it. We're back to days and nights scared stiff of a return visit from the zombie dog-men. To add to the ignominy, at night the neighborhood rats congregate at 11 Mill Lane, climb up the chimney and through the fireplace into our room. As soon as the lights go out we can hear them scuttling up the bricks and flues. Makes it a bit hard to nod off when you hear vermin afoot. Someone, maybe Pepys, maybe not, once said that in London you are never more than six feet away from a rat. In 11 Mill Lane we'd love the luxury of a six-foot radius.

I take to boiling a pot of water at night and keeping it bedside. At the first sound of vermin I leap out of bed and pour it down into the broken brickwork of the fireplace. Brady and I delight in their scalded squeals. It works for a while. Ten minutes at best. Long enough to let us get to sleep. There are more of them than there are pots of boiling water.

My tiny little insular world, replete with its in-granite preconceptions and tailor-made prejudices, steps on a landmine. The top of my skull is blown to the rafters. Here I be, sunk in my cinema seat, legs over the one in front of me, mid-afternoon, staring at the screen. Watching a musical.

With no bus in sight I came in on a whim, to get out of the rain. Now my eyeballs are on stalks, popping out of their sockets. I'm alternating between fever and chills. I keep having to remember to breathe. Every frame is sumptuous, delicious. Every note of music is perfect. The stage lighting on the musical numbers is simple and simply stunning: blues and reds and white spotlights.

What more could one possibly require? I don't want it to end. I want to remember every detail to tell the boys. I want to steal everything. I can even stomach watching Liza Minnelli.

I end up watching this film four times in a row. I haven't done that since *A Hard Day's Night* when I was thirteen. What is happening here? Who is Christopher Isherwood? Who is Bob Fosse? I want the Hollywood Brats stage show to look exactly like this. I want to purloin every lighting idea. We've got to find someone to help us with this.

Next day, after much evangelical blabbedy-blah, I drag the lads along with me to watch it again. And again. They get it. The experience inspires us, eases our disappointment, drags our spirits out of the gutter.

And then, wouldn't you know it, that very night we receive top-drawer news. Stein gets a call from Mr. O'Leary's office saying we're playing the Speakeasy, Saturday night, July 28. And not only that, but we can go to the Speak whenever we want before then, special invitation, drinks on the house. It is barely believable.

Tomorrow belongs to the Hollywood Brats.

XIII

Sometime in 1968, having survived a palace revolution or two, the King of Rock 'n' Roll, Elvis Presley—freshly trimmed, newly drugged, and bedecked in black leather—blasted back into contention via a televised affair that came to be known as the *'68 Comeback Special*.

There, on a small square stage, surrounded by a sea of beehived American babes sitting close enough to be perspired upon, Elvis declared to all whipper-snapping pretenders that if they were looking for trouble, they could once again look right in his face.

He teased, he tempted, he sneered, he smiled that knicker-elastic-melting smile. He fell to one knee and dabbed his brow with a proffered unmentionable then handed it back to a twenty-one-year-old stenographer who looked forty and who shed silent tears as she was led away to an institution for the psychotically infatuated.

He crooned, they swooned—that was the deal. His Lloyd's of London–insured pelvis still had all the power and crushed-chicken-bone voodoo it had once wielded. It was as though he'd never been away. Sure, there were concessions. He strummed an electric guitar, not acoustic. Brylcreem was out, shampoo was in. But there was no doubt about it: the King was back.

His subjects were mightily impressed. None more so than sixteen-year-old Stein Groven back home in Trondheim, Norway, watching on a black-and-white TV. This was, coincidentally, the night Stein learned the English word "comeback."

Stein keeps saying, "Let's have a comeback; the Hollywood Brats comeback." It does no good whatsoever to explain to him that in order to have a "comeback," you have to have been somewhere. We've never been anywhere, we haven't done anything, and we certainly haven't had the luxury of going, or even fading, away. So how can we have a comeback? Where did he come up with that word? He remains undeterred. His description of a comeback is vague, but the rest of us get the impression that a comeback is somehow wild, raucous, and decadent, the last thing anyone would imagine and the first thing they'd never like to experience again. Or something like that. Also, you have to dress up.

It's Friday night and Stein has designated it our "comeback" night. We've rehearsed for five hours and we have never sounded better. This is the sound we've been looking for. We are still bugged that we haven't got it down on tape but, oh my, in our West Hampstead kitchen we're untouchable.

We play like we're in some wild club in front of an audience we're not even sure exists. We're convinced that the Hollywood Brats are the greatest band in the world and that it's only a matter of time before everybody else catches on.

There is no escaping the fact that, since Mick came aboard with that lightning bass, our rhythm section is buzzing like a boomtown sawmill. The downside is that he dresses like a bus driver and he's always having to dash back to Hemel Hempstead to his girlfriend. In our religion these sins are cardinal.

Tonight is no exception: last chord and cymbal crash on the Kinks' "I Need You," and Mick's out the door, down Dog Shit Lane, heading for the Tube.

We're in the big room, sharing two tall Carlsbergs, the Pretty Things yelling "Rosalyn" from the pile of junk Brady calls a stereo.

One mirror (mercifully missed by the club-swinging apes), four Brats, plenty of makeup and finery. We've got bracelets, red fingernails, black fingernails, skyscraper heels, plexiglass bangles, a dress, a bodice, a waistcoat, and more—always more. Brady's in black from barnet to boots: black velvet, black satin, black leather, black scarf and shades, boot heels worn down, toes so pointy that cockroaches in corners are cowering.

I'm in topper and tails, red strides, and white shoes. Silver-topped cane, nails are black. We are ready to foist ourselves onto the London night.

Then Stein reaches into a satchel and pulls out two bottles. Says it's what Norwegian fishermen drink. Says it's 98 proof. We are neither discerning nor fussy. We each have a swig. Wow! It tastes like fire, like petrol, and goes down the throat like contaminated gravel. In ten minutes we're smashed.

This stuff's a blowtorch in a bottle, a flamethrower on the tongue, a napalm cocktail. Brady dances over to the stereo and screeches the needle across the grooves. He skims the Pretty Things like a Frisbee into the far wall. We applaud so he kicks a speaker to the floor, where it lies humming loudly in protest. He doesn't need much prompting these days. Got to admit, this lad's loosening up. He shuffles through a stack of records until he finds what he's after, plops it on the turntable, and drops needle on vinyl.

The record sounds like whisker rub then it's Long John Baldry growling Willie Dixon's "Hoochie Coochie Man."

Stein leans over to me, all shifty-eyed and conspiratorial, breath like industrial solvent. "Andrew, I've thought of a new name for me."

"Yeah? What is it?" I inquire, leaning upwind. The guitars and howling harp of "Hoochie Coochie Man" ensure confidentiality but still Stein and his breath lean closer. He sighs. Take it from me, a sigh isn't always just a sigh. Close to my right ear, he hisses something that sounds like "Steel Casino."

Wow. That's not what I expected and it's not bad. But I want to alter it a smidge. "How about flipping it around . . . Casino Steele?"

"Steel?"

"Yeah, Steele."

"I said Steve."

"Casino Steve? I thought you said Steele?"

"No, I said Steve Casino. But Steel's good."

"Steele's good? Steele's great. That's a great rock 'n' roll name, Casino Steele, with an 'e.'" I write it out for him. Stein nods. He loves his new handle. And why not? "Casino Steele," now that's a classic name. Then he holds up a finger and says, "I don't want that last 'e.' I don't want to be connected to Tommy Steele." Fair enough, squire, nor would I. We tell the boys and they agree it's a great name. From this moment on there is no Stein Groven. Arise and go forth, Casino Steel.

Casino has a few quid in his pocket so we go out to celebrate. Tonight, we'll go to the Speakeasy for the first time. Shame Mick can't come with us (cue meow and sound of whip). The boys want to hit the Marquee first, which is a bit dodgy for me, considering I was shown the door the last two times I was there. Brady was turfed once too but he doesn't seem to give a toss. Either that or he can't remember.

We catch a bus, grab the top pew, and away we go, sharing tugs on the second bottle of Norwegian barnacle remover. We are flying and decide to get out of the bus at Marble Arch and walk the remaining two hundred miles to Wardour Street.

We stroll along Oxford Street, north side, swigging on the bottle. Tourists give us a wide berth as though we carry bubonic plague. Brady has to slash so we pop into the first convenience we find, a ladies' public loo. Women scatter. It is all very dignified and elegant.

We finally arrive at the Marquee criminally, toxically drunk, and yet we are allowed in. Oily Jack must be out for the evening. While the rest of us head to the bar, Brady goes to check out the band. He's soon back with a babe in tow, the kind he favors: petite, dark, heavy on the eyeliner, half-undressed, and not fussy.

Soon, though, it's time to split. It's time to head to the Speakeasy, the blessed Speak—and by special invite, too. On Wardour Street rubbish bins set out for collection the next day prove too tempting a proposition for Brady and Lou, who set about kicking them to smithereens and throwing them into the street.

The sound at this odd hour of the night is deafening, and a solid citizen yells something about the police so we leg it until we hail a cab.

We've never been to the Speak. Well, of course we've never been to the Speak. We live in a rat-infested squat. We eat rice and, on a good day, wash our hair with Fairy Liquid. And you can't just go to the Speakeasy. You can't just show up and sashay in. You have to be somebody to go to the Speak; you have to have been on *Top of the Pops*; you have to have hit records or you have to be in films or you have to be a BBC slash Pirate DJ or something like that.

Goes without saying that John, Paul, George, and Richard Starkey, MBE, have been to the Speak. The only other way to get in the Speak, which goes without saying too (so excuse me while I say it), is if you are a gorgeous chick.

We fit none of the above criteria. And yet, after one phone call our carte is apparently and unbelievably blanche.

The entrance to the Speakeasy is at Margaret Street level, then a dozen or so steps down to the first landing, then a tight right-corner turn and down another dozen steps to the foyer. There, a kiosk with a couple of central-casting heavies at either side, beyond them the entrance and on into the club itself.

I'm first out of the cab, first through the door, and—having only been here once and at the time gone upstairs to Mr. O'Leary's office and also at the time not been sozzled on Norwegian nitroglycerine—one of my feet goes for the upstairs flight and the other, acting independently, decides on the downstairs. My legs get tangled up and I plunge headfirst in a tumble like a Romanian gymnast and land with a splat at the first landing.

Summoning a facsimile of dignity, I attempt to reassemble myself vertically, only to lurch in a spine-crunching backward plummet down the next flight of stairs, spilling like a trunk from Granny's attic into the lobby of the Speakeasy.

Eyebrows shoot upward, eyes pop, mouths are agape. I'm lying facedown, arms stretched out. Not my best look, first impressions and all. I'm rescued by the none-too-soon arrival of my three best pals, who can barely stop laughing for long enough to feign concern. They get me to my feet, rearrange my garb, straighten my scarf, check for protruding bones. All squared away.

Lou addresses the doorman with two magic words: "Hollywood Brats?" And wonder of wonders, the doorman checks a list and then says, "Right, this way, sirs."

A long rectangular room, stage at the far end. To the right as you enter there's a wraparound bar. Elevated tables and booths at the back, round café booths dot the floor leading to a twenty-foot semicircular parquet dance floor in front of a low stage. To the left of the stage, a curtain, which, when pulled aside, reveals a small dressing room.

But that's not the point. The point is that out there in the club, lounging around the tables, leaning at the bar and posing, always posing, are the glitterati of the London music scene. They judge and criticize, beaming supercilious smiles out of both sides of their faces, digging daggers in the backs of best buddies. They pretend not to read the *New Musical Express*, *Sounds*, *Record Mirror*, *Disc*, and the sainted *Melody Maker* every week, but in fact devour every page of them (except the jazz sections, of course) as soon as they hit the newsstands, scouring them for any snippet of a mention of their fabulous, shiny little lives. Doing this, signing that, and trying to make some girl.

We may be zonked out of our minds but we've arrived.

A short conga line later, we are shown to a fine table. We sit back and spy, among other fascinating things, Messrs. Stewart and Wood—Roderick and

Ronald, respectively—at the bar having what appears to be a conversation of sidesplitting hilarity, featuring much slapping of the bar top and bending down laughing at one's shoes. Mr. Wood's hairdo is particularly startling. It's like he's got a dead porcupine dyed black and plopped on his skull. It could poke your eye out.

Bryan Ferry from Roxy Music is in a booth not far away, with a companion as glamorous as she is gaunt. For Christ's sake, buy the bird a burger, Bry. Then again, perhaps he is entranced by the allure of her emaciation.

This is a million miles from our world of squats and slums. We're not walking the late-night streets of West Hampstead with our drummer eyeing the pavement for cigarette butts. This really is the Speakeasy, and that really is Bryan Ferry sitting not twenty feet away. He is nattily attired, naturally, in a shiny gray double-breasted number, cigarette dangling from his pout. His music may be rubbish but I must say his hair is fab, all floppy and blackened.

We'd better get used to breathing in this rarefied atmosphere.

A waitress arrives with an unordered tray of drinks. Just what we need. For some reason I'm drinking Southern Comfort for the first time in my life. She announces that the drinks are compliments of the management. This brings forth a chorus of appreciatory, drunken hurrahs. As the waitress leans over, distributing beverages, Casino, in the manner of a farmworker testing the ripeness of a grapefruit, reaches up and squeezes her breast.

This is not well received. After a sharp intake of breath she jumps upright and delivers a stinging slap to Casino's hand. Not overly perturbed, Casino shrugs, sits back, and smiles like a glassy-eyed Buddha.

Affronted, not to mention tested for ripeness, the waitress jiggles off in the direction of officialdom. I'd say our evening is getting off to a roaring start.

The DJ plays the usual tripe, perhaps slightly more upmarket tripe, more Floyd than Cassidy, more Focus than Sweet, but who cares, it's all dross. We are not short of a derisive jibe, the odd hiss, the succinct boo. This milieu is amazing, though, and it's undeniably where we should be.

A new pair of grapefruits arrives with yet another tray of drinks. She says that they were sent by someone at another table and points a fingernail in the direction of our benefactor. Good Lord, it's a famous television personality whose name we can't remember.

He waves. We wave back. He throws his head back showbiz style and laughs, displaying many fine teeth. We do the same.

'Tis a panorama of music bizzers. Top of the Popsters mingle with power-trio bass players, girls hanging off their elbows. Quasi-sensations abound. Seen 'em once, can't wait to never see them again.

A beefy guy comes over to make disapproving noises about our treatment of the staff and our disapproving noises. We all point at Casino. It won't happen again, guv.

What on earth is his name? That chap who sent us drinks? He charms the babes and catches the bad guys every week on ITV. His mustache, karate chop, and god-awful neck jewelry are his trademarks. He has a devilish smile and a suave macho charm that women seemingly can't resist.[*]

We are beyond drunk. Casino lays his head on the table to either die or go to sleep. You can't always tell with a Norwegian. Brady leers at women who thus far seem uncaptivated, some looking actually repelled, by his Irish charm. Lou is heavy-lidded, chain-smoking, and cheerful. I desire nothing more than to go somewhere and throw up. I try to focus on the blond haystack on the table.

I poke him in the shoulder. "Casino, are you okay?"

One of his key factors in making a band truly successful is if one of the members dies. Beatles, Stones, Doors, Glenn Miller—they've all done it. But he can't choke to death on his own vomit yet. What's the point? We have to at least record an album first.

Three pokes later, he sits up slowly, mascara smeared around his eyes. He's smiling, which I suppose is an encouraging sign. He slurs, "Fucking great. What a comeback."

Great it may be, but I've had it. I've reached the end. The beers, the Viking moonshine, the Southern Comforts, and the no food are not getting along at all well. I barely make the stagger to the loo. I barge into a stall, lock the door, and fall to my knees. Scarves and brown tresses frame the porcelain as I regurgitate again and again all the liquid excesses of the last few hours.

---

[*] All of which will remain intact for two more years, until he is discovered by the police late at night in a public toilet, trousers resting jauntily down around his ankles, and charged with "gross indecency."

I then want nothing more than to die in shame and squalor right here on the floor of the loo in the Speakeasy.

Lou, out of concern or a need for entertainment, has climbed up the side of the stall and is hanging over the edge, urging me to breathe. I now have another wish. I want not only to die, but to kill Lou before I do. He persists, keeps telling me to bloody breathe, and finally, twenty minutes later, he convinces me to exit the stall and wash up at the sink. I do, splashing my face and rinsing my sour mouth.

After a few more minutes devoted to regaining equilibrium we head back to the club proper, just in time to see Casino and Brady being yanked from their seats and escorted out the door.

That actor is sitting in our booth. Right next to where Casino was. He has a wistful smile on his face. My brain is too fuzzy to sort it all out so Lou and I leave the club right behind our comrades and their muscle-bound escorts. We hear something about Brady throwing an ashtray. An hour ago we were given a golden ticket, allowed into the Speakeasy for the first time with free drinks and all, feeling as though we'd arrived. Two drinks later, we've been kicked out. My head's killing me.

Poured into a taxi on the way back to the squat, my head hanging out the window, painting the streets of London, it hits me. Peter Wyngarde, that's his name.

Next day is a dead loss: massive, hellish headache; more nausea (the sensation, not the Sartre book); lying in bed, moaning; staring queasily at the phlegm wall and cursing Norwegian fishermen.

Lou, for some reason a touch perkier than Brady and me, finds a can of black paint and a paintbrush in a cupboard. He spends the day painting his room—walls, ceiling, door, floor, window frame—pitch-black. Looks great. But at night, after lights out and a couple of pans of boiling water down the fireplace to boil the vermin, we're nodding off when the door opens and it's Lou, dragging his slab behind him. His room is too scary to sleep in.

We are teeth-grindingly worried that getting turfed from the Speak might have jeopardized our upcoming Saturday-night engagement. How could we do that? We seem to have a death wish, constantly flirting with bandicide. However,

Casino shows up for rehearsal on Monday at noon with news direct from his hall phone. We've got the gig. O'Leary's secretary has called with all the information so, incredibly, for once it appears we haven't blown it.

Mick rolls in on the dot, daily, from Hemel Hempstead and we rehearse relentlessly, driving each other on. In the kitchen, I'm leaning on the sink, singing away into the microphone. Lou's set up over by the dead Norton motorcycle; Casino's got his back to the window, tempting snipers; Brady and Mick ponce around in the center.

"Courtesan" has come together, rolling and snarling beautifully along. Ultimately, I hear a Hammond in the mix, but right now this baby with its sleazy third-gear tempo is perfect for strutting around onstage, annoying people.

Cas and I introduce another new song to the boys, titled "Drowning Sorrows." We wrote it with Rod Stewart in mind. He could use it, we reckon. The man's showing distinct signs of going off the boil. Learning it allows us to jettison "Confessin' the Blues" when we need to slow things down in a set that is getting increasingly frenetic. "Drowning Sorrows" is a stirred-up mix of bluesy drum pattern, regret, baby grand piano, alcohol, crawling around on a floor trying to make that late-night phone call. It's got it all.

Lou and Casino want to do "Hoochie Coochie Man," and they finally break me down. My one concession is that I don't want it to plod along in drab, hackneyed blues fashion. If we are going to do it I want it to be unrecognizable. I want it to sound like it was done by mental patients on amphetamines.

We give it a whirl in the kitchen, and three tries later it is a suitably frantic mix of sweat and decibels.

And I can't help but notice that Lou and Mick are turning into a rhythm section made in rock 'n' roll Valhalla.

XIV

Ken's Tale

So, maybe my story starts in 1967–8, no, '67 for sure. Immediate Records bought the Small Faces contract from Don Arden but forgot to pay him, so I'm at the office, it's 7 p.m., when two gorillas arrive. I get introduced to Wilf and Arnie. They sit me down in my office with a sawn-off pointed at my knees and tell me to call Andrew Loog Oldham, who's with Allen Klein at the Dorchester flogging the Stones and not to be disturbed.

So we wait for two hours together—nice guys, they're very reassuring and tell me they don't want my kneecaps but biz is biz, no hard feelings. Finally, ALO returns with promises of 30 or 40K. So that's how I met Wilf Pine. He was a collector for Don and very good at his job. With Wilf holding your ankles out a window five or six stories high and threatening to clap his hands, you come to an arrangement.

When Immediate folded I worked for Don for a few months and got to know Wilf. Then I went to the States with ALO—Rare Earth, Bloody Marys in Connecticut, then Greece. Upon my return Wilf contacts me. He's stolen some group from a Birmingham schmuck, sold them to Patrick Meehan Sr. & Jr. and kept a bite of the action. Enter Black Sabbath.

Like many people, Wilf fell in love with the myth that was Immediate Records and wants his own record company, Patrick also. So I start at Worldwide Artists, new label stabled with the Sabs, Yes, Groundhogs, Stray, Jimmy Helms, etc., an inspiring bunch.

Then, I remember, back in Connecticut with Andrew Loog Oldham, Sean

Kenny says to me, "What the fuck are you doing, Ken? Piss off and find your own Rolling Stones."

Next, I must introduce Laurie O'Leary. He was a "business manager" for the Krays while they were enjoying Her Majesty's pleasure and accommodation. Laurie comes to Dover Street in Mayfair, says he's put this group, the Hollywood Brats, on at the Speakeasy and why don't I have a look?

Says, "Bit flash, they'll need a smack but have a look."

Ken Mewis, Bali, 1989

XV

The day has finally dawned, July 28, 1973. This is the day we have been aiming for since the church hall in Stanmore. This is the day when our fortunes take flight, when all the rats and rice and rubbish and boos and spitting and crabs and knob-warts will be deemed to have been worth it.

This is the day of the night that we play the Speakeasy. We have rehearsed a million hours in the kitchen and we are, in our utterly biased opinions, white hot. We don't know if they are ready for us but we're ready for them. It's Saturday night at the Speak. Who cares what picture you see?

Laurie O'Leary has let it be known via Casino Steel that tonight there will be a special someone in the audience, in attendance for the sole purpose of checking us out and deeming whether or not we are worthy of a record contract. Simple as that.

We can take the heat, so we're getting out of the kitchen.

It's 9:30 p.m. Here we are, nervous and edgy, in the tiny room curtained off behind the Speakeasy stage. No sink, no mirror, benches on three sides, cheap lamp on a cheaper table, stained carpet floor. Lovely.

We hear the club slowly start to fill up; we listen to and mock the crap music the DJ foists upon the punters. There is nothing to say but Lou insists on saying things anyway. A fidgety chatterbox, he's keeping everyone loose, I suppose, but if this constitutes loose I'd hate to try wound up tight.

Matted red velveteen bench, the five of us seated in a rough horseshoe. Casino, bless his foresight, has brought a bottle of Old Grand-Dad, Kentucky bourbon, and we pass it around, looking for a jolt of 80-proof courage. We feel the weight of it all, the monumental importance of the occasion, the worries about performance, individual and collective, all of it coming down from the low pyrofoam ceiling, pressing on our skulls.

And the biggest worry of all? The biggest worry is not that we'll be bad, because we're razor-edged, direct from the sharpening stone—we're kitchen honed. And we don't particularly care if the exalted Speak audience does not immediately like us, because that's what usually happens anyway and we've been trained to musically machete our way through hatred. It's not even the fear that Mr. Mysterious Magic Music Man with his powerful wand won't show up, or even if he does that maybe he won't like us. Nah, it's nothing like that.

Our biggest worry, number one with a bullet, which we can't even talk about, so as not to invite the evil mojo, is that our beyond-decrepit equipment will die, expire, explode at the very worst moment. Because you know what? Every moment that's about to happen is the very worst moment.

Out there onstage awaiting us are our weak amps, crackly microphones, buzzing speakers, clapped-out leads, and loose, sparking, arcing plugs. Little red lights are glowing. Intermittently. The low, threatening, sporadic static of the amps; every one of them, except Mick's, says we're on borrowed time.

And dare any of us? Dare any of us sitting here on the chewing-gummed, stained, stinking, beer-drenched Speakeasy bench remember the last do-or-die moment? The last time we played a venue of similar import? Dare we remember the Marquee?

Dare we remember the singer walking out, grabbing the microphone, and yapping like a sap in a silent flick? No, don't you dare think about that, laddie. Do that tonight, and what? If you stride to the mic and it's conked out, well, then it's you that is conked out, matey, not the mic. If that happens on this night at the Speak you may as well just walk offstage, through the club, out into Margaret Street, and either throw yourself in front of a bus or peel off the false eyelashes and get a job in an insurance office. Pass the pills, the rope, and razor blades, please.

The trash music gets steadily louder as more and more people fill the club. Another tug on the Grand-Dad. Brady peeks through the curtain. He reports that the joint's jammed. The tables, booths, banquettes, bar, aisles, and entranceway are full of London's finest drunken, stoned, and impartial critics. The glitterati of the biggest music burg on the planet have shown up on a Saturday night to see and be seen. They're dressed up to the eights. They give not the slightest toss about who's onstage tonight.

Oh, yeah? Watch this. Roll them dice, boys.

Some guy pops his head through the curtains—"You're on at the end of this song"—and then he's gone. No "Good luck, chaps" or "Have a good show" or "Break a fucking fibula" or anything like that. Just, "You're on at the end of this song."

Mercifully, the song in question is "You Can't Always Get What You Want" by the Stones. Not that it's good—it's okay—it's just that it goes on forever and is nod-off-to-sleep boring, so we know we'll come out and wipe the floor with it afterward. The "goes on forever" aspect is handy, too, because it allows for a few more good gulps of Old Grand-Dad. Still, nerves abound among the five of us.

We're standing up, punching each other, getting the marching order straight: Lou, Casino, Mick, Brady, Me. Another slug of Grand-Dad.

The song goes to double time and dies its slow, dull death. In the awkward silence that ensues, we walk in predetermined order onstage with no introduction. There is no such thing as stage lighting so it's as though we've strolled into a particularly dire cocktail party.

This is as far from *Cabaret* cool as it can get. The crowd shuts up momentarily, though, when they get a look at us, which I take as a good sign. Then, as usual, the snickering starts. We don't care. They can't intimidate us. We stared down the RAF so this is nothing. These people are dinosaurs. It's just that no one's told them yet.

I stand stock-still, arms crossed, at the microphone, looking out at the enemy while the boys get plugged in, situated, and comfy. This takes its usual eternity, of course. Just when it reaches its most painful point I glance over my left shoulder at Cas. He nods, and I count all the way from one to two.

The boys are in on the three, and for the umpteenth time I wonder what we would do without "Melinda Lee." One of the first songs Casino and I ever wrote, and we use it to kick-start every gig.

She slips up to me easy
She's holding my hand
She says my every wish is her command

If they're noisy, Melinda shuts them up. If they're ignoring us, Melinda gets their attention. If they're heckling, Melinda drowns them out. And if they want to dance, Melinda tickles their tail feathers. She's tailor-made for the minefield that is a typical Hollywood Brats gig.

But eventually, as all good things must, "Melinda Lee" ends, with . . .

I'll see you in the sheets, Melinda Lee

Crescendo, sustain chord, screeching high note and earsplitting feedback, courtesy of Brady, followed by the definitive cymbal crash. Crowd response: not much. To call it a smattering of applause would be to, well, lie. There are murmurs, titters, and laughs. Sod 'em.

Next song, "Running Wild," smack 'em between the eyes. And so it goes. Three minutes of mayhem followed by three more minutes of even worse mayhem. We've got the action so we couldn't care less about the reaction.

We're walking the stage like we own it and acting like they love it, and you know what? Soon they seem to fall for the deception. Soon they start to believe it, too. In the microsecond we give them to respond between songs they are starting to loosen up, slap palms together, and whoop a little. Maybe their alcohol intake is kicking in. Who cares? Enjoy yourself.

Sure, we still have the budding Oscar Wildes that can't help but yell out their carefully rehearsed ad-libs, some of them coming right up in front of us, but all in all we might just be winning these suckers over.

I give 'em the verbals and the boys hit 'em with the noise. That's our formula and we're not changing it for these exalted tossers.

There is, however, one slight hiccup, and it's Lou's hiccup, and one more like that and I'll strangle his scrawny throat. We're in the middle of Randy Newman's "Gone Dead Train"—why we're still playing this song is beyond me—and there's an eight-beat stop in the middle, straight in on the nine, and

Lou decides he'd rather come in on the seven and a bit, which doesn't exist, so we're screwed for the ensuing twenty excruciating bars or so.

We stagger to the end of the song like punch-drunk punks. That's it, we're never playing this song again. I turn to give Lou a withering look, but for some reason he is fervently fiddling with the butterfly nut on his ride cymbal so he doesn't see me.

No troubles, though. Brady kicks in to "Sweet Little Sixteen" and suddenly she's really rockin' in Boston and Pittsburgh, PA, and we get to the end of the first set and, glory be, the aforementioned glitterati blow their carefully considered cool; they yell and clap and indicate by various other verbal and nonverbal means that they'll miss us a bit while we're gone. We leave to a modest sitting ovation.

Exit stage right into the little velveteen sanctuary. We've done okay and yet a toss I do not give; I'm seething about the "Gone Dead Train" screwup and I let Lou know it. No skimping on the syllables, either. I'm standing up and doing an Adolf H. to the boys on the benches. When I've finished the rant I lie down on the floor and stretch out on my back with my arm over my eyes, like a particularly peeved Marlene Dietrich.

The DJ cranks up, what else, bloody "Superstition" by Stevie "Ray-Bans" Wonder, and all gets back to normal in the Speakeasy world. In the dressing room, where nobody's heard an encouraging word, they're just bent over, just catching breath, just dripping sweat, that's all.

And then, it's one of those moments . . . the curtain is pulled back and, good Lord, a vision from rock 'n' roll managerial heaven enters. This thing is five foot ten, maybe eleven, gray pin-striped suit, sunglasses (in a club at 10 p.m., mind you), white shoes, spiky blond hairdo, fag drooping out of pouty lips, looking for all the world like James Dean's sexually confused cousin.

Our piano man, aka Mister I'm All Business, leaps up, sticks out a mitt, and does the old chitty-chitty chat-chat. After a beat or two he says to me, "Andrew, this is Ken Mewis, from Laurie's office."

I don't move. From the floor, on a sweaty hot night in July, I say two words: "Merry Christmas."*

---

* Ken Mewis, Bali, 1989

"I went backstage, a trifle apprehensive, and spoke to the only one that would speak to me, the keyboard player. So I thought, if nothing else I've met this tasty Norwegian. Days later I sussed she was a he."

* * *

Second set, we murder 'em. We've saved up "Chez Maximes" and a few other choice incendiaries, and we smack 'em like cattle with that stun thing used in only the most discriminating of abattoirs.

This club is nothing really when you get right down to it. It's like every other club we've encountered and probably like every other club on the planet. It's no different from a biker club in Southend or Redhill, or the Railway Hotel in Harrow, or anywhere else. The true difference, the mind-boggling, or should I say remotely interesting, aspect is the clientele.

Bryan Ferry's here again (doesn't he have a home to go to?), so is Keith Moon and Rod, and at one point even Jeff Beck (pint in hand and not looking a minute older than when I saw him doing "Shapes of Things" on *Hullabaloo* in '66 with the Yardbirds) wandered down stage-side to clock us. Imagine: Jeff Beck at the side of the stage while we do "I Ain't Got You."

Thank Christ the Irishman was too busy concentrating on running his bottleneck up and down the neck of his Strat to see him, or I'm sure we would have had another "Gone Dead Train" moment.

And then that's it. We've done it. We've played the Speakeasy. If we haven't knocked 'em out, we've at least smacked 'em to the canvas a couple of times, so maybe we can call it a split decision. Who knows? We're in good shape afterward, though, packing up, laughing, and bopping around. The gear, bless it, didn't let us down.

The manager comes up as we are packing to say thank you (imagine that?) and that he hopes he'll see us again (imagine that?). Then, on a night made of miracles, up walks Keith Moon, carrying a tray of pints. He hands the tray to Lou and bows.

"Dear boys, dear boys. Hollywood Brats. Drink up, chaps. And well deserved, too."

Five jaws hit the floor. Unintelligible words are stammered. Keith Moon turns to the manager and says, "The Hollywood Brats are the greatest band I've ever seen." Then he bows again and strolls off through the club and out the door, stopping only to allow a blonde to take his arm.

XVI

Sunday, we lie around the squat, drained, on edge, wondering what our fate will be. Monday, down Mill Lane to the phone box. I call Casino at a prearranged time and when I return through the smashed front door, running up the rotting stairs, past the wallpaper penicillin, I am able to report that the guy who came in the dressing room on Saturday night is called Ken and he wants to see Casino and me tomorrow for a chat.

Tuesday, 2 p.m., Casino and I—scrubbed, brushed, and in full makeup—enter a restaurant in Mayfair that is beyond fancy. White tablecloths, exotic greenery, knives, forks, and spoons that look like they may be worth pocketing, bow-tied waiters, nimble and agile, looking like dancers from silent films.

The maître d' is a dead ringer for a snooty, past-it Rudolph Valentino. He also looks like he has been waiting for us, because as soon as he claps eyes on us he does not call the police. Instead, we are whisked away to a corner table where sits the man who just may change our lives forever.

Ken Mewis is slouched back in his chair, tie askew, dark gray suit, pink shirt, glass of red wine halfway to his lips, hair stunning, eyes heavy-lidded like he's about to nod off. Maybe he is. What do I know? Or maybe he's just louche, cool. Maybe he's self-assured. Maybe he's going to carve us up like a couple of roast pigeons.

Ken orders a bottle of red, and when it arrives there is much staring at the label and murmuring with the waiter. It is deemed worthy of decanting. Then Ken starts to chat, telling us a bit about himself. He was with Immediate Records, for Christ's sake. He drops names like the Small Faces, the McCoys, Humble Pie, and nearly man Chris Farlowe. And, get this, it scarcely seems possible but he says he personally knows the great Andrew Loog Oldham. I lean my jaw on my fist to stop it hitting the table. Two or three punches and the man has knocked us out.

He orders another bottle of red. I note that less time is spent label staring and waiter murmuring. We haven't eaten in a day and a half, and we are certainly unaccustomed to this standard of intoxicant. It all begins to go to my cerebral cortex, or somewhere equally discombobulating. Everything he is saying is so unbelievable; I have to state our case, rouse myself, counterpunch.

I am about to tell him that Keith Moon thinks we're great when Ken says, "Keith Moon seemed to think you were quite good, but then again he was smashed on rum and coke and whatnot."

He then spends some time extolling the many virtues of his new company, Worldwide Artists: record label, publishing, films, the works. At the moment they've got Black Sabbath (hate 'em), the Groundhogs (hilarious), and Stray (never heard of 'em), among others, and Ken makes it clear they want to offer us a deal. My contract-signing hand begins to quiver with excitement.

Another bottle is ordered, and this time the label is not so much as glanced at and the waiter is completely ignored. To the brim, *garçon*, and *vite* about it.

It slowly becomes clear that we are not going to be ordering food. For once, we don't care, though, and content ourselves with surreptitiously gnawing on the breadsticks that are poking out enticingly from a white porcelain container. We dip them in the wine, bite off the end, use the stub to illustrate a point, and dip again. It's all very classy.

When the third bottle is drained and our heads are filled with a few more fantastic stories, Ken sits back, runs his fingers through his immaculately tousled hair, and says, "Right, you've met the brains, now let's meet the brawn."

What this means we have no clue, but we follow Ken out of the restaurant.

Blinding afternoon sunlight as we walk north along beautiful, posh, rich Dover Street. Ken stops to put something in his car. Gadzooks! The man drives a purple MGB. This guy just keeps getting better.

On we tread, until we reach number 27 and in we go, through a beautiful entryway and up a sweeping staircase to the offices of Worldwide Artists. They have the entire gorgeous floor, with vast windows overlooking Dover Street. The receptionist, Mandy, stands up and shakes our hands, says she's heard so many good things about us. I am glad I'm still wearing my sunglasses as it enables me to ogle her rather curvaceous exterior while maintaining a gentlemanly veneer.

Ken leads us through the busy office to the rear, where two immense white doors open into what must be the inner sanctum. We go into a large, beautifully appointed office, cluttered, yes, but with only the most important, expensive-looking clutter. A white leather sofa and matching chair face a desk the size of a modest aircraft carrier.

And behind the aircraft-carrier desk sits a man who looks like he could bite a chunk out of an aircraft carrier and chew it like an hors d'oeuvre. He looks B-movie menacing. He looks like he very well could have been at the other end of a leash with a club, smashing a radio a couple of weeks ago at the squat. Ken introduces him as Wilf. Wilf, it turns out, is the boss.

Wilf stands up slowly. The altitude doesn't decrease the impression of menace one iota. He sticks an arm like a tree trunk across the desk. I shake his hand. It is a hand with tattoos. Four of the fingers that subsequently crush mine spell "LOVE," only not that neatly. More tattoos crawl up his arm. He decided on the matching set for his left arm, though the letters on his left hand spell, and this is a surprise, "HATE."

Casino and I sit on the sofa, Ken sinks into the armchair and lights his four hundredth cigarette of the afternoon. And baby, this is living. This is the culmination of everything we've been working toward. I drink it in, head on a slow swivel, eyeballing the hideous though no doubt pricey art on the walls. This is one exciting afternoon. This is where we belong.

Then Wilf says, in a voice you'd never, ever want to hear in your life, "Andrew. It's Andrew, right? Andrew, take off your sunglasses."

As it happens I was just about to but now, for reasons that can only be associated with red wine intake overriding any basic survival instinct, I come up with this riposte: "No." Silence.

Ken starts to make some light comment but Wilf holds up the "HATE" hand and Ken obligingly shuts up. Wilf hasn't taken his eyes off me. "I said take off your sunglasses."

"I like them on."

More silence. Casino doesn't move. He stares intently at his knee. His foot taps slowly, nervously, to some music in his head. Chopin's "Funeral March," perhaps.

"You like them on, do you?" Wilf's voice goes down a decibel or two, and then a couple more, so that he's almost whispering. "You like them fucking on, do you?"

Funnily enough, when his voice gets quieter it doesn't get more reassuring, as you might ordinarily think. It gets bloodcurdling. Deep in my underwear my nuts begin to shrivel like I've just seen a girl from Sheffield.

Wilf says nothing. Second after eerie second ticks by. Then he slowly reaches out the "HATE" hand, switches on a desk lamp apparently equipped with a surplus Second World War antiaircraft searchlight bulb, and twists it round so that the beam is directed right at my face. I am six feet away and I can feel the heat. Even with sunglasses on I can't see a thing other than the planet Scaldo heading straight for me. Does he keep this blinding contrivance on his desk in the slim chance that just such an occasion might one day arise? If so, well played.

This is how the scene stays for the rest of the meeting. We chat cordially enough, and the battle of wills fights it out with the battle of won'ts. Despite it all, at the end we are told that Worldwide Artists and something with the unlikely name of Gladglen want to sign us up. Wilf comes around the desk, smiling, and crushes both of our hands. He laughs and punches me lightly but meaningfully on the shoulder. "Andrew, Andrew," is all he says.

Ken sees us out. When we part company he is shaking his head but smiling. He hands us an envelope and says he'll call tomorrow.*

Down on Dover Street, we open the envelope to find five tenners therein.

Fifty quid? We're on our way.

On the way back to Mill Lane, in a taxi, I'll have it known, we stop and pick up loads of lager, a bottle of whiskey, and chicken and chips for four. At the squat, where Lou and Brady have been anxiously awaiting our return, we

---

* Ken Mewis, Bali, 1989

"A phone call to Mill Hill or wherever they lived and Andrew and Casino let me buy them a few drinks. Then they got to meet Wilf, who I remember tried to intimidate Andrew (unsuccessfully), and later referred to him as 'that arrogant sod.'"

scream the news at their pale, needy-urchin faces and we all begin to bounce off the walls with excitement.

We've done it. The Hollywood Brats have got a record deal. And Ken Mewis, incredibly, is exactly the manager we've been craving. Can you believe it, he even knows the sainted Andrew Loog Oldham? This is science fiction. I hate science fiction, but what else can it be compared to? Maybe a Sal Dalí painting?

On the spot, a unanimous decision is made that the best course of immediate action is to crank up some rock 'n' roll and get disturbingly, irretrievably, obnoxiously drunk. This we proceed to do.

Twenty minutes later there is a knock on the door and we freeze in terror. Brady scratches the needle across *Bo Diddley Is a Gunslinger*. Lou timidly opens the door a crack. Turns out it's just Zlatan the Mysterious, inquiring as to, in his words, "Why the maximum merriment?" When told, he says, "I've had occasion to hear you playing in the kitchen. You're groovy, very groovy. Crack me a lager, gents, and we'll celebrate with a couple of monster jays, featuring narcotic ingredients recently delivered from my ex-accountant, formerly of Wapping but now in exile in Bangkok."

Later—an hour, three minutes, I don't know—through a cloud of blue smoke I begin to ask Zlatan about the recent visit from the bruisers with the canines. From his position, flat on my bed, staring out glassy-eyed and uncomprehendingly at the phlegm wall, he interrupts, raising a hand and waving languidly as if to brush away a moth. "Did I not tell you things would be cool?"

"Yes, you did, but we were just . . ."

"And things, how would you describe them?"

"I'd describe things as, well, so far, so placid, but those dogs . . ."

"Ah-ah-ah." He holds up a forefinger. "Are things or are things not . . . cool?"

"Well, yes, I suppose they are."

"Well, cool, man."

And that was that.

I raise my can of Long Life. "Lads, here's to Zlatan rendering the situation cool."

We all raise our cans and toast: "To Zlatan."

He acknowledges the praise, drinks a long drink, then belches a long belch. Lou replies in kind, only more dramatic, and we all roll around laughing, like carpet hyenas. Finally, we recover somewhat and are all catching our breath, sighing contented sighs, when I ask Zlatan, "What is your last name, Zlatan?"

"When?" he replies.

"Now. What is your last name? Just curious."

"Can't tell you."

"Why can't you?"

He looks at me blearily, meaningfully. "Because it's a mystery, innit."

Oh, yeah.

Two days later we take our remaining cash, as well as Mick's (well, he's in Hemel Hempstead), and, at Brady's behest, go to this club we've been reading about in the music press. It's at Hungerford Arches, beneath Charing Cross, and it's called Global Village. Sounds like a hippy commune, I know, but despite that crippling handicap it turns out to be rather lively, with pounding music, a cinema, and maximum opportunities for posing. Also, it is jammed with attractive girls.

Onstage tonight is a band operating under the severely daft name of Silverhead. Despite the risible handle they are getting great press. We've been reading about them more and more, and we wonder if they are in any way to be considered competition. The singer is called Michael Des Barres and he looks half-decent in a pinched, vulpine sort of way, but I've seen pictures of the rest of them and there appears to be a mustache or two in evidence and maybe even a goatee.

They come on and yep, Des Barres looks good, and yep, a mustache and goatee pop up elsewhere. Des Barres is the real thing in terms of a front man, and he has great hair, all fluffy, bouncy, and photogenic. But not for long. One song into the set and the great hair of three minutes ago is hanging soaked like a hundred rattails clamped to his skull. I've never seen anybody outside of Louis Armstrong perspire this much. This guy is drenched.

Verdict: a not bad, if sweaty, front man, an ordinary band, and naff songs. Dreck.

Good club, though. Lots of action. We stay late and drink much.

Two young ladies from New Jersey are kind enough to offer Brady and me lodging for the night. Wonder of wonders, they have a car to get there, too. Outside, we pass by a queue for taxis. A hundred-odd souls are hunched in the light drizzle of predawn London. Who should we spy in the middle of the line, about number 68, but none other than Jimmy Page from Led Zeppelin? Imagine that. Jimmy Page, wealthy beyond wealthy and standing in the rain in a fifty-yard-long queue for a taxi outside a poxy club at three in the morning. Call yourself a rock star?

After the Volkswagen Beetle, suicidally driven on the wrong side of the road by one of the drunk American college students, screeches to a stop in front of their pad in, of all places, Kangaroo Valley, we discover that, alas, there is only one bed. And, as everybody knows, to the singer the spoils. So the guitarist and his get the floor.

Next morning, I don't know what's the matter with my guitar slinger but he looks deathly ill. He's got a face like a haddock, talks in feeble grunts, and walks like a gimp. I immediately begin thinking of replacing him, but when we are finally sitting on the upper deck of the bus home his color seems to improve a bit. That is, until the bus stops adjacent to a butcher's shop, and Brady catches a glimpse of today's special, a huge tray of offal: brains and pig heads, tripe and trotters. All good stuff.

Brady groans and then explosively pukes everywhere; people are ducking for cover and I am vehemently denying ever having met the disgusting creature. I get off at the next stop and take another bus home.

XVII

Life picks up speed. Coincidentally, so does Brady, twelve tabs from Zlatan, and we stay awake and whacked out of our brains for two straight days and nights, playing records, singing songs, yelling and screaming, adding to the rich tapestry of the phlegm wall, and fighting the urge to scrub the stove.

The following day we pull it together, spruce up till we look like 1940s department-store mannequins, and go to the office to meet again with Ken Mewis. This time we bring Lou along because he doesn't believe it when we tell him how frightening Wilf is. Five minutes into the meeting, and Lou and Wilf are jabbering away, laughing like old army buddies. I don't get it. Too bad there isn't a lock that needs picking so Lou can really win his heart.

Ken wants to stick us into a studio and throw some tracks down, in one take, just to see where we are. Bring it on, oh man in a suit. So he does. Says it's already booked.

Gooseberry Studio, 19 Gerrard St., W1, at 1 p.m. on August 9. Right back where we were in the Dark Ages, in another life, with Chris Andrews. A tube full of Long Life and Ken leaning back in a leather chair beside the engineer at the console, as if to the mannerism born. We set up what's left of our rubbish gear, nix the engineer's suggestion that I go into a booth, push aside the screens he has hidden Lou behind, and let them know, through the glass, that we are ready to go.

We can't hear them, but we see the engineer and his tape-op speaking to Ken with earnest, imploring looks on their mugs. Ken is nodding, smiling, drinking, and waving an arm languidly in the air. These are good signs. Finally, with a slight, uncomprehending shake of his hairy little bonce, the engineer presses the talk-back and announces, "Right, then. Shall we start?"

Start we shall, and start we do. One take, the lot of them. Just to set the tone, we kick it off with: "Kiss My Ass." Followed by: "Nightmare," "Southern Belles," "Courtesan," "I Want to Be King," "Son of the Wizard," "I Ain't Got You," "Chez Maximes," "St. Louis Blues," "Drowning Sorrows," "The Boys in Blue," and "Tiger Lily."

Ken seems to absolutely love every note he's hearing. We see him laughing and bopping around the control room. Many times the engineer tries to say something to him, but he just keeps smiling, shakes his head, and sticks his hand in the engineer's face, palm at a right angle like the Supremes when they do "Stop! In the Name of Love." This is scarcely credible. For once, someone is standing up for us, fighting our battles.

Afterward, I see some notes he's made beside the track list. His handwriting is terrible, scratches like a drunk chicken wading in ink, but I see he has scrawled one star beside "Southern Belles," two beside "Courtesan" and "I Want to Be King," and three stars beside "Chez Maximes."

There is no discernible star beside the Matheson-Brady opus "Kiss My Ass." I wonder if this has anything to do with the fact that, at one point in the recording, Mr. Louis Sparks went off on a rather mad tangent.

While the rest of us were hurtling through the coda, Lou, oblivious to the dark glares from yours truly, came out of a drum roll thumping away at an entirely different song. One could sense the panic, the dread, the sheer loss of talent as the boy fought to regain the beat. Alas, as all drummers can attest, once the beat is lost it is one hell of a slippery eel to get back. He dragged the beat but the slow must go on, so the psychotic Micmac did his best and plowed "Kiss My Ass" steadfastly through to its grim conclusion.

In the vinyl analysis it's no big deal. It's a rubbish song, really.

At the end of the session Ken hands us an envelope with another fifty nicker. What a pleasant habit this is getting to be. He does something else, too. He reaches into his leather bag and pulls out an album—it's the New York Dolls. We step back like it's radioactive.

In the taxi on the way home we pass the album back and forth, checking it out microscopically. This is nerve-wracking and has certainly dulled the celebratory edge of the session. But, for all the trepidation about what awaits us inside the cover and deep in the vinyl grooves, there are positive signs.

For a start, it is produced by Todd Rundgren. Who came up with that bright idea? What does he know about rock 'n' roll? Rundgren has never made a rock 'n' roll record in his life. He's a soppy balladeer singing sweet songs to sad girls, a self-styled "genius" hooked on layering track over track over track. Millions of harmonies, saccharine sentiments wrapped in spotlessly clean recordings; that's Todd Rundgren.

Give him David Cassidy to play with, someone safe. Must be Mercury Records scared stiff of a little rough stuff erupting and spilling into the tracks. Can't have that now, can we? This does not bode well for the Dollies but it's good for us.

The picture on the cover, though, is the aspect that is the most encouraging. In every picture we've seen of these guys they've looked great. On the cover of this, their debut album, they just look plain ridiculous. They look like they're commiserating backstage after placing ninth to thirteenth in America's Hottest Transsexual Contest.

They don't look chic or edgy or like the look is natural to them, which is how they've looked in every shot we've ever seen of them before. Here, in black and white, beneath a stupid high-school lipstick graphic, they look like some art department's idea of what the Dolls should look like. They've been around for five minutes and they've already caught the down escalator and descended into parody.

The singer, who has until now made a living out of looking like Jagger's mutant kid brother, now looks like Jagger's elderly auntie from Palm Springs looking down the back of the sofa for a gambling chip. He's got a perm. A perm, for Christ's sake.

They should have just lined up in an alley in the Bowery, handed a Kodak Instamatic to a wino, and said, "Here's ten bucks, take some shots, buddy." Would have been a million times better. Hey, if they'd called I would have told them.

Back at Mill Lane, we top up on the studio suds and drop the Dolls disc onto the turntable. Six, eight, ten bars in, we're smiling, thumbs pointing to the floorboards.

We listen to both sides, relief growing with every track. When it's over, the verdict is in: good band, weak songs, horrible production.

No contest.

* * *

Our presence is requested in the office at 2 p.m. on August 13. And here we sit, splayed on the couches in the big room, young lords enjoying the freedom of their new manor, eyeing Mandy and a couple of other secretarial tartlets as they scour the music papers and clip out articles about the Groundhogs, Black Sabbath, and all the rest of our talented stablemates. Then we pick up the clippings and mock every syllable.

We point out the curious blue vein running down the left side of the Groundhogs' Tony McPhee's never-ending forehead and decide that it would be staggeringly funny to refer to him from now on as Tony McVein. We pass around the photo from *Record Mirror* of the long-fringed white leather vest worn by the chubby Sabbath singer Ozzy Osbourne. It looks like something Martha or a Vandella would wear on an outing to Kentucky Fried Chicken.

The wisecracks are instantly papered over and the smiles wiped off our faces—replaced by frozen, dumbstruck expressions—when the big doors open and in from the outside world walks Ken Mewis, looking sharp and talking sharper. But that's not what shuts us up. Behind Ken is none other than the great man himself, our unattainable ideal of a manager, the Svengali who practically invented and definitely sassed-up the Rolling Stones—our hero, the sainted Andrew Loog Oldham, in the flesh.

We are introduced, which to us is a mildly religious experience. Oldham says he's just been listening to the tapes with Ken and he likes what he's heard. Bloody hell.

He reminds me of Ken, actually. They could be brothers or maybe sisters. The Oldham and Mewis show is quite something, too. They seem not just related but rather members of some alien species who communicate in fey gestures and witty camp chatter. They laugh at each other's comments, collapsing damply into each other's shoulders and hanging on to a lapel as though they would otherwise fall flat on the floor. Perhaps they would. The pubs have been open for hours.

Both of them try to outdo each other, spouting quadruple entendres replete with flouncing wrists and madly gesticulating fingers daintily clamping half-smoked cigarettes that they use as exclamation points. They are like a pair of dotty maiden aunts left too long alone in the garden on a hot Sunday afternoon with a bottle of cooking sherry. They are absolutely great.

Ken hands over a little brown envelope containing fifty quid, and in addition gives me a copy of *The Wanting Seed* by Anthony Burgess. Suggests I have a glance at it.

As we are leaving, Andrew Loog Oldham says to us, "Your music's good, really good. If you don't make it, don't worry. The music will still sound great five years from now." Then he walks away.

Casino and I look at each other. What did he say? Five years from now? Five years from now we'll be on our fifth album! Five years from now we'll be suing each other in court or, best-case scenario, be dead. What is he talking about? Not make it? Five years. The great man has obviously lost the plot.*

Lou's birthday—he is twenty. We receive, by special delivery, the acetate from the Gooseberry session. The package also contains a note from Ken saying that Mandy and the tartlets have been given the task of finding a suitable flat for us so we can exit the squalor of the squat.

Three reasons to celebrate as life just keeps getting better and better. We crank up the music box to ear-bursting decibels and play the acetate deep into the wee hours.

Casino shows up at the squat with even more good news. He's heard from the Musicians' Union and they say that, on the basis of the letter I wrote yonks ago, he can stay and work in the United Kingdom. He even brings me a gift in appreciation, a book by Nik Cohn, *Awopbopaloobop Alopbamboom*. I remember those eight pages I anguished over, rewriting them four times, and, finally, the late-night walk to the postbox in Bushey. They probably just got worn out reading it. Who cares? It worked.

To celebrate, pockets all a-jingle with Worldwide Artists' cash, it's off to the Markham Arms in Chelsea for a baker's dozen of pints and perhaps the odd whiskey.

---

* Andrew Loog Oldham, Bogotá, 2012

"I cannot recall exactly when I met Ken Mewis. Somehow this former hairdresser from the North became the head of A&R for Immediate Records, the company I founded in '65 with Tony Calder. Ken rolled a good spliff, had a winning way and good ears. He was pale as a pit boy, good-looking, and his hair was always immaculate. So were his ears.

He went to work for a puffed-up would-be gangster who fancied himself as an impresario. And why not? Helps to have ears, though."

Afterward, out on the quiet streets of Chelsea, Lou and Brady get a bit rambunctious. They're just revved up—we're signing contracts tomorrow—but reprehensible behavior, nonetheless.

The office sends Casino and me a "standard" contract to look over, and we repair to the French House pub in Soho to do so. The contract weighs a pound and is as thick as a *Vogue* magazine. We order a pint each, sit at a corner table, and start flicking through the pages. It might as well be written in Korean.

We understand nothing.

A scruffy old chap at the bar sends us a round of drinks. Thanks, mister. We find out later that he is Francis Bacon, a painter of some renown. We find out later still, from the barman, that Mr. Bacon brushes his teeth with Vim.

That's nothing, mate. I clean my balls with Dettol.

It's August 22, 1973, contract-signing day. We sit at a huge table covered with pages and pages of documents, which Ken and Wilf and some other mysterious somebody in a suit keep shuffling around from Brat to Brat. We all sign our names dozens of times without reading so much as one word on any of the pages. Joviality is being kept to a maximum by all and sundry of the Worldwide Artists/Gladglen employees, and somewhere not too far off champagne corks pop in quick succession, exciting much girly giggling from Mandy & Co.

A blizzard of papers. Sign here, initial this, in triplicate please, there we go. What is it? Oh, don't worry, just a formality, it's a standard contract, completely standard, no tricks, ha, ha, ha. Lawyer? What would you need a lawyer for? We've had our lawyers go over these contracts dozens of times. Just sign here, boys. You're going to be huge, boys, huge.

After signing their names, Lou, Brady, and Mick are whisked away by Mandy to Champagne Town. Casino and I, being writers, are special and we also have to sign publishing contracts. We are introduced to a jovial fellow named Malcolm Forrester, who apparently has a publishing company that goes by the snappy name of Panache, and they too are part of this cheerful, helpful Worldwide Artists/Gladglen gang.

Then Casino and I sign another contract with some company called Hemdale. When we ask they say, "Yeah, it's Hemdale, films. You know, David Hemmings. Remember him in *Blow Up*? The Antonioni film? Yeah, that's it. Sign here.

There is much chuckling and back-slapping as it is explained to us that, in order for them to sign us, they have to adhere to a legal formality and offer us a monetary advance, which for reasons far too complicated to explain they can't really do. Therefore, in order for the signing to be completed, we will be asked to make a gentleman's deal to forgo any immediate recompense and accept the token amount of one shilling each.

One shilling? Five pence? Yes, that's just the way it has to be, but don't you worry, soon enough you'll be receiving royalty checks that will make your heads spin. You boys are going to be massive. Let's get these contracts signed and join the rest of the lads with the bubbly, shall we?

Where do we sign?

XVIII

Two days later comes the blissful news that the company has found us a suitable flat on Bishop's Road in Fulham Broadway. We're scheduled to move in four days. Finally, we're going to blow this doss-hole. Cans of lager are cracked and tipped down our throats as the three of us resolve to spend the evening in the squat congratulating ourselves, playing the acetate endlessly, and getting politely hammered.

This we do for seven straight hours until, at ten o'clock, we decide it would be an excellent idea to jostle around the mirror, slap the makeup on, slip into our finery, and toddle off to the Black Lion on West End Lane for a nightcap. I'm sporting my top hat and walking stick, and the lime-green clogs I inherited from Sonja. Off we go.

It is a warm summer night, lots of people about as we make our way eastward on Mill Lane. The Black Lion, when we arrive, is jammed, with patrons spilling outside and sitting at tables under Cinzano umbrellas or milling about, jabbering. We can't help but make an entrance, with Brady uttering loud inanities about the Hollywood Brats, his arms spread wide as the crowd parts to let us through. Not for the first time lately do I wonder where Dr. Brady Jekyll got this personality. There was neither Mr. Hyde nor hair of it a mere ten months ago in a bedroom in Bushey. The timid, quiet little Irish wallflower has metamorphosed into quite the obnoxious, lippy piece of work. You get what you ask for, I suppose.

One junior office boy makes a drunken move toward Brady, until I poke my walking stick up around the knot of his tie and he comes to a surprised halt, waving his pint, pointing at me, and spouting some common-or-garden vitriol. We leave them muttering outside and enter the pub proper.

Inside, we are received in much the same manner. Brady continues going for the Mr. Congeniality award, talking loudly to people who look like they want to kill him, telling them how great the Hollywood Brats are, charming none and sundry. One pint later and the barman refuses to serve us any more, and as the crowd don't seem overly enamored with us I suggest to my two cohorts that it might be time to exit.

Lou needs no persuasion—he's all for it. Brady protests, saying he's got three-quarters of a pint left. Nonetheless, he follows us, pint in hand, out the door. The crowd parts, the jeering starts, we haven't broken any hearts. Dickheads take swipes at my topper, somebody spits, women are swearing like fishwives. All in all, quite a nice outing.

Somehow, we make it through to the curb on West End Lane, at which point the mob seems content to let us leave with just a bit more baying and howling. Fair deal, I say.

Alas, Brady is not of the same mind. He chooses this exact moment to hurl his three-quarters-full pint glass in a high backward arc over his shoulder. It smashes dead center among the crowd outside the Black Lion.

Well, we don't need to hang around to see how this is received. We leg it up West End Lane, turn left on Mill Lane, and run until we can run no more. We stop, gasping for breath and looking fearfully back for signs of pursuit. Thankfully, all appears peaceful, so we continue our way slumward, breathing heavily and castigating Brady for his psychopathic behavior.

Lou and I can only castigate for so long, however, before dissolving into laughter at his rare brand of insanity. What a complete nutter. We laugh some more, increasingly so, until we are actually bending over at the waist, laughing hysterically.

In fact, we are laughing so hysterically that we don't even notice the mob that has caught up with us until it is too late. We are surrounded on the corner of Mill Lane and Narcissus Road. Now there's poetic justice for you, or irony, or some bloody unpleasant thing. There are at least twenty-five of them, not to mention three carloads of extras, just in case they need them. And this rabble do not seem to be amused. They want justice, and not the sort delivered by police and courts and such. And none of this poetic rubbish just mentioned, either. They seem to be unquestionably leaning toward the vigilante variety.

They separate the three of us. Brady, though, is the villain that commands their most vigorous attention. Three thugs have him bent backward over a hedge, and while two of them bravely hold him down, the other courageous fellow cocks and lands a vicious fist right in Brady's face. This momentarily distracts the Neanderthals holding us two. They begin yelping encouragement to the puncher. I catch Lou's eye and he gets it, and we take this split second of inattention to break free and make a mad dash for it. He heads south, down Holmdale Road, and I head north, up Aldred Road.

This breakout briefly confuses our sharp-minded assailants and gives us a few precious seconds' head start. Have you ever tried running for your life in a top hat and clogs? I wouldn't advise it.

I find myself on Agamemnon Road, then take a sharp right onto Achilles Road. Behind me, I can hear yelling, the grinding of a gear stick in the palm of an idiot, and the loud revving of a car's engine. I leap over a stone wall into somebody's garden and crouch with my back pressed against the rough stones, trying to stifle my loud breathing. Summoning a thimbleful of nerve, I peek through a small gap and see about six hod carriers jump out of a car—a forties Chevy, weirdly—and scout around, trying to find me. After a couple of agonizingly long minutes laced with profanity of a decidedly low order, they climb back in the car and reverse with squealing tires back down Achilles Road. Over the wall I clamber and continue my escape up to Ajax Road, where I dart left onto Ulysses Road.

And what's with these names, anyway? I'm trapped in the middle of my own personal Greek tragedy maze.

Leaning on a garden gate, I catch my breath and listen for any sound of the Black Lion Bricklaying & Motoring Club. Nothing. So I begin a slow, careful, circuitous—not to mention cowardly—route around the back streets, through hedges and gardens until, finally, I arrive at 11 Mill Lane and scurry in through the front door.

Fifteen anxiety-riddled minutes later, Lou arrives, telling a tale of how he ran through some gardens with a mob in pursuit until, in terrified desperation, he pounded on the door of a house and some Chinese guy came out and immediately went into a karate stance and made some weird barking noises, and the thugs ran away. That cat was apparently fast as lightning. After that, he let Lou in and gave him refuge until the coast was clear. This could only happen to Lou.

A solid hour later, Brady makes it home. He crawls up the stairs. His eyes are swollen shut, he's got bruises everywhere, and they robbed him of all his money.

One quid.

XIX

After hiding indoors for three days, we go south in the city and up in the world. We move into 26 Bishop's Road, Fulham Broadway, the ground floor of a house. What a palace. Not a rat in sight, a large front room with fireplace, a large rear room, a kitchen with table and chairs, a bathroom complete with tub, and even a glass conservatory leading to a small garden. We have a telephone and, wonder of wonders, a television.

Within an hour, charming Lou has obtained credit at the shop across the street and comes back with Pepsi, chocolate bars, crisps, and cans of lager.

We have landed in heaven.

Just like the Monkees, the four of us move in together, including Mick, who arrives from Hemel Hempstead and sits on one of the beds for fifteen minutes before sighing, standing up, and saying, "I'll be right back, lads."

Ken assigns us a road manager named Louie. He's a cockney, five foot seven, tops, shoulder-length hair, mustache, Buddy Holly glasses, and a leather trench coat. He's a bundle of nervous, chain-smoking energy. Ken has previously described him as "an obliging little ferret," but we like him instantly.

Two days later, the three of us are in the big room at noon watching TV, riveted to a kiddies' show about the difference between a square and a circle and how to draw them, when Lou says, "Anybody seen Mick?" Only now do we notice that he never came back. Like that chap with Scott of the Antarctic, he just walked off into the night and never returned. Perhaps he thought our rations were running low and that we were almost out of whale oil. It's strange, anyway.

But we can't dwell on it because today Louie is taking us shopping. That's why we got up so early. He picks us up in a van that already contains a Norwegian keyboard player and drives us to Shaftesbury Avenue, home, as previously noted, to the best music shops in the universe. Seems like five minutes ago we were staring in these windows, coveting and drooling. Now, we can't really believe it but we have been told we can have whatever we want. Imagine that.

The van takes us through Piccadilly, up Shaftesbury Avenue and Charing Cross Road, pulls up outside Sound City, and in we go, the "obliging little ferret" leading the way. As soon as he's through the door he announces in a loud, cockney, town-crier type way, "Ladies and gentlemen, these are the Hollywood Brats and they are going to spend a lot of money."

You'd be surprised at how quickly this announcement gets attention and a truly superior brand of service. This happens in every shop; we are treated like royalty.

For a band that has existed for so long balanced on a knife-edge of decrepit instruments and junk gear held together with gaffer's tape, the sheer wonder of this afternoon cannot be adequately described.

Casino, his little sperm microphones and red-painted two-ton upright confined to the Dark Ages of memory, gets a Fender Rhodes electric piano, a Hammond B3 organ with Leslie speaker, Orange amp and speaker cabinet, and a Yamaha acoustic guitar.

Brady, his face still puffy and a lovely shade of purple from the Black Lion beating, gets a '68 Gibson Firebird and an invitation to travel by limousine to the Hiwatt factory to custom design his own amp.

Lou selects a set of Gretsch drums with Zildjian cymbals and a year's supply of sticks.

I content myself with a Gibson J-200 acoustic. In addition, Casino and I each get a tape machine to help us with the writing process.

On top of this, and under the watchful, demanding eye of Louie, technicians buzz around getting us microphones, stands, leads, speakers, and all the rest of the mountain of boring bits and pieces that a band needs to perform at top whack.

At Macari's, I forlornly search the walls crammed with beautiful expensive guitars. There is no sign of a black Vox teardrop.

That night, after one of the greatest days in the history of Western civilization, we finally head off to the land of Nod, drunk and exhausted. I lie there in my lovely new bed, complete with sheets and pillows, afloat in that mysterious, blissful stratum twixt consciousness and sleep.

Then, against all of my better inclinations, I am struck in the brain by a lightning bolt of pure inspiration. I fall out of bed and grope around in the dark for my brand-new tape machine, purchased for just such a moment. Kneeling there on the carpeted floor, I sing, quietly and hoarsely, into the small microphone for a minute or so, add some slurred spoken instructions, then back to bed. Two seconds later, I'm out cold.

Next day, my birthday, as a matter of fact, I check out the nocturnal recording and it's not only good, it is in fact quite good and just might be the best thing the Hollywood Brats have got. I have to get this to Casino as soon as possible. I toy with the recording throughout the day, throwing on a couple of guitar chords and a few more lyrics.

That night, the three of us pop down the road to our new local, the Greyhound on Fulham Palace Road. Casino joins us and we hang around, lording it over any musicians daft enough to come near us. And whom should we run into but Mal? We last saw him, ooh, when was it? Oh yes, being stiffed by yours truly outside the Café des Artistes way back when. He seems to have forgotten, or at least he's not bearing any discernible grudge. We rather enjoy catching up with him, telling him what's new.*

Ken calls to inform us that Mick has quit. Actually, what he really says is, "Mick cracked up." Well, we can have that effect on people. Truth is, he wasn't a good fit anyway. Great bass man and classic chap, but he wouldn't immerse himself in our culture so what's the point? It does, however, mean that we're back to the soul-torturing drudgery of looking for a bloody bass player.

The office sets up a rehearsal studio for a week in Wood Green, where the four of us get to work introducing our songs to all our lovely new equipment. Not only that, but in these weeks of wonder there is yet another stunning

---

* Brady's Diary, September 2, 1973
"Went to Greyhound with Andrew, Lou, and Cas. Met Mal, of all people. Chatted up American girl he was with. I think Andrew might have shagged her in the loo. Andrew's got a new song. Great title. 'Sick On You.'"

development. Ken has got a recording session booked for us, September 27–29. And what studio has he booked? Just Olympic Studios, that's all. We can't believe it. The Stones recorded *Beggars Banquet* at Olympic. Everybody who is anybody has recorded at Olympic and now it's our turn.

We are, of course, need it be said, of the firm conviction that we thoroughly deserve it and that it's about time, too.

Ken has this idea that he wants us to record a single: A-side "Chez Maximes"; B-side "Nightmare." He also says he wants to have a shot at producing. By all means, squire.

Two dozen idiots show up at Wood Green to audition for the role of Hollywood Brats bass player. These morons have obviously not actually read the ad we put in the *Melody Maker*. Awful-looking bunch. All they've done is read the magic words we now add to the description of ourselves in the ad. We now put "with record deal." That draws them like flies. So, small wonder they seem as appalled to see us as we are to see them.

Ken sends a session bass player to Wood Green to cover the upcoming Olympic recordings, in case we don't find anyone in time. He keeps telling us to just get someone to play bass. He doesn't have to be part of the band, says Ken. We'd prefer a permanent player but we have to reluctantly admit that this advice makes sense. The chap he sends along is a nice-enough guy but he's a hippy and he must be forty years old, at least. He looks like he's come to mend the fence. He asks for charts as soon as he walks in. Charts? Why, are you sailing to Tahiti, mate? Turns out he's no Mick, but it must be said the man can play and it's refreshing to hear that great bottom end in the sound again.

Truth is, the music is sounding different with the new gear. Lou's snare sounds like a machine gun, cymbals like "The Sorcerer's Apprentice," bass drum like Hercules's heart beat. Casino is a great organ player (who knew?) and we stick his Hammond on every song, trying it out. It's perfect on "Courtesan" and "Drowning Sorrows." But it is Brady on the Firebird that is the real revelation. His sound and playing are starting to match his new psychotic personality. Finally.*

---

* Eunan Brady's Diary, September 8, 1973
"Andrew and I go to see the Stones at Wembley. Block E, Row 24, 3 p.m. show, £1.65. Great 'Street Fighting Man.' Buy *Goats Head Soup* afterward.
Derek called, asking about the bass gig. No chance."

XX

Number 117 Church Road, Barnes. South of the river. We make it a point not to venture south of the Thames. What's there, after all? Battersea Power Station? Battle of Hastings? Lou's got a girl in Clapham, but that's his problem. He got shot in the arse in Clapham and that's south of the river. Says it all, really.

Ah, but Barnes is a different south of the river. This is west of Putney Bridge and here all is verdant and leafy, with nice cars and pubs and Victorian houses and bright-red double-decker buses and tourist-brochure pubs. It's English, here.

And, strangely enough, this beguiling little corner of this green and pleasant land is where you will find the undisputed greatest recording studio in the world. You want to dispute? Okay, muggo, which studio is better? Abbey Road? Go to a grip shop and get one. Abbey Road is famous because of five guys and one of them is named George Martin. That's it. Move on.

Well, how about somewhere in New York, the Record Plant, for instance? Or Los Angeles, the Record Plant, for instance? Or Sun Studio (museum) or Muscle Shoals (banjos and catfish)? Or how about Motown in Detroit? Sure, but where are you going to park your car? And who is going to escort you to and from your wallet? Even Berry Gordy hit the road and took the first Greyhound bus leaving for LA.

How about some European studio mecca? And where would that possibly be? Perhaps some Swiss place or Parisian rock emporium or any Continental *salon de musique* where they record only the most cutting-edge discotheque? Where does Sacha Distel record his stuff, anyway? Or Johnny Hallyday?

Still need convincing? Twit. Try this for a sample Olympic Studios client list: Yardbirds, Troggs, the Rolling Stones, Led Zeppelin, Small Faces, Who, Dusty Springfield, Jimi Hendrix, and Faces.

Still not convinced? Well, get this: Procol Harum skipped the light fandango at Olympic. The soundtrack for *The Italian Job*—brilliant Michael Caine flick—was recorded at, where else, Olympic. Even the Fabs did parts of the yawn-inducing "All You Need Is Love" at Olympic.

Need more? Well, on top of all that, try as we might we can't forget that the utter cinematic wankery of Jean-Luc Godard's *Sympathy for the Devil* (*One Plus One*) featured studio scenes, mostly illustrating the sad downward spiral of the blessed Brian Jones, shot at Olympic.

Brian Jones: "What can I play?"
Mick Jagger: "I don't know. What *can* you play?"

Chilly stuff, Michael Philip.

But, get it straight, when it comes to "Roll tape . . . take one," Olympic Studios is *the* place to be on planet Earth.

And this is where the Hollywood Brats are on the evening of September 27, 1973. We are also in awe. We are afforded a quick tour: first, Studio C, small and well-appointed, mostly for vocals; Studio B, intimate, opulent, but still big enough to rock; and then there's Studio A. Studio A is huge and, in fact, looks like the cinema it once was. It is big enough to record an orchestra, which is, of course, why the Beatles used it for "All You Need Is Space."

We try to affect an attitude of cool and not look like four rubes fresh off a tourist bus, but it's difficult to pull off. This place is amazing and because of its history, a history with which we are all too familiar having read about it in liner notes for years, any young musician would crawl across a hundred miles of broken hearts just for the pleasure of collapsing on the doorstep. And the Hollywood Brats get to plug in and roll tape.

Ken introduces us to our engineer. He is not exactly an inspiring sight: tall, head to toe in denim, sandals, long haystack hair, beard like a young Santa, and untrimmed mustache so long it seems like he doesn't have a mouth.

This looks promising.

We set up in Studio B. The engineer puts me in my own little vocal phone booth, okayed as a favor to Ken who spoke to me about it earlier. And they surround Lou with his own personal Berlin Wall. Now, I know Lou doesn't like this because since we started playing together way back in Stanmore, July 1, 1972, he likes to check me out for little signals about this and that, and over time it has become almost second nature to us; just a glance and he's on the ride, a nod and it's hi-hat time. And he lets me know, with a raised eyebrow, when he's going to roll. Like that.

But this is the big league, so we'll listen to the big-league boys. After a bit of engineer-type messing around for levels, we start to play. Nothing serious, just a little workout based on St. Chuck, just to warm up.

Sounds terrible through my headphones and I wonder how things sound to the rest of the lads. Not so hot, judging by their expressions. Still, when the talk-back button clicks and the control room says it's take-one time on "Chez Maximes," we count it in and away we go just like we've done at a dozen gigs and a hundred kitchen rehearsals. Three minutes or so in, right on schedule, it comes to its cacophony of a climax and then everything goes quiet. We look at each other, those of us that can see each other, and shrug our shoulders.

Through the glass, we can see the big brains in the control room, heads bent in earnest discussion. Take two, they say, and away we go again, then, same comforting train-crash ending, followed by the same silence. What we're doing sounds like rubbish to me but what do I know? This must be how things are done up here in this rarefied atmosphere. I notice, also, that Brady is playing just like he did back in a certain bedroom in Bushey. And that's not good.

Finally, the engineer asks Casino and me to come into the control room. When we get there it appears that he and Ken have arrived at the conclusion that "Chez Maximes" needs a riff. A riff? What are we, Hot Chocolate? A riff? We want a tornado of guitars smacking you in the gob if you're daft enough to play the record. That's what we want. Not a riff.

Casino has a quiet word in my lughole, giving me a concise version of his treatise "Politics in the Latter Half of the 20th Century," and convinces me to ignore every instinct I hold near and dear. I try to do the one thing that is most alien to me. I try to get along. You want a riff? You, sir, shall have a riff. I point to Brady. Let me introduce our resident riffster. But, apparently, he is not needed.

We all traipse out to the grand piano and stand around it like we're going to sing a chorus or two of "Swanee River," but instead the engineer sits down on the piano bench, cozies up to Casino, and hums a riff he thinks will be just dandy. Casino tinkledy-tinks until he sorts out the notes. Brady copies it on the Firebird. It is awful, an embarrassment. A ten-note riff over two bars. Repeat as necessary. It is everything we are not. So let's give it a try, shall we?

Two, three more bashes at this thing and we lay down what the mega-minds in the control room say is the "perfect" take.

Next, we tackle "Nightmare," and this goes much smoother, no riff required, apparently.

After we get the basic track it's back to "Chez Maximes" to overdub the dreaded riff. Brady is alone in the studio while we are all in the control room watching. The riff is rubbish and, just to complete the package, so is Brady. With talent like he's putting on display here tonight he could easily play for, say, Lieutenant Pigeon or, at a pinch, Love Affair.

Our hippy bass player sits in a corner—unconcerned, uninterested, uninvolved—drinking grape juice and staring at the Page 3 girl in the *Sun*. She's quite tasty, actually.

Over the course of the next two days we overdub this and that. For instance, three of us—me, Lou, and Ken—in a stairwell around a microphone doing handclaps. Only trouble is, gee whiz, only two of us can do handclaps in tempo. Exit Ken.

On day two I lay down the vocals and then the producing wizards settle in to knit their brows and mix the thing. The final product? The engineer loves it. The boys and I are ashamed of it.

Ken knows it.

Back to Wood Green and back to bass auditions. The office has thrown a net far and wide and yanked in everybody in England who has ever played bass anywhere. Somebody from the band Jonesy, whoever they are, shows up, plugs in, bores us to tears, and is given the boot. Most of them can play but the problem is the look. Well, that and the age. Don't forget, we are appalled that Brady is twenty-three. We want a certain look and age, and we are not going to compromise. But this bass situation is getting dicey.

Lou and I meet with Ken at the office to talk about a clothing budget, a wheeze we dreamed up the night before. By the end of Lou's imploring speech even I'm ready to dig in my pockets and contribute a couple of quid. He really does have the gift of the gab. At the end of the meeting we walk out with a little brown envelope containing £125. You can do a lot of damage with that kind of money in a half-decent secondhand shop.

Time at home is spent playing music, larking about, and, above all, watching TV. We love television. We are severely TV depraved, because we've been severely TV deprived.

So, now that our ship has finally come crashing into the dock, our TV is switched on from the moment we crawl out of bed until ITV, BBC1, and BBC2 close down for the day, usually at the ridiculously early hour of 11:45 p.m. It ends most nights with some bonkers white-haired fat chap in an ill-fitting blue suit telling us about stars and planets for fifteen minutes. Some nights, it ends with a prayer or an orchestra playing "God Save You Know Whom."

Sometimes, on Wednesdays, TV viewing ends with Rod Serling's *Night Gallery*, which we love. It's all earwigs crawling into brains and laying eggs and things like that.

Guy Fawkes Night is somewhere off in the near future, and we buy strings of small red firecrackers at the shop. These wee, red, cigarette-shaped firecrackers pack a surprisingly huge and nasty wallop for such a modest-looking incendiary. We sit around watching TV, surreptitiously lighting firecrackers and throwing them at each other. You act nonchalant, seemingly transfixed by the telly, but really you're just waiting for the chance to blow the other chap up. Makes for some hilarious leaping and yelping. Out in the hall, you tape one to the front of a teacup, light it, then hand the cup to the agreed-upon sap, handle first. He takes it, thank you very much, ta, goes to take a sip, and *kaboom*.

One night, due to rampant firecrackery, Brady's bed bursts into flames, which we don't notice for the longest time, since our eyeballs are glued to Reginald Bosanquet reading the news plastered on TV. There's a huge black hole right in the middle of Brady's bed. He doesn't seem unduly concerned.*

---

* Eunan Brady's Diary, October 19, 1973

"Still looking for decent bass player, i.e. one who doesn't look like Hoss (Ponderosa). Derek phoned twice last week looking for bass gig. Ha, ha. Sap."

The acetate of our single arrives at 26 Bishop's Road. We don't exactly rush to the turntable like we did with the Gooseberry acetate. We are wary about this one. And we are right to be wary. It sounds competent, professional, and interesting, but it certainly doesn't sound like the Hollywood Brats. It is smooth, tidy, and tame, three words that will never be associated with us. That stupid riff makes toes curl and balls shrink with embarrassment.

It's great to see the Brats on a 45, though.

XXI

Yet another ad in the *Melody Maker*, yet another audition. Now the office handles all phone calls and sets up the audition at the Pied Bull, scene of one of our former crimes against entertainment. Auditions are boring but it will be a nice change to be on that stage and not be detested.

The bass players are rubbish. But it's my attitude I'm worried about. I don't even expect anything anymore. They all look like they should be in Jethro Tull. The Hollywood Brats, however, look great after taking their wardrobe dough for a walk around town. Lou's got a ladies' flower-patterned blouse knotted across his skinny ribs and great shoes that he must need a stepladder to climb into. Cas has nabbed a gray zebra-stripe jacket with black buttons and bangles to match. Brady has been to see his mate Gerry in Kensington Market and come out with the exact snakeskin boots Keith wears in the *Let It Bleed* era.

I bought white lace-up boxing boots in a fight shop in Soho and I'm wearing red strides, courtesy of Sonja, with a purple velvet frock coat.

I spoke too soon about the stage at the Pied Bull, by the way. We've been on it for three hours and every bass player leaves detesting us.

Then Brady comes up with one of his typically bonkers concepts. Out of the blue, he says he knows the bass player from Silverhead. Says his name is Nigel Harrison and they've been mates for years. He and Nigel had a pint yesterday, and Nigel might be interested. I never noticed Nigel at Global Village and Brady sure as hell never mentioned they were buddies. I can't conjure up an impression of Silverhead's bass player, and neither can Lou or Cas. That can't be a good sign.

Nevertheless, Silverhead are playing in Birmingham on October 23 and the office hires us a limo to go up and see what's what, make an offer, as it were, poach the lad if need be. So the four of us, plus Ken and the obliging little . . . sorry, Louie, sit back in the tooled-leather upholstery of a top-of-the-line limousine and head up the M1. This turns out to be a ride of luxury and laughs. For a start, there's a bar, and Brady doesn't even have to search for it. Ken offers up its intoxicants within the first thirty seconds. The driver rolls down the don't-bother-me window and hands back a small zippered leather bag containing four square inches of dark hash, a vial of white powder, and a mirror. The Hollywood Brats grab for the mirror to check out the eyeliner.

After a two-hour mobile drinking/smoking/snorting session, we arrive at the gig just fashionably late enough to see nothing of the show and are escorted to a private box to do just that. A young lady shows up with a tray of lager.

Brady goes backstage and, after a bit, returns with Nigel. Bloody hell, Nigel's got curly hair. Back in the limo, back down the M1.

On the way back to London, on the limo radio, we hear that David Cassidy has reached number one in the charts with "Daydreamer."

Grim gets grimmer.

We are also bored to death. Auditioning bass players day after day saps the spirit of a band. We're completely sick of it. We should be in Olympic recording a classic album, not trooping off to Wood Green to play "Johnny B. Goode" a hundred times.

As a distraction, Brady, our social convenor, directs an outing to Imperial College to see Queen, the bunch that got into a snit over our old name. The teeth that launched an unprovoked attack on my fist. I was fed up with the name, anyway. It's a daft name, truth be told. A cheap laugh at best.

They seem to have survived their early nonsense and onstage appear fine, if ordinary, to me, like a clean-shaven Silverhead, albeit with Mal's twin brother on guitar.

Backstage afterward I wonder why I'm here, since I want to go home or to a pub or to the Red Cross to donate blood, anywhere but backstage at a Queen gig. We nonetheless kiss and make up and lie through our teeth about what a marvelous performance we've just witnessed. It's pathetic but it works, because we get invited by the towel-draped punchbag and Mal's doppelgänger to attend a Guy Fawkes party at their place three days hence.

So, on Guy Fawkes Night we travel for thousands of miles on the Tube from Fulham Broadway to Acton and show up at a very nice house indeed on a very nice street indeed. Inside, it's crowded but you can't really say the joint is rocking. The joint's not even swaying—it's more like flinching. Student types are standing around chatting, holding drinks politely and talking earnestly. One couple are holding hands and doing a sort of Tourette's twitch to the naff music on the stereo.

So muted and tweedy are the crowd that, for the first couple of minutes, we think we've got the wrong house and instead have stumbled into a retirement party for a particularly dull Ecclesiastical Studies professor. But no, soon enough one or two of the Queensters come over with beverages and bonhomie. Not to mention loon pants and cheesecloth shirts. Spare me.

I find a mantelpiece to lean on near the stereo and immediately wish I hadn't. It is nonstop prog rock, Genesis, ELP, and unidentifiable others of the same pretentious ilk, interspersed with Queen, Queen, and more Queen. Casino can't stand it either and takes a much more aggressive approach to the problem, rifling through the LP stack until he finds something palatable. He commandeers the stereo, tosses Genesis aside, and puts on Mott the Hoople. I don't particularly like Mott, but Cas does and it's a huge improvement on the progs. What isn't?

There are precisely no attractive women at this party. None. Not even sort of. Not even a halfway reasonable looker to whom one would, out of a sense of Christian charity, administer even the most perfunctory of porkings.

Even the firework display turns out to be a damp squib. We've got way more exciting fireworks, competitive fireworks, dangerous fireworks every night in our front room. Early on, we take our leave and start the long journey back, trying to make last call at the Greyhound. As we walk the dark streets toward the station Lou lights the way with a torch he has conveniently brought with him.*

The next day, Guy Fawkes plus one, the office sends us to Camden to meet a "highly rated" bass player for a pint and a chat. I don't know who rated this

---

* Eunan Brady's Diary, 5 November 1973

"Firework party at Queen house. Freddie Mercury and two others there. Andrew refuses to acknowledge them. Lou nicks a torch."

guy "highly," probably his foster mum, but when we meet him he reeks of patchouli oil and is wearing patched denim jeans, an Afghan coat, and a hat. And we all know why he's wearing a hat.

Right, Brady is, I'm told, under siege. He is being bombarded by calls from the shag-rug Siamese cat man. He wants a meeting about this Derek character. The four of us convene at the Mitre pub at the corner of Bishop's and Dawes Roads, and over a pint we debate the pros and cons of the man. The number-one consideration on the agenda is that the endless search for a bass player is grinding our spirits into dust. Why can't we find a bass player? It is four strings, for Christ's sake, and they're big, too. You can't miss them. You put a finger down and there it is, E.

Anyway, from what we remember, Derek does fit the bill looks-wise, sort of. His clothes are pitiful but what can you do? And Brady claims he can play.

The main grudge all of us have against him, one we each bring to the table separately, is that we offered him the gig when we were starving, living in a squat, and had nothing but an idea, a concept, and he turned us down flat. Now that we've got a contract and money and new gear, and are about to start recording in Olympic Studios, suddenly the chump's had a change of heart and is on the phone, pleading, every five minutes.

We get a couple of other things off our chests: the white shag carpet, the Siamese cats, things like that. Then we take a vote, outcome 3–1 in favor of his admission. We discuss things some more, each Brat making his case, and then we vote again, outcome 2–2. Three more pints go down the hatch before we come to the realization that time is flying by. Mainly, we're sick of auditions. We have to get back into Olympic.

Another vote is taken: outcome 4–0.

Back down Bishop's Road. Here we come, walking down the street, we get the funniest looks from everyone we meet. We stop and admire a beautiful '72 lime-green Lotus Europa. One day, when I'm rich . . .

We open the door of number 26. The phone is ringing. Guess who?

Ken sets up an audition at the Pied Bull in Islington, and on November 22, 1973 (ten years to the day since Lee Harvey Oswald shot that policeman in Dallas), we put Derek through his paces. He turns up looking not a million miles removed from one of the chaps in the New Seekers. Nondescript hair, tame threads, but his bass case contains a Fender Precision and there are hints that the man might have a sense of humor. He's familiar with the Kinks' "I Need You" so we give that a bash, along with the obligatory Chuck Berry, and we even have a go at "Nightmare." He's okay. He's not Mick or the session guy, but he's okay.

We all repair to the nearest rub-a-dub-dub where pints are sunk and Cas, Lou, and I continue to inspect the man over the rims of our drinks. He likes a pint, he knows "I Need You," he can hold his own in the chat department, and he has some kind of rapport with Brady. What the hell? Three rounds down five throats and Derek's in the band. Ken will work out what to pay him and whatever bass and amp he wants.

This guy's not backward about stepping forward. Next day, he rushes out and picks up a Rickenbacker 4001 Fireglo bass then pops over to Roxy Music's house and from them buys a Fender setup with reverse eighteen-inch speaker and an extra twelve-inch cabinet. Says send the bill to Worldwide Artists. He's not shy.

No more auditions, thank Christ. Now the office sets up block time for serious band rehearsals at a great facility in Walthamstow. The studio is spacious and carpeted, with fantastic acoustics, an in-house roadie to assist Louie, and best of all, it comes with a complete bar and bartender. There is only one problem. Where's Walthamstow?

A quick scour of the *A–Z* and there it is, way out at the end of the Victoria Line, last stop, past Seven Sisters, Tottenham Hale, and Blackhorse Road.

We arrive to find our equipment set up perfectly, the keyboards, the Gretsch drums, the Firebird, the microphones—and this time they are joined by a certain bass man's Rickenbacker/Fender ensemble.

Thus ensconced in deepest Walthamstow, we begin the task of teaching the Hollywood Brats repertoire to Derek. Day after day, working hard, getting better and better. He's starting to fit in, starting to give lip back when he gets it, which is often.

Ken wants to come and see us but we tell him to forget it. We'll let you know when we're ready. And the thing with Ken is that he loves that kind of attitude. He says he'll wait. Don't worry, squire. We don't need much time.

Thank you for the days in Walthamstow. Four days, six days, it's starting to sound like something interesting is going on here. More and more often, in the middle of a song Casino and I look at each other and give a slight nod. There's no denying it. This thing is starting to cook, just like Bo Diddley backstage with his chicken and his frying pan.

Casino and I have a new song we are working out with the boys called "Tumble with Me." It's not entirely finished lyrically but we've got the musical arrangement sorted out. This must be a relief for Derek because he gets to learn it from scratch along with the other lads, for once. I've written all the lyrics except for the chorus. I haven't yet come up with something that fits the rest of the mood of the piece. Stay tuned, I'll figure it out.

But then suddenly I don't have to. We run it through again and, when it comes to the stop at the chorus, I'm just about to mouth some gibberish when Casino leans into his microphone and sings:

So wake up little Susie
Stop picking your nose

We all break up laughing and the song clatters to a halt, but when we settle down I tell Cas I like it and we're going to use it. He can't believe it—he was just joking.

XXII

The New York Dolls are on *The Old Grey Whistle Test* tonight, November 27, so we wrap up the rehearsal at Walthamstow and Louie picks us up in the van. He lives in one of the delightful tower blocks nearby and has invited us to go there to catch the program. Derek declines the invite. Eyebrows are raised, glances exchanged, but we leave it at that. So it's just the four of us, as usual.

The tower block in which Louie resides is right out of *A Clockwork Orange*. A bleak concrete maze with nary a sprig of greenery in sight. Broken glass, underground walkways full of debris swirling in the wind; all it lacks is a soundtrack featuring the lovely Ludwig Van.

Up the creaking, stinking lift we go to the fifteenth floor. The lift doors open to reveal five skinheads standing there, bored stiff, smoking, waiting to descend. One is having an unabashed slash on the wall opposite. Judging by the stain and the stench it's not the first time this has occurred.

They seem as surprised to see us as we are to see them and, because the lift doors are beginning to close, for once it's a draw. They all hurry to get in and hold the door while the urinating chap shivers, zips up, flicks his fag end down the hall, and saunters in to join the droogs of the Walthamstow chapter. He must be their Alex.

Once safely, mercifully, inside Louie's flat, we are introduced to his missus, who is gracious and welcomes us into her home and serves us as many beers as we like. She's a good lass. We settle down with our usual Doll trepidation to watch *Whistle Test*.

We can't stand wheezy Bob Harris, his beard, his asthmatic whisper, his clobber, his program, his phone-perv voice, or anything else about him. But, as

British viewers, we're condemned to this monopoly. It's this or *Top of the Pops*. These two programs have UK music sewn up—we've got no choice. We're doomed to watch them.

The difference is, though, that *TOTP* has no pretensions. Absolutely none. If you're in the charts this week you're on, simple as that. Plus, they've got Pan's People. Cue coyote howl. *Whistle Test*, meanwhile, is nothing but pretension. It is the hippy ideal of what music should be. And into this nuthouse stagger the Dolls.

Roberto del Wheezer introduces them with some preamble claptrap, something about comparing Monkees to Beatles, a "pale and amusing derivative," he says. What? What a dink. But I don't have time to reflect on it. The Dolls kick off with "Looking for a Kiss." Brady is familiar with it. I look askance at him. He must be secretly listening to the Dolls album. Still, on TV it sounds okay to me. And I can't help but be transfixed by two things: firstly, the rhythm guitarist's a Lilliputian; secondly, where do you get a set of pink drums? And, speaking of drums, given our recent bass woes, look at these guys. Their drummer dies in a bathtub in London and five minutes later they've got another one, plays fine, looks fine. What's New York got that London hasn't?

The four of us give the TV screen serious lip while they're playing—sneering at this, deriding that—but really, what a relief. These guys no longer present a problem. Later in the program they wrap up their *Old Grey* experience with "Jet Boy." And oh, my, does "Jet Boy" love the spotlight. "Jet Boy" can't get enough of itself. "Jet Boy" goes on forever. I sniff Todd Rundgren's overkill influence here. Any normal rock genius would have edited this baby at the three-minute, twenty-second mark, if only to maximize the two ounces of dynamics it possesses, but no, on it plods to just short of five minutes.

That's verging on prog rock. Cue catcalls and boos from the Walthamstow Tower Block Chorus.

As they finish we sit back, yak away, and relax in the knowledge that this band we had worried so much about is in no way a threat. We are about to give them a couple more verbal jabs, kick them when they're up, when something happens that shifts our allegiance like only an 8.6 Richter-scale earthquake can shimmy, shimmy, ko ko bop a tectonic plate. As the last note dies away, wheezy Bob sniffs, chuckles, goes to pick his nose but deflects his finger at the last second, and then dismisses the New York Dolls as "mock rock."

Mock rock? The New York Dolls may not be my cup of hemlock but let me tell you this: they are great compared to most of the navel gazers I've seen on *Old Grey Whistle Test*. Mock rock? Go rinse out your beard and buff your incisors.

The Hollywood Brats don't consider the New York Dolls musical rivals, but this is different. Maybe now we see them as philosophical allies aligned against all the dinosaurs of this world.

Oh, there is one supremely annoying thing. The Dolls' bloody guitarist has a Vox teardrop.

We rehearse diligently and effectively throughout the first two weeks of December and are actually beginning to sound like the Hollywood Brats should sound. One night, on the wheels of a whim, we decide to pop out and find a pub, just for a break. The nearest one is a beauty, a throwback, prewar time capsule. Not fancy in the slightest, in fact Edwardian dowdy, twenty or so customers, coal fire blazing away at one end. Six patrons standing, pints in hand, around an old upright piano, singing "All of Me." We love it. Publican and patron alike treat us better than we get treated in Chelsea or Oxford Street. Friendliness, politeness, and good humor are the order of the day.

After the first pint we can't resist joining those at the piano in a bit of a singsong. You took the part that once was my heart so why not take all of me? Brilliant. What an interlude here, far away from the Speak, the Marquee, and all the ultrahip rest of London.

On a freezing night, while we're watching *Parkinson*, the kitchen ceiling at 26 Bishop's Road collapses with a mighty, dusty, terrifying thump. This is how we get the distinct pleasure of meeting our landlord. Two days later he comes over to inspect the damage. He is a drunk, stoned, pleasant-enough Jamaican fellow called Jasper Beauregard III, who finds the scene hilarious and can't stop laughing. He has to sit down on a kitchen chair amid the chaos and ask if we have a beer we can spare. I can barely understand his charming, musical patois and have very little interest in doing so. Just fix the ceiling.

Next day, three more Jamaicans arrive, waking us up at the crack of 2 p.m., to sweep up the plaster and broken bits of wood lathe and such, rabbiting away the entire time and taking many "tea" breaks. In a mere three hours they get all the rubble out the front door, into the boot and backseat of a beat-up Ford Cortina, and drive away.

The drummer, the guitarist, and I spend our evenings throwing firecrackers at each other, watching TV, drinking cans of Long Life, and gluing together and painting plastic models. Lou buys a '55 Chevy, Brady a '31 Model A Ford, and I, a Stuka dive-bomber.

Ken has booked us into a rehearsal space on King's Road on December 16 so he can see what we've been getting up to out there in darkest Walthamstow. We get in, set up, give it a bash to get loose, down a tube or two to get looser, then send Louie to retrieve Ken, who is also warming up, after a fashion, down the street at the Chelsea Potter.

He arrives, the epitome of cool: just nudging drunk, ten-foot-long white wool scarf wrapped around his throat, and, dragging across the floor as he walks, a gray overcoat; Ray-Bans, plimsolls, ever-present fag, and, as always, killer hair. He refuses to sit, insists on standing, or rather leaning.

We then proceed to pin him to that wall he's leaning on and knock him completely dead. "Tumble with Me," which he's never heard, kicks off proceedings, then, whammo, "Sick On You" has been distilled into the raw essence of the Hollywood Brats. This is custom-made mayhem. The drums are primal and pounding, the vocals sneering, retching, the guitars finally at maximum razor howl. We've created a perfect, snarling, four-minute chainsaw symphony. This is it. This is what we are.

Two songs later, we wrap things up with a blistering, not to mention entirely riff-free, "Chez Maximes."

Ken's cool has evaporated. He ceased leaning about ten seconds into "Tumble with Me." He can't stop talking. He loves it, he's got plans, Wilf has got to see this, the world has to see this. He pulls out a notebook and scrawls something unreadable down. It's plain, he's slain. This ain't the Speakeasy anymore and this ain't Gooseberry and this sure as hell ain't last month's Olympic Studios riff-stravaganza.

This is the Hollywood Brats plus one in Chelsea, December 1973.

XXIII

Ken is so pleased with his pilgrims' progress that he hands over £30 for us to go have a drink after rehearsal, a rehearsal that ends, of course, within two seconds of him leaving the building. The poignancy of the moment falls somewhat short of poignant, but I nonetheless recall that this marks the second time we've been given £30 by a manager after seeing us rehearse on King's Road. The first episode seems like it occurred a century ago. We've come a long way since Chris Andrews, good chap though he was.

And there's another key difference between that time and this. Along with thirty nicker, Ken also hands us an invitation for the Hollywood Brats to attend the *Penthouse* Christmas party at their eponymous club in Mayfair on December 21.

Life just keeps getting better and better. *Penthouse* magazine, created by Bob Guccione, the Mafia's answer to Hugh Hefner, is a magazine much revered in Bratdom. The young ladies featured in the pages are distinctly attractive and don't appear to have the slightest qualm about not only disrobing, but also contorting their bodies into various gymnastic poses so as to give the viewer maximum visual advantage when it comes to perusing every square inch of their delectable selves.

Now *Penthouse* is throwing a Christmas party, and the Brats are invited? If this is a dream, for Christ's sake don't wake me up.

Of late, Brady has been spending time with some minx named Lynn. I've met her; she's generally drunk and her top half is blonde. Seems all right, I suppose, except of course for her appalling taste in men. I would ordinarily not give her another thought but the boy has developed a whining tendency, when drunk, for moaning about her and pleading for her attendance and suchlike. This behavior is utterly unacceptable in our world.

On the day of the *Penthouse* party we pop into the office on Dover Street for a quick meeting with Ken to discuss progress with Derek and, more importantly, to pick up another of those little brown envelopes stuffed to the gills with tenners. The plan is to then scarper back to Bishop's Road and get ready for the party. Alas, Ken, the consummate host, brings out a bottle of gin and pours us all a stiff one. Brady, though, cannot let it be. He commandeers the bottle and upends it down his throat, an act he repeats two or three more times. On the way back home he halts the taxi outside an off-license and buys his own personal bottle of Gordon's, which he proceeds to crack open and gulp all the way home.

Thus, at 5 p.m. he has turned himself into a vaudevillian Irish-caricature drunk.

I am repelled. Lou, on the other hand, is kind and helpful and packs the moron off to bed, telling him to get a couple of hours' sleep and then we'll head off to the party. Brady gets into his fire-blackened bed but doesn't shut up, baying non–Hollywood Brat sentences like, "Oh, where's my little Lynn? I must talk to my little Lynn." Then he passes out.

Three hours later, Lou and I are looking sharp and ready to roll. I'm in a tux with tails and Lou is the epitome of drummer chic, pardon the oxymoron. Shamrock Seamus, however, is dead to the world, in a nasty yellowish singlet, arms spread wide, pits on hairy display, and snoring like a bent trombone. Not his most attractive look.

But worse is yet to come. He awakens and drunkenly pleads for the phone to be brought to his bedside. Lou obliges. Brady then calls his "little Lynn" and mews drunken inanities to her while Lou and I look on, appalled. However, I'm not quite so appalled that I don't go to get my tape machine and sit on Brady's bed taping this ridiculous, embarrassing conversation for future blackmail.

"Lynn, Lynn. Oh, my little Lynn, I miss you. What, what? No, I do, really. But I have to go to this party, this situation. What? No, no, purely business. I could come by later. Oh, don't say that, my little Lynn. What? Oh, sorry. What? Two pints, that's all. What? Maybe three. We've been up late, I'm tired. What? Of course I do." This Shakespearian repartee could theoretically go on forever and, compelling though it is, I reach over and disconnect the phone. Brady collapses back on his pillow and falls instantly asleep.

Forty-five minutes after this, Lou gives him a shake, says, "Come on, man, it's the *Penthouse* party. Let's go." I'm watching this pathetic scene. We're leaving in fifteen minutes with or without this clown, and I know what my vote is. Lou, though, is persistent, pleading with his guitarist.

Finally, I've had enough of this crap. I grab a bucket from the backyard, go to the bathroom, and fill it with cold water. English December cold water. As I enter the front room Lou catches a glimpse and says, "Uh, oh." I walk to Brady's bed, where he lies splayed in drunken Irish oblivion, and hit him right in the face with an entire bucketful of frigid, wet wake-up.

Twenty minutes later, the three of us are in a cab, heading for Mayfair.

The Penthouse Club is beyond fab. We are disgorged from the cab and walk, with the help of our pink *Penthouse* invitation, through a gauntlet of beefy security into a party palace, a glittering expanse of revelry and excess. Tables full of exotic grub, bartenders dispensing every drink known to man, celebrities kissing each other's every visible upper cheek and making arrangements to smooch the lowers later.

The centerpiece of this hedonistic playpen is a ten-foot-high pyramid of a thousand crystal champagne glasses atop a table surrounded by hundreds of bottles of Moët & Chandon. Must have taken an age to get it right, and it looks amazing in the lights.

Thespians and pop personalities abound, stuffing their gobs, glad-handing and gushing compliments to one another while all the time looking around for somebody more important to talk to. The funniest looking among a funny-looking lot is Rick Wakeman, from the dreadful Yes. He does not remotely have the physique to pull off the head-to-toe tight-red-leather abomination he's wearing. His doughy nether regions look particularly distasteful.

Suits everywhere, rich-looking corpulent coves standing around, smoking cigars and slurping champers. Beefy Italian types are also in evidence, including, unmistakably, the man himself, Bob Guccione: beige lounge suit, ridiculous lapels, peach shirt open to the navel, worse lapels, gold medallion like he just won Best Extortionist at the Cosa Nostra Olympics, thick gold rings, bracelet, chest like an oily welcome mat—he's got it all. Everything you need to be a caricature of an Italian-American porn king.

Best of all, of course, are the women on display. The joint is dripping with gorgeous babes in all the three main hair colors. I've never seen so many knockouts all in one place. And that extends to the waitresses, too. The Penthouse waitresses, dipsy-doodling around with trays of champagne, are even better than the civilian babes. They're stunning, and they're dressed like extra-saucy French maids, with dresses so short they make a miniskirt seem positively Amish. Frilly little hairpieces, lace cuffs, and underneath those ultrashort skirts, checked underpants trimmed with frothy white lace, designed to be glimpsed.

As soon as we get situated, one of these serving wenches comes over with a tray and hands us all drinks. Casino is so pleased and grateful that he pats her on the rear as she departs. This is not as well received as he possibly might have hoped for. Second round, new waitress, same pat on the checked white-froth undergarment. Cas considers this a compliment, not to mention top-drawer funny as well, but this girl begs to differ, complains to management, and soon enough a side of beef in a bad suit arrives and delivers a short, polite, but firm lecture. Basically, saying hands off the merchandise.

We're eating smoked salmon on baguette and knocking back the champagne like it's the eve of Prohibition. Brady, still soused on gin from earlier, looks as though he's out of his tiny little raving mind. His mascara is smeared across his cheeks, he's giggling hysterically and shouting at people. He and Casino head out to the small dance floor near the champagne glass pyramid, holding on to each other's lapels and laughing. Horrid American dance music blares annoyingly from huge speakers.

A little bloke shows up at my elbow. Even in platform shoes a carnival freak would die for, he still winds up talking to my pocket-handkerchief. I can't picture where I've seen the top of his head before, but that's no problem as he's quite prepared to tell me at length. He's Jack Wild and he played the Artful Dodger in *Oliver!* Oh, of course you did. One of my favorite films. Can you sing me a chorus of "Consider Yourself"? He says funny I should say that as he's about to launch a pop career. I start to edge away.

But things can change rapidly, can't they? First, the Artful Dodger's eyes get very wide, then there is a lady's horror-film scream followed by an almighty crash that sounds very much like a collapsing table, the shattering of a ten-foot-high pyramid of crystal champagne glasses, and the smashing of dozens of

Moët & Chandon bottles. This is instantly followed by the synchronized gasp of five hundred guests, the sound of running feet, and a huge fist with ostentatious ring protuberances smashing unannounced into the middle of my unsuspecting face, sending me flying backward across a table for eight. Glasses, tablecloth, napkins, cutlery, and various wine bottles travel messily and noisily with me as I slide across and fall off into a painful heap under the next table.

I am not allowed long to reflect upon this sudden, confusing turn of events, as I am grabbed under the armpits by two large chaps who have quite obviously performed this sort of task before and dragged between the tables, across the floor, through the entrance to the club, and tossed arse first onto the freezing Mayfair pavement. Two seconds later, Casino lands in a heap beside me.

I lie there on my back, stunned, bleeding heavily from my nose, eyes watering, my face one big pain zone, and every other part of my body hurting from the various iniquities visited upon it in the last ninety seconds. I finally open my eyes, squint, look up, try to focus, and finally see there, leaning over, staring at me, well, who else could it be, really? It is none other than Andrew Loog Oldham. He peers down, shakes his head, adopts a disapproving look, and says, "The last time I witnessed a display like this it featured Brian Jones."

Then he kindly steps over me and continues on his way into the party.*

A Yuletide get-together at the office on Dover Street on a wintry December 23 afternoon. Everyone is here, all the bands—Hogs, Sabs, something called Stray—friendly Mandy and her friendly friends, Wilf and Ken, Patrick Meehan, various other liggers and scoundrels popping in and out.

Miraculously, my eyes were not blackened in the *Penthouse* sucker-punch incident, but my nose and right cheek are red and puffy and my lower lip has never looked so pouty and sultry. I'm wearing my tails again, but with a red paisley bow tie to match a long red silk scarf. Wilf catches my eye, crosses the room, and stands in front of me, looking me up and down. He says, smiling, "Andrew, you look like a fucking waiter." I hand him my empty pint glass.

"Give this a top-up, will you, Wilf?" Astoundingly, he laughs and does just

---

* Andrew Loog Oldham, Bogotá, 2012

"Ah, Andrew, you on the pavement at the *Penthouse* party. I was the pot calling the kettle beige. Or whatever."

that. We even have a good conversation when he comes back. Must be the spirit of the season.

Ken introduces me to Jimmy Helms, who has scored a top-ten hit with an irritating number called "Gonna Make You an Offer You Can't Refuse," sung in a falsetto that makes the fillings in your teeth vibrate. Dead fish handshake, but other than that he seems harmless enough.

There's a weird fat man with a greasy comb-over, resplendent in polyester leisure wear, swanning about, annoying the secretaries, and blowing cigar smoke everywhere. Ken keeps trying to avoid him.*

He takes us in the other direction and introduces us to Mike Faraday, a friendly sort dressed in wall-to-wall denim who is, we are told, from this moment on our "personal" roadie. I take Ken aside and ask him to clarify this word "personal," and he explains simply, "Louie handles the gear, transportation, and all the organizing. Whatever else you need, ask Mike." Crikey, what did poor Mike Faraday do to get this assignment?

Near the end we are each given some cash as a Christmas present. Four seconds later we bid everyone goodnight, Happy Christmas, and make our way by cab to the Greyhound, where we get legless, sing naughty Christmas carols, stick sprigs of mistletoe in our hair and in the waistband of our trousers to lure in the cute, the curious, and the seasonally soused.

Christmas Day, and what a difference a year makes. Last Christmas, in Bushey, we were hungry and freezing, huddled around a one-bar electric heater with barely a gas-meter shilling to our names. This year we have it all. Sure, we've got a hole in the ceiling but Lou, not only a drummer and lock-picker but also a naturally talented chef, cooks a full roast-turkey dinner, and we've got bottles of whiskey and wine, umpteen cans of beer, mince pies, trifle, the works.

Later, we watch Christmas telly until late in the eve then, last thing before we go to bed, we load the turkey carcass with all our remaining firecrackers and blow it up.

---

* Ken Mewis, Bali, 1989

"Erwin Schiff. A Jewish heavy who's not talking. Difficult when you're sucking in cement in Brooklyn. A nice enough guy who threw Viets out of helicopters. Loved his work."

I visited Ken one day in Olympic Studios.
He was producing the love of his musical life,
the Hollywood Brats.
I came up the stairs and perched outside
the door of Studio A. Ken was doing me,
and his band was doing the Stones. I
suddenly felt very strange.

Andrew Loog Oldham
Bogotá, 2012

1974

I

Okay, now. To hell with auld acquaintance. It's already forgot. This is 1974. Let's go. Back to Walthamstow to blow away the Christmas cobwebs. It doesn't take many minutes of rehearsal to realize that we are ready. Let's get this noise on tape. The office has block-booked Olympic Studios, starting on January 17, and we can't wait.

Casino and I have decided two things. We don't want the engineer twiddling the studio knobs and we want Ken to gracefully retire from the producer's chair. The second part is easier to arrange than the first. Ken gets that he is not a producer, and he gets that Cas and I understand completely what we're going for and that we'll figure out how to get there. Ken wants the engineer on the sessions but says he'll keep him in line. Yeah, well, if you say so. We have just one ultimatum.

Get us a young engineer that will follow orders.

There is a design meeting: the band plus Ken plus art director to discuss a poster and album cover. Some stupid ideas come up but at least the poster concept looks good. The art director brings with him an impressive full-size mock-up: the five of us standing in front of a night cityscape, black skyscrapers with glowing yellow windows and yellow sky, buildings a cross between Art Deco and Surrealvador Dalí style.

Two o'clock on a frightfully cold January afternoon, Louie pulls the van up in front of Olympic Studios in Barnes. The five of us pile out and bundle through the doors to a surprise the surprising Louie has awaiting us. Expecting to be led to the cozy confines of Studio B, where we endured the riff debacle, we enter the cavernous, mighty Studio A and, behold, there is our equipment, set up perfectly in a neat, carpeted semicircle just below the elevated plate-glass windows of the control room. Mike Faraday, personal roadie, kneeling down, adjusting Lou's hi-hat, stands up and smiles at us. Wow, can it be? Yes, it can. The Hollywood Brats are in Studio A.

I notice, far away in a back corner, equipment stacked fifteen feet high with the stencil "The Eagles" plastered all over it. Who are they? Then I notice their huge, idiotic brass gong. Drips, whoever they are.

Into the control room we venture, goggle-eyed, each of us a stranger in paradise, and there, awaiting us, Ken and the engineer. Ken is pouring a lager down his throat, as a gentleman should, while the engineer is dicking around with a couple of sticks, shoveling brown rice into his beard. Mate, the British invented the spoon a millennium ago. Give it a try.

Out in the studio, roadies strum things, poke this, smack that.

And just look at the control room, will you? I don't know anything about the capabilities of Studio A's recording desk, but have a gander. Look at it. It's five feet by fifteen feet, loaded with row after row of knobs, dials, and mysterious meters. Look at all those needles whipping back and forth on all those channels. What are they meant to represent? All I do know is that, when we crunch a chord, whap a snare, or coax a little feedback out of the speakers, those needles whip into the red zone and engineers go into panic mode.

But what Casino and I have learned to be Brats' gospel—from Alvin's toxic marital-hell studio in Hackney Wick through Chris Andrews to one-take, to-heck-with-mistakes Gooseberry—is when those needles are zapping back and forth, like when a psychopath is strapped to a polygraph machine, *that's* the sound we like. When those little needles are bashing into the red zone and making the engineers weep, only then do we like the way the band sounds.

So Ken, just keep those needles in the red zone, will ya?

From the first moment we hit a chord in Studio A in 1974, we are on fire. We knock down the takes, the tracks, the songs, one by one. Brats cruise, engineers seethe.

Next day, next formula. We shake this up and move that around. The engineer maintains his seat at the desk, just about, but now Cas and I have moved in either side and we talk across the beardo. Also, Ken has hired a new lad as tape operator. He's young, with good hair, and he's ambitious—three admirable traits in Bratdom.

We lay down a second day of tracks, each one sounding nastier than its predecessor. Late that night, after the session, we grab a bottle of cheap cognac and four straws at an off-license and head to a cinema Brady has sussed.

Throughout January, recordings are going fantastic, with minor, acceptable irritants. In Studio B, Donovan is recording an album with the great Andrew Loog Oldham at the helm, but we haven't seen the Sunshine Superman yet. Andrew Loog, that is. Sometimes, during the session, I walk down the corridor and press my ear to the door.

I used to quite like Donovan when I was a lad. "Catch the Wind"? Brilliant. Not to mention "Hurdy Gurdy Man." But no note can I hear through the door. Back to the big studio; I wonder what Oldham's doing over there in Studio B.

We nail the basic tracks to "Chez Maximes," "Nightmare," "Southern Belles," "Drowning Sorrows," "Courtesan," and "Tumble with Me."

David Bowie is spotted lurking about in the halls and pops in to say hello. He hears a bit of "Nightmare" and says, "Luv it, luv it." He looks great, naturally. We've heard his new single blaring out of Studio C for the last three days: "Rebel Rebel." We "Luv it, luv it." Excellent riff, best I've heard in years. Go, Bowie. Everything else in the charts is utter rubbish.

Need I remind you, children, that on this day something called Mud is number one in the charts?

Just saw the Eagles. They are a Californian caricature. A band full of roadies, all hair, beards, and denim. The drummer's got a perm. They'll never get laid in England.

Brill, our pal, benefactor, and former life-support system, comes by the studio with his dog Max. We want to show off for him, impress him. Max, that is. Brillo couldn't care less. "Running Wild" is next up. It's a typical Brats song, maximum attack, breakneck speed, noise, nihilism, and nuisance. The usual. But for some reason we can't even nail the basic track. Time and again it eludes us.

We give it go after go but there's always something wrong—usually Lou, not that I'm pointing fingers. So we decide to take a break and head down the street to the Red Lion, where all life's problems take on the rosiest of hues.

Part of the Hollywood Brats' philosophy is never to do more than two or, at the maximum, three takes on any song. And if we do three takes we can't look at each other, we're too embarrassed. We consider it an insult to the music, slovenly musicianship. But on "Running Wild" we end up doing twelve takes before we finally get it. Like we're Pink Floyd or something.

Next day at Olympic, it's vocals, more vocals, and a bit of this and that. Ken wants handclaps on "Chez Maximes." Didn't we try this joke last year? Anyway, a microphone is set up in a stairwell, just like for the Elvis vocal on "Heartbreak Hotel." Cas and I nail it then nix it. It was a dopey idea anyway.

The heating has been off at 26 Bishop's Road for almost a week and our entreaties to the office have had no effect. The weather's frigid, so when I find an ax in the backyard we start chopping up the furniture and burning it in the fireplace. A chair or two a night generally does it. Burning varnish does imbue the room with a certain iffy smell, but the resulting flames are blue and cheery.

Lou picks the cellar lock and we lug up a workbench that I chop up in the garden. This lasts us quite a few nights. Later on in the week I am swinging away like a lumberjack, hacking apart the kitchen table, when there is a loud exclamation behind me. It is our landlord, Jasper Beauregard III, who has let himself in to try to figure out the heating problem. I stop chopping and ask if he's come about the ceiling. The obvious humor in the situation entirely eludes him and he storms out, threatening to call the office and then the police. Yeah, right. The police. Go ahead, Mr. Beauregard.

Brady asks me to help him out in the backyard. He brings a whiskey bottle, matches, string, a file, and a candle. All very voodoo. While I nervously hold the bottle, he scores the neck with the file, lights the candle, ties the string around the neck, and sets it on fire. While it burns he drips candle wax over it and mutters something in Latin. Ten seconds and three twists of emery paper later, Brady has a bottleneck slide. He uses it on "Ain't Got You" that afternoon at Olympic.

Brady decides to move out of Bishop's Road. He explains that he really needs some private shagging time with a new bird he's picked up from the Greyhound, Tina, and he's tired of Lou and me watching them at it, not to mention occasionally taping proceedings to play later over the Olympic sound system. Spoilsport. Anyway, he sells his Strat for £110 and moves to a rented room in one of London's more dodgy locales.

Olympic, Casino and I doing all the vocals. Sometimes our noggins are together on the microphone, sometimes one of us in the control room producing. The engineer is becoming entirely marginalized.

On a wander during a break, I see the Bee Gees enter Studio C. Later, I can't resist loitering outside the door to try to hear what they're doing. It is a beautiful version of the Beatles' "Sun King." The harmonies are amazing. The Fabs' original version is no slouch but this is positively ethereal. The door opens and Maurice comes out into the hall, followed by a billowing cloud of marijuana smoke. He coughs "hello" and walks off down the hall. How can they sing through all that?

The day comes when we are going to record what has become our favorite song, "Sick On You." "You want to know what it's like, condemned to live with you?" Well, do ya, honey? Anger, aggression, and attitude out to here. And, as if that weren't enough, thanks to Mr. Steel it is in the suitably psychotic key of F-sharp.

Lou kicks things off and we run through it, instrumentally, to warm up and let the tape-op get some levels. Get those needles bouncing to the extreme right, sonny. Then the engineer comes on the talk-back and says, "Take one." Away we go at full throttle. Somewhere around the first chorus we see him standing up, staring slack-jawed through the glass. He looks at Ken then presses his little talk-back button again and says, "Wait. Stop, stop, stop." We stop. Reluctantly. That sounded good—what's the problem?

"You're kidding, right?" he continues. "I mean, that's not it, is it? That's a joke, right?"

Well, cue a collective Vesuvius. We down tools and explode into the control room, ready to boot the beard back to Woodstock. Ken gets between us, waving a £20 note, knowing from previous experience that cash hath charms to soothe the savage Brat. He sends us off to the pub, says come back in half an hour.

When we return, half an hour times two, we are drunkish, angry, and resentful, all of which can really help some songs. The engineer sits at the console with chopsticks, staring resentfully into the middle distance eating a bowl of brown rice. We go back in the studio, strap on the weaponry, and nail "Sick On You" in one take. Through the glass, Ken gives us an enthusiastic two thumbs up.

Someone presses the talk-back button. We see the engineer slowly stand up, shaking his bison head back and forth. He says, "I'm sorry. I just don't understand this." Then he walks out of the studio.

We never lay eyes on him again.

There is only one photographer, at least only one photographer Casino and I want, to shoot the Hollywood Brats. Gered Mankowitz was eighteen years old when he was chosen by Andrew Loog Oldham to go to the States with the Stones. Eighteen, and official shutterbug to the Rolling Stones. Imagine that. He shot the covers for *December's Children* and *Between the Buttons* (after a session in a park near Olympic Studios). That's all you need to know. We tell Ken that's who we want, and guess what? That's who we get.

Casino Steel's birthday, February 22, 1974. He is twenty—ha, ha. We rendezvous, done up and dandified, in Piccadilly Circus and make our way to Gered's studio. On the short walk a Stuka-inspired pigeon makes a white splattering deposit on Lou's head from a great height. Lou curses in disbelief and wipes the top of his skull with pages from a discarded newspaper, while the rest of us are bent over, convulsed with laughter.

The photo studio is fantastic, just what you'd imagine, and Gered is everything we thought he'd be: professional, creative, bursting with ideas, and crazy-focused when he's framing a shot, with a look in his eye that Charlie Manson would get stupid middle-class girls to kill for.

Four members of the band bear an uncanny resemblance to the Hollywood Brats but, as usual, the bass player needs serious attention. The only thing Derek brings that passes muster is a Maltese cross around his neck. So we get to work on him. Casino contributes a studded leather wristband, and Brady gives him a blue paisley silk bolero blouse. I chip in a blue scarf with white polka dots.

Casino is in a black leather shirt, fingering a genuine swastika armband belonging to yours truly, black satin strides, four-inch black belt with Johnny Reb brass buckle, wristbands, silk scarf, rings, tattoos, and red nail polish.

Lou is wearing a gold lamé choker and dangling necklaces, silver bracelet, red silk chemise, skinny jeans with silver studs and turned-up cuffs, and the highest, wildest pink stack-heeled shoes in the world.

Brady's in black satin with junk jewelry, a silk top from Chinatown, Kensington Market boots, and a red patterned scarf borrowed from the lead singer.

I'm in my Mr Fish chemise, black-and-white polka-dot trousers by Sonja, red satin coat, black fingernails, and sporting a silver-topped Edwardian walking stick all wrapped up in a fourteen-foot-long pink ostrich feather boa.

Follow that, pussies.

After an hour of studio shots under the lights and in front of a backdrop, Gered moves the madness outside up some stairs to the roof. I take the opportunity to ditch the Mr Fish for a mauve top and blue velvet ladies' jacket, hand-painted in Ireland in the thirties, a couple of bracelets, and a black leather Jayne Mansfield belt with silver-star studs.

It's Arctic cold and Gered's not shy about putting us through our paces: climbing up stairs, running down stairs, bursting through doorways, etc. When we plead the need for cognac he sends us to a nearby pub and lends me a huge full-length bearskin coat in which to warm up. It weighs about fifty pounds and makes me look like a glam camera-hog Sasquatch.

While at the pub it crosses my mind that this coat is tailor-made for a spot of pilferage. But, as Chad & Jeremy mentioned, that was yesterday and yesterday's gone.*

After a couple of decidedly non-VSOPs, followed by a pint or two of best

---

* Gered Mankowitz, London, 2013

"It was lovely to hear that the Hollywood Brats were so enthusiastic to work with me and I was thrilled to know that the Stones covers had such an impact.

I had known Ken since he started working for Immediate and we always got on well. I expect he thought he could score some points with the Brats by setting up the shoot.

My studio at that time was at 41 Great Windmill Street, on the third floor of a pretty run-down building a few doors up the street, opposite the infamous Windmill Theatre. The floors above us were abandoned, used by whores and pigeons and me and the Hollywood Brats. It was February and it was freezing.

We certainly had a great session and the photos do still have a freshness to them."

bitter for good luck, it's back to the photo studio for more lurking about meaningfully on freezing stairways.

When it's over, we know it's good. Can't wait to see the results. Gered's the guv'nor, just as Casino and I always knew he would be.

Back in Olympic, center of the Universe. It's March and this album is taking shape. Ken is exuberant. He says the Brats are going to be massive. Couldn't agree more. And now that the engineer isn't grassing to Wilf on a daily basis, like our own internal Stasi mole, things are moving along.

Casino and I know that guitars must take center stage and we spend hours working with Brady, goading him to get wilder and wilder. We layer the tracks, learning as we go, making a million mistakes but, often as not, using the mistakes. Sometimes we go for that Hackney-Wick-Alvin studio sound. We overdub Brady's guitar without letting him hear his original track. It works wonders. He's never in sync. Thanks, Alvin, for your general hippy ineptitude and please do say "hi" to your lovely missus for us.

We put an amp on its back, mic it up pendulum style, with the microphone swinging back and forth, tell Brady to rock and see what happens. We record entire tracks on the screaming edge of feedback, then tuck it deep in the mix, just to see the effect. We like it. Now that the brown-rice man is off the premises we are completely free to do whatever we want. And that's exactly what we do.

One day, we're just about to run a playback on "Sick On You" when the door opens and in walks none other than the ever-so-famous Tommy Steele. He must be working in one of the other studios and just can't resist foisting his wonderful famous self on everyone else in the building. He hops around, shaking hands, teeth protuberant and gleaming, the epitome of the "cheeky chappie." Couple of hits, I suppose; how would I know? Mostly, we've seen him on TV being showbiz daft, a pantomime figure, singing chirpy duets with Twiggy, things like that. Still, he insists on sitting down and listening to the mix. Fair enough, mate. Buckle up.

After "Sick On You" comes to its conclusion Tommy stands up, stammers "Yes . . . well . . . all right, then. Ta, ta," and then scurries out the door.

* * *

We are rehearsing at a place called Dragon Studios in Shepherd's Bush and, midway through a song, Brady breaks a string. He bends down to pick up a replacement when the dangling end of the broken E string, waving about hither and thither, pokes into the hole of an electrical outlet. There is a huge bang, a blinding flash, and the sight of a guitarist momentarily airborne before smashing backward into a brick wall. He crumples to the floor and lies there, moaning, trembling, his face red, his arms marble white, fingers even blacker than usual. The Gibson Firebird, clenched in an almost-death grip by those blackened digits, lives up to its name, for once. It is ablaze, flames ten inches high burning away, varnish crackling, like a kitchen chair in a fireplace.

The rest of us dissolve into convulsions of laughter, complete with finger-pointing and back-slapping. Finally, exhausted, we go over to see how Brady's doing. Casino unplugs him, Derek and I help him to his feet, and Lou pours a lager over the guitar, putting out the fire.

It takes a long time for Brady to truly appreciate just how fortunate he is to have been able to provide us with this hilarious slice of entertainment. He spends the night in hospital and his hair is never the same again. He's luckier than Les Harvey of Stone the Crows, though. Poor fucker was fried to death onstage a couple of years ago.

Monday, March 25, we spend a few hours with Kentucky Fried Brady in Olympic doing guitar overdubs with a rented left-handed Gibson 335. While we're sitting back on the leather sofa, there's a knock on the door and some bald guy who says he is in Family (the band, not the social construct) as though this info is supposed to make us shiver with excitement, tells us he's recording next door. He has obviously somehow clapped eyes on the Gibson and, just as obviously, must have a southpaw guitarist, or be one, because four seconds after our last take he shows up and hey, man, asks to borrow it for half an hour.

In the spirit of musical solidarity we say, "No."

After this intrusion, it's a quick tart-up at home and the band plus Ken, minus Derek, are off to the Rainbow Room at Biba in Kensington to see Bill Haley and the Comets.

The Rainbow Room is straight out of a thirties movie. Beautiful, ultra-stylish (well, of course it is, it's at Biba), jammed with that unique London chic, tickets impossible to snag, best gig in the world. The Dolls played here, annoyingly enough, just before their drummer went to heaven on a lifetime's supply of Nescafé. This could be Rick's place in *Casablanca*. If ever a venue was custom-made for the Hollywood Brats, this is the place.

Ken has us displayed for public viewing at a primo table, the best in the house, in fact, front row, ten feet from the bandstand. The place is gorgeous; the audience is gorgeous. Bill Haley, while not quite what one would describe as gorgeous, nonetheless looks exactly as a Bill Haley should. He and the Comets deliver. They put their glad rags on: gray suits, pink shirts, bootlace ties, black patent-leather shoes, twirling stand-up bass, they've got it all. We're going to rock around the clock tonight.

At the end of the evening I'm like a one-eyed cat creeping in a seafood store. I bid adieu to the lads and am driven to a mews house in Chelsea by a dark-haired woman in an E-Type Jaguar. Next morning, I open my eyes and a little boy is standing by the bed, holding a teddy bear, sucking his thumb and staring at me.

I can't get back to Bishop's Road quickly enough.

But, oh, it's a social whirl. The Fulham Broadway Three meet up with the London Street One at the Greyhound to see the Tremeloes. Not remotely our cup of char, but we have to admit they are note perfect. "Silence Is Golden," "Here Comes My Baby," and all the rest are spot on. They do seem like animated creatures in a noisy, smoky museum, though.

Brady confesses that his daft experiment with actually paying rent in Maida Vale has lasted less than four weeks. The man is like a murky, malodorous liquid that can't help running downhill until it reaches its natural level. He's moving to a squat on Boundary Road.

Casino and I work late into many nights at Olympic Studios, finishing up the mixes on all the tracks. Ken always accompanies us, staying in the background, looking sharp, solving problems, standing guard at the castle gate. He always protects. He never interferes.

Lou often comes along to act as the deciding vote on sticking points. But Cas and I are soaring along in smooth sync. There are no sticking points. We created this thing. We've nurtured, honed, coerced, and whipped this nag from mere to eternity. We agonize over this, don't give a toss about that. There are differences of opinion, sure, but no arguments, no snits, no moods.

A heartbeat ago one of us was looking up, scared, covered in muck, three thousand feet down a mine shaft deep in the guts of the pre-Cambrian Shield. The other guy was desperate and down in a charming town at the end of a fjord in Northern Norway. We both had skulls full of ideas that were driving us insane.

Now look at us. We've just finished the record we always wanted to make. The desired noise, bouncing around our brains for years, is sizzling right there on the two-inch tape.

We finesse that vocal, rough up that guitar lick, sprinkle a little something on that one crash cymbal, just one last time, change a couple of bass tracks from Derek's to the old session guy's. Finally, we push the chairs back from the console. Ken and his legendary ears are called in. Our record is done, completed and, modesty tucked in a back pocket, we think it's pretty good. An hour later, Ken's smile says it all. He does, too.

Great. So, over to you, squire. Get it out there, Mr. Mewis. Do whatever it is you and Wilf do. Grease DJ palms, break legs, get hookers on retainers—just get it on the radio. Sic 'em, Ken.

III

Brady spends more and more nights with us back on Bishop's Road. The shagging is better and certainly more private on Boundary Road, but you can't beat the laughs, fireworks, and TV in Fulham Broadway. For instance, one night we get two bottles of vodka to try to reach a state we've only read about—I think it was Roman emperor Nero who mentioned it first, or perhaps it was Charles Laughton, whatever—something called "delirium tremens." After an hour we're well on our way and, when a Jamaican in a porkpie hat suddenly appears in front of the TV, we think we've actually achieved it.

But no, it is merely the ubiquitous Mr. Beauregard, our landlord, even drunker than we are. He is so plastered, unlike our kitchen ceiling, it's a wonder he can get his key in the door to enter our home unannounced whenever he pleases. He is babbling incoherently, even going up an octave every now and again to squeak for emphasis. I haven't a clue what he's on about and tune him out, leaving it for Lou to deal with.

He translates that Mr. Beauregard would like an advance on next month's rent. The reason? It is the opening night of a new brothel in Tooting and he doesn't have the cash, man. Well, why didn't you say so? It is quite obviously a worthy cause, and more sympathetic we could not be as Lou steers him kindly out the door and advises him to call the office with the same story.

Back to sprawled about on the floor, casually catatonic, we watch an odd television play called *Shakespeare or Bust* about three working-class Derbyshire chaps who rent a barge to sail the canals and waterways of England in order to get to Stratford-on-Avon.

That's it! By the end of the night we have cooked up a caper that Lou will present to Ken tomorrow: we have wrapped up the album; we are exhausted and need a break; a week away on a barge would be just the tonic.

It works. Well, of course it does. Lou's got the gift. So, three days later, the four of us plus Derek arrive at a canal near Watford, where a rented narrowboat awaits. It's a lovely craft, ornate and beautifully painted, which sleeps six and has a kitchen, shower, strange toilet affair called a Portosan that requires emptying every day (boy, does it), lounge area, and fridge. All in all, it's far more luxurious than Bishop's Road.

Derek and I get a lesson from the harbormaster. He is a gruff old bird who teaches us the finer points of sailing the thing and, at 4 p.m., in freezing drizzle and with a wind out of the northeast, we cast off. Away we sail, north, I think, under a low bridge and off into the gray, drenched English countryside.

Lou has painted a sign, "HMS *BRATS*," which we hang off the stern.

Shipboard duties are delegated according to our various talents.

Andrew: Pilot, captain, on the bridge, ship's wheel always in steady hands.

Derek: Backup pilot.

Casino: Navigator, map reader, locating ports of call, most importantly pubs, along the way.

Lou: Chief Cook and Bottle-washer, responsible for supplies, in charge of the galley.

Brady: Portosan patrol, emptying and cleaning toilet.

Half an hour into the voyage, all of us are blind drunk. Half an hour after that, Casino falls overboard. Well, he was tearing about the deck, in the rain, leaning over the railing swearing at swans, swigging from a bottle of Old Grand-Dad, singing, and all this while wearing six-inch heels. Of course he went overboard.

It is a well-documented scientific fact that it is almost impossible to pull a fully clothed, hyperventilating Norwegian out of a canal in a storm when one is laughing uncontrollably. All of us take turns trying but it is just too much, and we're about to give up and unwittingly fulfill Casino's desire for a death in the band when, with one last desperate heave, he flops on deck like an exhausted tuna, gasping for air.

Eventually, with great effort, he turns over and, on his elbows, begins crawling toward the cabin. He travels no more than fifteen feet before we regain our composure enough to mosey on over and assist him through the doors and on to a bunk.

Once we have stopped giggling and Casino is wrapped up dry and groaning, we assess his physical state. Turns out he has suffered a broken ankle and a badly ruptured ego. There is no choice. He must be marooned at the next pub.

The night is spent bobbing up and down on the waves, comparing Casino's rapidly swelling purple ankle to how it looked an hour ago, taking photos of it for said comparison, watching Lou do amusing impressions of Cas falling overboard, and getting even more sloshed.

The next day, from his bunk, Casino plots a course for the Fisheries Inn, many leagues hence, where we have arranged for Ken to meet us so that we can offload our wounded comrade. And so, after a hearty breakfast of four aspirins and three bowls of Frosted Flakes each, we set sail. Late in the afternoon, the Fisheries is spotted off the port bow, so we take 'er in and drop anchor.

Ken has brought a mock-up of the poster with him and it looks great. At least the local lasses seem to think so, as Brady shows it to them fifty times. Many pints are sunk, tales are told, more photos of Casino's ankle are taken, and finally Ken, drunk, staggering, and barely coherent, loads our gimp keyboard player into his MG, grinds a few gears until he locates what at a pinch might charitably be called "first," and swerves off jerkily down the road toward London.

The rest of the voyage is nothing but worsening weather, thousands of back-breaking locks to traverse, much drinking in many pubs, and random attacks from the savage tribes we encounter along the way. At one point things get so desperate that Mike ("for anything else, call Mike") is summoned from London to meet us at a pub near where the Zambezi River intersects with Leighton Buzzard locks and deliver us a brown envelope of tenners and a modest square of hashish.

We come to, of all things, a totem pole. Our resident Micmac gets off the boat and does a ceremonial dance around it, just like I always imagined our drummer would.

Old salt though I am, I'm finally convinced to take a break after countless hours of sailing through sleet, rain, and occasional hail. I hand Brady the wheel while Lou serves us a quick cup of tea and beans on toast in the galley, a much-welcome respite. A respite, however, that lasts a mere four minutes before the door opens and Brady calmly announces, "Ah, chaps, we're going to crash." A prediction that proves uncannily accurate, as one second later he sails us head-on and at full speed into the side of an ancient stone bridge. Dishes, bottles, Hollywood Brats, beans on toast—everything flies everywhere to the outraged yells of fellow canal enthusiasts, smoke filling the cabin, and a nasty smell from the Portosan. The last of which, as soon as things are wrestled under control and once again calm, Brady is sent to deal with, following his demotion from pilot duty.

Finally, a week later, soaked, hungover, and having suffered 20 percent casualties, we limp back to Watford, bruised but not broken, where a welcome-home party breaks out.

But something has gone awry in the music realm. Hollywood Brats momentum has slammed into a wall. Life is still a blast, but intense rehearsing and swanning around town socializing can't disguise the fact that we wrapped up the album a few weeks ago and thus far there are no plans to ship it into record shops and get it zapping up the charts. This calls for a meeting with Ken.

Casino and I meet him for a glass or two at the Warrington in Maida Vale. After our senses are suitably softened Ken lets us in on a little something we didn't previously know. Worldwide Artists is not, in fact, a record company.

Wait a minute.

We thought it was. In fact, signing those recording contracts they put in front of us gave us the distinct impression that it was, indeed, a record company.

But alas, no. They are a production company. Sort of. They produce the records and then lease the tapes to real record companies who turn them into vinyl and finagle them into the charts. Oh. While this is sinking in, Ken says we're going to play some gigs, and he hands us an envelope containing £250, which is £50 each for clothes. This has the desired effect: distracts us, shuts us up.

One of the bands under Worldwide Artists' banner is a four-piece leaden rock outfit called Stray. They come replete with the usual hair, denim, and solos. They're probably saving up for their first gong. The pecking order at 27 Dover Street seems to be Black Sabbath, the Goundhogs, and then Stray. I don't think the Brats are actually on the pecking order.

Stray appear to be a pet project of Wilf's, and he even produced their last album, *Mudanzas*, which, if my Spanish serves me well, means, "Hey, Pedro, the basement's flooded."

Nonetheless, the album went goldish and now they are doing a short tour in England. Ken wants us to be the support act. First gig, Cleethorpes. Never heard of it.

Ken scoops us up in a hire car and drives for what seems like hours to Cleethorpes, which turns out to be a seaside town in Lincolnshire. The hall is big and the gig is well advertised around town. Well advertised if you are Stray, that is. There is no mention of the Hollywood Brats on any of the posters.

Still, we don't give a toss, really. We're just here to please Ken, shake off the ring rust, and get ready for our next chapter. We waltz in and Louie and Mike have got us set up and ready to shake. Ken asks if we'd like to meet Stray. What a comedian.

In our dressing room there is beer and whiskey that we are compelled to taste test at length for quality assurance. Quick soundcheck, with Stray standing at the back wall checking us out, muttering into each other's ears. Who cares?

Back in the dressing room, we drink and show each other the glad rags we all bought with our fifty-nicker clothing allowance. Everybody has purchased fantastic threads, shirts, scarves, jackets, junk jewels, strides, and daisies. Everybody, that is, except bass boy.

Derek has had specially tailored a two-piece white silk disco atrocity with bell bottoms and scoop sleeves that even Björn and Benny from ABBA would find embarrassing.

Showtime. *"Mach schau,"* Brady and I say to each other, a good-luck charm we learned from reading about the Beatles in Hamburg. Out of the wings and onto the stage. It's hard to believe, but this is the first time we've hit the boards since the Speakeasy. That seems like an ice-age ago.

That was then, this is wow. "Melinda Lee" is yesterday's papers. It's "Tumble with Me" time. Casino starts it off on piano, followed by the thud of Lou's bass drum. The curtain opens, the place is packed, yokels drop jaws, then we're all in and socking 'em between the ears. We play for half an hour and the sea-siders don't have a clue what's going on. If you're a bloke and you wear makeup in this town, you're facedown under the pier with a mouthful of seaweed next morning.

It's obvious some of them like us, but the majority don't know what to make of "Sick On You" or "Then He Kissed Me" or anything else we play, for that matter. We like it, though. That's what counts. All that rehearsing has paid off. We're confident and cocky.

We keep going. No chitchat, no attempt to engage, just keep smacking 'em around the chops with our particular noise. And what do you know? After the last number Cleethorpes is baying for an encore. We don't do encores but it's the thought that counts.

They don't stop. It's early evening so it's not like they just don't want to go back to their fishing huts. They're stomping and yelling. They want the Brats back onstage.

Stray? Hey, we're your warm-up act. So they're warmed up.

Follow that, pussies.

Ken is rather pleased by our efforts. In fact, he's frothing-at-the-mouth rabid. I've never seen him so excited. He does a bit of redecorating.*

We hear from Ken that Stray hate us. Hate is such a withering emotion. All we did was ignore them. Still, they're stuck with us. We're playing another gig with them a few days later at Plymouth Polytechnic. It's a long way to Plymouth so Louie arrives to pick us up in a campervan complete with bunk beds, a couch, and a sink. It is 10 a.m. Casino, bless him, has brought along a couple of bottles of Old Grand-Dad for stage props. By 11 a.m. one bottle has been drained dry and we are on the lager, utterly crazed.

I am armed with a crocodile water pistol and, from my vantage point on the top bunk, I squirt the chaps as they whip out their tackle to slash in the sink. Drinking, singing, pissing, and squirting in such manner, to the delight of passing motorists, the miles go whizzing by.

We stop for petrol and Louie takes a photo of us in front of the pumps, Old Grand-Dad and water pistol in evidence. Life is but a frolic.

The polytechnic has a big auditorium and a stage to match. The accountancy student with the clipboard and Castro beard lisps that the place is sold out.

---

* Eunan Brady's Diary, May 9, 1974

"Played Cleethorpes. We were great. Stray were shit. Ken went wild, wrecked the dressing room."

Good. So it should be. We head to the dressing room and, horrors, it is just that: a dressing room, singular. We are sharing with Stray. Nice room, though, a long rectangle with actual makeup mirrors all along one wall, surrounded by lights. Stray is down that end and we, by process of elimination, are up this end.

Stray's stage denim, as opposed to their street denim, is hanging up neatly, and there is a large crate of bottled beer on the floor in front of the mirror. That's it.

We watch their soundcheck and they do go on a bit, kindly using up most of the allotted time and leaving us a miserly ten minutes. This drives Mike and Louie crazy but it doesn't faze us. We run through a quick "Tumble" and then escape the polytechnic to find a pub.

Hours later, we get back to the dressing room in plenty of time to get all mugs slathered and finery fitted. Stray lurk in their end of the room trying desperately to be the headlining act, but we refuse to play along. We are loud, politely inebriated, whipping each other up, fighting for mirror space as usual, even though there's miles of it, stepping into outlandish outfits, and just generally acting as though we are marvelous. Our worst crime, though, continues to be that we completely ignore the headlining act.

Ken stations himself between the two camps, making with the nonstop chatter peppered with the occasional apologetic shrug.

Then it's "Mach schau" time. And this week "Melinda" gets a reprieve. The set is tailored for end-of-year students who might want to strut their West Country stuff, such as it is: "Melinda Lee," "Sweet Little Sixteen," "Tumble with Me," "I Ain't Got You," "Another School Day," "Chez Maximes," "Then He Kissed Me," "Southern Belles," and "Sick On You."

The first song seems to smack them stupid. They stare, they gawk like we're a five-car pile-up featuring decapitations. After "Melinda Lee" we go straight into "Sweet Little Sixteen," and I can spy in the audience a little shake here and a little shimmy way over there. Some dig it. Most don't get it. Beautiful. Just like old times.

"Then He Kissed Me" drives the straw-chewers and the rugby players and the straw-chewing rugby players mad with bloodlust. And finally, Plymouth Polytechnic seems to take "Sick On You" as a personal critique. At the last thundering note and crash of the cymbals, things get flatteringly dangerous and then we're off.

Behind us we can hear that the audience is split: the 40 percent comprised of hicks with chicks appear not only to detest us, but also to think we should be beaten up immediately; the 40 percent made up of wine-soaked single babes are agitated, on estrogen overload, and squealing; the remaining 20 percent, the repressed, suicidal, leather-jacketed, night-crawling loners (our core audience) are howling for more. So we conclude, all in all, a job well done.

We pass Stray in the hallway and it takes a monumental humanitarian effort for me not to quote Casino and say, "Follow that, pussies." However, I'm not a monumental humanitarian so I can't help it. "Follow that, pussies," I say out of the side of my mouth as we pass them in the narrow hallway. They go crying to Ken.

Then Stray limp onto the stage.

Back in the dressing room, we discover that squirts from the crocodile water pistol make the lights surrounding the mirrors explode with a satisfyingly noisy bang, tiny shards of glass flying everywhere. There are dozens of lights. Everybody wants a go.

Once we are cleaned up and just about to leave the now near-dark dressing room, Casino walks over to Stray's beer crate, sitting on the floor, bottles chilled and awaiting Stray's triumphant return. He straddles the crate, whips out his Nordic joy-bringer, and urinates back and forth over all the bottles.

When we stop laughing long enough to be able to walk, we head out to the campervan and the long haul back to London.

Next day, Ken wants a chin-wag so we all meet at Casino's local, the Sussex, down the end of London Street. Casino has preceded us there and is suitably lubricated when we arrive, telling a ribald tale of an afternoon in a brothel called "The Oak Room," nearby in Lancaster Gate. Perhaps we should alert our landlord.

A couple of pints in and Ken, with maximum wrist-waving and hair-tousling, finally gets to the point. And what a point it is. He tells us that we are a hair's width away from a deal with Atlantic Records. Well, this causes an eruption of unhatched-chicken counting. Celebratory cognacs are ordered on

Ken's tab and excited babble ensues. What color is the label of an Atlantic record? Lou knows, red. Who's on Atlantic that we like? Humming and hawing, staring at ceiling and beer-stained carpet until Lou, again, remembers J. Geils. Yeah, we like J. Geils, fat, fuzztop harmonica player and Peter Wolf's beard notwithstanding.

The Hollywood Brats on Atlantic Records. Yeah, that'll do.

Yet another gig with the increasingly morose Stray, this time at a college in Yeovil. What's with these guys? How can they stand us? We're wiping the floor with them every night. Why haven't we been sacked? And where on earth is Yeovil? Nobody knows for certain. What's near there? Nobody knows. There must be some recognizable town near there. We look it up on a map. Oh, sure, there's Odcombe, Over Compton, Barwick, and Clifton Maybank. Why didn't you say so?

Yeovil is almost as far away from London as Plymouth. Same campervan, same shenanigans, only this time our mate Brillo is along for the ride. To keep our spirits up Ken shows us a letter that the office received from Plymouth Polytechnic. Stray are being billed for seventy-two lightbulbs and "janitorial services."

This college in Yeovil is the same gig as Plymouth, really: Che Guevera with a clipboard; same drama backstage, same set, same audience reaction. Stray even have a crate of beer in the dressing room. Didn't they notice?

On the trek back to London we tell Ken, "That's enough." The way we're going, the next gig will be in the Outer Hebrides. We were doing better playing the Café des Artistes once a week. At least we were in London, music capital of the planet, building momentum, playing to jammed houses, signing pink plastic Japanese handbags for pink plastic Japanese sex bombs.

That's it. We're not doing this anymore. Stray will be heartbroken, but we can't help that.

Next afternoon, we hear from Atlantic Records. They have somehow managed to resist the urge to offer us a record contract. How can this be?

The drunken, stoned, unannounced midnight visits from our landlord, Mr. Beauregard, are taking on downright Tonton Macoute overtones. And he's starting to ask where the furniture went. So we scarper. Brady squats contentedly on Boundary Road while Derek throws in his lot with Lou and me, and the office finds us a great pad on Fordhook Avenue in Ealing.

Casino and I don't spend as much time together as we once did. We used to write all the time and walk around, broke, for hours, planning and scheming, nursing a cup of coffee, listening to music. Those days are gone. The album is written, produced, in the can. These days, when we get together it's only to worry and bicker and wonder what's going on with Worldwide Artists. We're frustrated and snarl at each other over the slightest thing. We've made the album we wanted to make. The one we've been working toward since the church hall in leafy Stanmore. So why is nothing happening? We're stupid. We take it out on each other.

I call him and tell him to grab Sonja and a few au pairs and come over to our new pad on Saturday night. It's party time. The only requirement for entry is that you must be dressed in a stunning outfit or you're not getting through the door. Unless, of course, you're an au pair, in which case you can wear whatever you want.

We concoct a fabulous bash. Great food, gallons of intoxicants, poundingly perfect rock 'n' roll, beautiful drunk babes in every nook and cranny, their own personal nooks and crannies on display for everyone's viewing pleasure.

Mirror, razor blades, and straws in the kitchen.

Brady rolls up dressed in black velvet with Tina, the tart he plucked from the Greyhound. She's dark and petite, with Cleopatra eyeliner apparently applied with a butter knife, pink-frost lipstick, and an overall suspicious look in her eye. He tells me he's just found out that she is considerably younger than he was first led to believe. Nevertheless, he somehow finds it in his heart to forgive her for withholding this saucy information.

Casino shows up with a couple of bottles of Norwegian Hell Hooch and a bevy of blonde beauties. Scandinavian au pairs, more than enough to go round. This man knows how to enter a party.

As one of three hosts for the evening, I'm resplendent in top hat, tails, and the ubiquitous Mr Fish blouse (35 quid well spent all those months ago). Ken and his missus drive over in the purple MG. He's wearing a white dinner jacket, sporting a pink rose in the lapel. Turns out he plucked it from a garden down the road. Ten minutes after he arrives, his lapel is green with ten thousand aphids abandoning ship, pouring out of the rose, and crawling down his front. The image of Ken's legendary sangfroid is forever ruined by his squealing Houdini-like contortions as he tries to rid himself of his jacket.

What follows is a bacchanal of Ancient Rome proportions: gyrating, fornicating, screaming, singing, smashing glasses, fighting, dancing, the obligatory puking—and then the party enters its second hour. Three times throughout the evening the police pound on the door; three times Lou uses every ounce of his statesmanlike skills to placate all and sundry, sending the constables away thinking the neighbors must be utter philistines to complain about this charming young man in the mascara.

Halfway through the festivities, we hold the world premiere of film footage shot on our barge voyage. Foul weather, larking about, swastikas, sailor suits, and a Wehrmacht helmet perched jauntily on Derek's bonce. Guests desirous of further unfettered bar privileges applaud loudly. Just like in Hollywood.

While Lou deals with the bobbies a second time, someone, who shall remain shameless, seizes the opportunity for a quick shag on the back porch with a mate of Brillo's. Brady catches them at it when he runs out the back door and vomits past them onto the neighbor's petunias.

The police show up a third time at 2 a.m., after Ken calls them to report that his car has been stolen. Hearing Ken's slurred, outraged complaint, the two bored but impeccably polite coppers turn around and point. "Would it be that purple MG over there, sir?" Ken is, in fact, so drunk that he merely forgot where he parked the sports car with the subtle paint job.

After the constabulary depart, Ken hooks his infested dinner jacket over the aerial like a flag of surrender, pours his sloshed missus in the passenger seat, sheepishly gets in the MG, and weaves his way back home, erratically, menacingly through the streets of Ealing at a stately two miles per hour. At 3 a.m. the girl from Clapham calls a taxi and goes home.

Finally, in the wee small hours, I conk out, flat on my back in bed up in my attic room: two walls pink, two walls and ceiling black, painted by my own hand. During the night, I go back downstairs for a glass of water and hear voices in the living room. Upon investigation I see Derek and Lou at the dining table with two blondes. They are playing strip poker. Derek and the girls are fully clothed.

Lou is stark naked.*

Back in bed, exhausted but awake, something nags. Earlier, when Ken was at that stage of inebriation that is pre–violent vomiting but post-discreet, he threw an arm across my shoulder (overly familiar—we're not on these terms) and, in a blaze of foul breath, began slurring away about hoodlums, mafia, Ronnie Biggs, organized crime, and other forms of general underworld skulduggery. He tapped the side of his nose meaningfully, or perhaps he was crushing a stray aphid.

"The Krays."

"What?" I ask, moving my ear politely away from his wet lips.

"The Krays, the Krays. You know." He widens his eyes for emphasis.

"Oh, the Krays, gangsters, sharp suits? Of course I do."

"Yeah, gangsters, sharp suits. Sharp suits, definitely. Gangsters? Hmm, yes and no, yes and no . . . but mostly yes."

"Are the Krays scary?"

"Scary? Nah, not as such. They're lovely chaps. Gentlemen, really. Complete gentlemen. Unless, of course, you actually come into contact with them. Then . . . well, yeah, perhaps they could be construed as being . . . ah . . . maybe just the slightest bit . . . ah . . . terrifying."

"They're in prison, right?"

"They are, they are indeed, serving at Her Majesty's pleasure. It's just that . . ."

"Just that what?"

"Well, it's just that, when it comes to Reggie and Ronnie, being in jail is just a . . . how shall I put this . . . to them it's almost a minor inconvenience."

"Inconvenience how?"

"Well, they wouldn't let a trivial thing like a life sentence for murder stop them running their . . . ah . . . various businesses."

"Who did they murder?"

"You know, the Blind Beggar thing."

---

* Eunan Brady's Diary, June 16, 1974

"Party at Andrew's gaff last night in Ealing. Terrible hangover next day. That night, we all go to see the Kinks at the Palladium. Trouble brewing between Andrew and Cas. Ego problems. Rehearsal next day. Mike fucking late as usual. Andrew and Cas both pissed off."

"Do you know these guys?"

Ken ignores the question and presses on. "This bloke, fellow villain, called Ronnie Kray a fat poof, which is just not done. Anyway, Reggie took exception, tracked him down to the Blind Beggar, demanded retraction and a pint of stout, and when neither were forthcoming he put a bullet through the bloke's skull. The barman was spared. Wet his drawers, though."

He pauses for what I assume must be dramatic effect then knits his brows over bloodshot eyes and stares at the floor, pondering. "Yeah. I think they took a blade to Jack the Hat, as well, but the point I'm making is . . ." Ken lowers his voice. "That business goes on as usual."

"Does it?"

"What I'm trying to say is *certain* people, here on the outside, *certain* people at *certain* companies, *certain* clubs, get it? *Clubs?* . . . wink, wink."

"Yeah? What's 'wink, wink' mean?"

"Well, you know . . . the Speakeasy?"

"Yeah, the Speak, of course. What about it?"

"And Worldwide Artists?"

"Yeah?"

"Well, a nod's as good as . . ." Ken taps the side of his nose again.

"As good as?"

"A nod's as good as a . . ."

"As good as a what? What are you on about?"

"As a wink to a blind horse, for fuck's sake."

"What is?"

"A fucking nod. A nod's as good as a wink to a . . . Oh, for Christ's sake. You're signed to the Krays, is what I'm trying to say. The Hollywood Brats are signed to the Krays."

Since George Raft was asked to vacate the Colony Club in Berkeley Square the "Italians" had problems getting into the UK. So now Wilf, infatuated by the Mafia, gets introduced by Laurie O'Leary to Joe Pagano, a capo in the Genovese crime family. They see I'm in with a UK public company, movies (Hemdale), rock 'n' roll, etc.

Everyone at Worldwide/Hemdale thinks Wilf's dreaming and indulge him until these sinister-looking characters begin to arrive at the office.

Ken Mewis
Bali, 1989

They were puffed-up would-be gangsters
who fancied themselves, along with so many
other striped-suited, greased-up spivs,
as impresarios.

But breaking people is not the
same as breaking into the charts.

Worldwide Artists did not know
what they were doing, therefore
the Hollywood Brats got lost.

Andrew Loog Oldham
Bogotá, 2012

IV

The following week, Ken tells us more about Worldwide Artists' business partners. They are twins, they look great, they dress sharp, they are terrifyingly lethal, they love their mum and Judy Garland, and they are currently banged up, doing Her Majesty's pleasure for life. Tales of swords and pliers, hammers, impromptu dentistry, and, of course, that old standby, bullets, and something called a "cigarette punch" abound.

Ken further asserts that Laurie O'Leary is part of the Krays' operation. Laurie O'Leary? Mr. O'Leary? That nice chap who made time to talk to us when we dropped in unannounced last year and then gave us a gig at the Speakeasy? The gig that changed our lives? That Laurie O'Leary? Oh, yes.

Ken also tells us the big news that Wilf is not only a certified villain (not quite with a diploma on the wall, but you get the drift), but he's part of the Krays' inner circle, a trusted lieutenant, if not more, he hints darkly.

Eventually, it begins to dawn on us. Perhaps this is why, or if not why then at least a contributory factor, people are reluctant to touch us with a ten-foot barge pole.

I'm a bag of nerves. Ken called on Friday to tell us that Wilf wants to meet me on Monday. Today. That made for a relaxing weekend. What does he want? What have I done?

I take Lou with me. Well, wouldn't you? On the bus to Dover Street we discuss the Mob. What images come to mind? New York turkey shoots; abattoir clam bars; the customers of restaurants—stuffed with fettuccine and lead—and barbershops—freshly coiffed and perforated—stretchered out into meat wagons. Marlon Brando; Guccione, the sucker-punch king; Charles Bronson in *The Valachi Papers*; Sicily; what do we know? It all blends in.

We come to the conclusion that this afternoon's agenda probably doesn't include a hit. We doubt I'm going to get shot. What we do think is that maybe we're in for a diatribe cunningly disguised as a chat. And soon enough, here we are, splayed on the white sofa. Lou chews gum and smokes. Off to one side, Ken is plonked in the armchair, sloe-eyed and smoking too. Chain-smoking, in fact. The scene is very smoky.

Wilf doesn't just sit at his desk. He wears it like King Kong's tutu. He thumps a fist upon it, making the perfectly sharpened, unused pencils jump in fright and cigarette butts leap in dusty terror from the heaped ashtray. Tattooed fingers drum on the desktop. One digit now points, Lord Kitchener style, at me. "A single. I've heard your tapes. We need a fucking single. Why can't you fuckers write a fucking single? Eh?"

"What about 'Sick On You'?" I ask.

Lou snickers and blows an insolent smoke ring that sails forth then dissolves in fright midair between the sofa and the desk. Ken wipes off the first trace of a smirk and fumbles in his pocket for another French fag. Unable to locate Jean Genet, he settles for Gauloises and does a palms-up shoulder shrug in Wilf's direction. What can I do?

But Wilf is in the middle of a speech. His mouth emits a sharp explosion of spittle-flecked air. "Do what? You fucking . . . that song's disgusting. Don't you come the cheeky bastard with me, Andrew. I'll rip your fucking intestines out, I will. That song's fucking profane."

Imminent disembowelment being something of a constant threat at Worldwide Artists, I let the remark pass and instead offer, "Actually, we consider 'Sick On You' to be our best song. Besides, we don't write singles. The word 'anathema' springs to mind and—"

"Ana what?" shrieks Wilf. The word "apoplectic" springs to mind.

"Ana fucking what? Fuck you and your fucking words, you little poofter shite. We need a fucking hit fucking single from you fucking nancies to get you on *Top of the* fucking *Pops*, and we need it in two fucking weeks. You got that?"

"But we hate *Top of the Pops*."

"We like Pan's People," Lou interjects.

"True," I concede.

A big vein, reminiscent of Tony McVein's, throbs hypnotically on Wilf's temple. He snarls, "Am I hearing things? Are my fucking lugholes deceiving me?" He looks over at Ken, exasperation laced with malevolence, and hisses, "Ken, can you talk to these fucking cunts, what you brought into our midst, and tell them if they don't stop playing the shite they play and write me a couple of fucking hit singles I will personally tear their fucking balls off, starting with you, Andrew, and give 'em to the fucking secretaries for fucking Christmas earrings. Can you tell 'em that, Ken? Eh? Can you fucking inform them as to this?"

Ken is slouched, legs crossed, shoes white, wrists delicate. He flaps one as if to demonstrate that it's broken. He opens his mouth, aims for laconic, and lands just south of coherent. "Welll, ahhh . . . it's cooool . . . I'lll jusss . . ."

Wilf's face gets even redder, his eyes narrow to slits, and his mouth opens wide. He is cut off in mid-bellow—face frozen, mouth agape—by the doors of the office swinging open.

No warning. No intercom beep from Mandy, one of the "fucking secretaries" whose lobes apparently await my globes. Through the doors stride two lower primates in double-breasted suits and sunglasses perched on noses obviously not unfamiliar with fists, with jowls wrapped in permanent five o'clock shadow.

They don't say a word. They stand to either side of the door and stare straight ahead at the far wall, past Ken's alarmed head. They clasp their paws together in front of their procreation equipment and stand deathly still.

Wilf's mouth closes with a wet clop, and in a voice mixing query, quandary, and threat, asks, "What the fuck?" Through the door walks a smaller and older, though no less menacing, version of the two doorstops. The guy is wearing a $10,000 suit, beige patent loafers, and dark sunglasses, and is smoking a cigarette in a whittled-down elephant-tusk holder. He stops just inside the room and looks at Wilf. Then he holds his right hand out, a ring glinting ostentatiously on his pinky finger. The rock responsible for the glinting is the size of a camel's gonad.

Wilf murmurs something unintelligible but reverent, leaps from behind his desk, and, before our astonished eyes, falls to one knee in front of the visitor and with another murmur kisses the proffered hand. He never greets us like that.

And I know why. It's because the guy who just wafted through the door is the real deal. If this guy isn't Mafia then he has missed his true calling in life. This is no cotton-in-the-jowls Brando goombah. This is one of those *made* guys, and judging by the reaction he is way up there, too. It's a sure bet no concrete gets poured, no liquor or gaming license gets doled out, no whore's legs spread, no garbage can gets emptied without this guy wetting his beak. *Fari vagnari u pizzu*. Whatever that means.

And what do you get for the crime lord who has everything? A slice of the British music industry. And, by extension, me and the boys.

Wilf heaves himself upright and begins spluttering about flights, schedules, and such, with a couple of "my apologies" thrown in for insurance purposes. The old guy withdraws his hand and, without looking, extends it to the gorilla on his left who, also without looking, places a silk handkerchief in the palm. With Howard Hughes–like attention to detail the mobster wipes his hands and, in a voice like a man swallowing a rusty hinge and asking for a glass of oil, says, "In our business sometimes it is unwise to stick too close to schedules."

Wilf, uncharacteristically flustered and grasping at cordiality straws, shuffles two steps backward, points at our manager, and says, "You remember Ken."

Ken is immobile, frozen in place, but he's a man who knows a *capo di tutti capi* when he sees one. He rockets from slouch to momentarily vertical, before lurching forward, tripping, and collapsing, prostrate and eating carpet at the old guy's loafers. The gorillas react as one, right hands disappearing under left armpits.

Ken bounces back up, bumping the back of his head on the old guy's now-outstretched hand. Grabbing the fingers for balance, Ken bends and pokes himself in the nose with the pinky ring before staggering backward to the safety of the armchair.

The dignified old gangster, trying to make sense of this spectacle, now repeats the silk hanky bit with the right-hand gorilla. The gorilla complies, though his trigger finger is still flooded with adrenaline. The old guy rubs, wipes, and polishes with true vigor.

Well, there is no avoiding it. Now Wilf has to, can't see a way not to, deal with the introduction of the two creatures from inner space sprawled on the sofa. I'm in red velvet strides, white canvas coolie shoes, and a fifties purple cocktail dress scissored up the middle. Lou sports black patent pumps, black denim pedal pushers, a pink sweater, a pair of Vincent Price in *The Fly* sunglasses, lipstick, and two red rouge spots on his cheeks. He looks like Annette Funicello on smack.

Now, this impeccably presented gangster has probably seen some odd sights in his long and colorful career, has probably even been responsible for some of the more colorful ones, but he is certainly giving us some serious eyeball at the moment. Almost horizontal in our recline on the big white sofa, in this increasingly film-noir tableau, we give him some serious eyeball right back.

Wilf, aghast and sweating a metaphor as appropriate as bullets, waves a meaty paw in our general direction. "Ah . . . these are two of our . . . artists . . . uh, musicians. Just leaving, in fact. Weren't you, lads?"

To Wilf's utter horror Lou and I simply stick our hands out, as does the old guy, and we shake. How you doing? Pleased to meet you. Musician to mobster. No ring smoochers, us. Wilf dry-gargles and regards us with a bug-eyed, ever-mounting fury.

"Yes, they're leaving. Good talk we had though, lads. Glad we got it all straightened out. See you soon, then."

Leaving? Now? Just when the show gets this good? Not likely. We refuse to be ushered. The old guy smiles and the hinge grates.

"Very nice meeting you, boys. I'd like to hear your music sometime. You got a combo, group, what is it?"

"Yeah, band," I reply. "The Hollywood Brats. I don't know, though, it's kind of wild. What do you listen to?"

Behind him, I see Wilf doing an impression of a man practicing semaphore while suffering from a hernia. The old guy strokes his chin. "Ah, you know, I listen to Dino, Tony, Vic Damone, all the paisans. Not Sinatra, though. Can't stand that pussy."

I'm just about to tell him that I love Dean Martin when Wilf interjects physically and tugs the sleeve of my dress. "Yeah, well, time to piss . . . uh, leave, lads. Don't forget that place you've got to get to."

"What place?"

"You remember. That place. That meeting. Ken, you go with them, will you? Make sure they get there." Then he turns to the old guy. "We love these boys. They're going to be huge. Bit cheeky, heh, heh, but what can you do?"

Wilf smiles at us. The scientific instrument has yet to be invented that could measure the lack of mirth in his arrangement of stretched lips and gritted teeth. Then Lou pipes up.

"What about the twenty quid?"

Much more accustomed to being the extorter than the extorted, Wilf is slow to get it, but get it he does. If looks could punch a guy in the guts while two other guys hold his arms, Lou would be puking his breakfast beer all over the expensive white carpet.

Wilf plunges a hand into his pocket, pulls out a fat roll of bills, peels off a purple one, and hands it to Lou. He smiles that frosty smile and looks longingly at Lou's bony kneecaps in the black pedal pushers, as though hoping to encounter them some other time, some other abandoned warehouse in the East End.

Lou and I stand up. So does Ken, unraveling himself upward until he's on his feet. Then, caught in that limbo zone between cool and irretrievably daft, he sashays toward the door blowing smoke like a camp locomotive, languid wrist holding aloft his hundredth cig as though he's fording a chin-high river and daren't let it get soggy.

He says, "Yeah, roight . . . it's, ah . . . yeah, roight, then."

Wilf does a pirouette, like the hippo in Disney's *Fantasia*, and grabs Ken's arm on the way by. He squeezes a squeeze worth at least a thousand words more than a picture. Ken nods. "Yeah. You got it, maaan."

Just before he reaches the lower-primate hanky dispensers, Ken turns and does an awkward salute-cum-genuflect curtsey at the dapper mobster, then dives backward through the door.

Lou pats the old guy on the shoulder. The gorillas tense up. Wilf steadies himself on his desk. "So, take it easy, sir," says Lou.

"Yeah, nice meeting you," says me.

The mobster smiles benignly, gives a little wave, and works the rusty hinge. "See you on the jukeboxes, boys."

See you on the jukeboxes.*

---

* Ken Mewis, Bali, 1989

"These characters kept showing up from the States. Like the fat guy who paced my office seven steps by seven. A lesson learned in the can for zapping Legs D. Kissing Mafia rings. Show a little respect. We were 'Family, man.' I liked the old Don. He'd talk to me. 'You're a son, come visit.' Yeah, great."

V

It is beyond frustrating watching the dross on *Top of the Pops* and *Old Grey Weasel Fest*. Why can't Ken get us a deal and get our record out there? Tempers are short. We're all arguing more and more.

Brady has bought a Vox Marauder guitar. It's an absolute beauty and he says he's written a song with it. Which means he's got a riff and two chords, tops. As suspected, it's a riff. Not a bad riff, though. I tape it, get the key, and tell him I'll have a bash at it.

Up in my black-and-pink eyrie, I have worked on Brady's threadbare little excuse for a song and managed to knock it into presentable shape with verses, chorus, instrumental break, and all the rest. The riff is the main attraction. It is more poppy than anything else we do, so maybe it will fit the straitjacket remit from 27 Dover Street.

It started life in my head as "Hello, Sailor" and almost immediately began veering off course and into a whining ode to camp androgyny. Sort of like something Cockney Rebel might lisp-synch on *Top of the Pops*. Can't have that. So once I get the structure I just start singing whatever comes out. What comes out is, "I just want you to be my baby," over and over again. Fits like a glove but I can't call the bloody thing "Be My Baby." It's not very Brat-like and, besides, the Ronettes have the "Be My Baby" franchise sewn up. I let it ride. I'll think up a snappier title later.

We rehearse it for two days in a rectangular, narrow room in King's Cross that stinks of fags and failed musicians. Casino doesn't seem overly thrilled with this Matheson-Brady interloper in the Matheson-Steel writing club. He works hard on it, though, and comes up with some interesting ideas for the arrangement.

Ken brings his ears in for a listen and likes what he hears. It is decided that the single we will deliver to Worldwide Artists will be Brady's new song, with a B-side of "Then He Kissed Me," the latter chosen because the flip-flop pronouns just seem to whip people into a lather whenever we play it live. I'm sure Wilf will love it.

Ken sets up a recording session.

On July 11, 1974, we venture south of the river once again, but not to Olympic. This time it is to dreaded Clapham, home of the buttock-blasting black guy who still has not been arrested. And, of course, Lou's got a girl in Clapham.

We head to 146 Clapham High Street and Majestic Studios. The place is not bad. Sort of a smaller version of Olympic. The horrible hit "Gonna Make You an Offer You Can't Refuse" by Jimmy Helms was recorded here, but we don't let that deter us. The engineers are sharp and friendly, and also we are no longer rookies. Casino and I know what we want and we have a much better grasp of how to get it.

For the last few nights I have been forcing my way through a dry-as-sawdust biography of Carl Jung. Finally, I can't take it anymore and toss it into the bin. But not before I get a title for the new song. I tell the engineer it's called "Zürich 17," and that's what he writes on the tape box.

We nail the basic track on Brady's song in a couple of takes, get the riff down, and move on to "Then He Kissed Me." We want a big, booming onslaught. Brady's ringing, slashing southpaw guitar chords kick-start proceedings then Lou comes in with a thudding neo-Spector bass drum/snare combo. We want this thing to be live, off the floor, like we're onstage poking the cage. Four takes later, we've got it. Embarrassing that it took so long but what can you do? Three to get ready then go, Brats, go.

Brady gets the backing-vocal duty for this one. It works well and, more importantly, looks good onstage so we let him give it a bash in the studio. His vocal is high-pitched, renegade, and not perfect, but when has that ever stopped us? We like it.

Next day, we tighten some things up and record the vocals. Casino has some excellent ideas for harmonies on "Zürich 17" and we layer them on. This is easily the most polished backing-vocal session we have ever done.

Lou completes a Spider-Man painting. He invites his flatmates for the unveiling. Derek and I, keen to the sense of occasion, pool our dwindling funds, walk to the high street, and buy six cans of Long Life, return home, sit on Lou's bed, and, in the company of the artist himself, marvel (small "m," obviously) at our drummer's talent. It is nothing short of amazing. On the east wall of his bedroom is a life-size rendering of the web-slinger, full color and brilliant. Almost 3-D. Where did he even get the paint? Seriously, if we could spare him we'd send him off to art school.

Word comes through from 27 Dover Street all the way to Brats headquarters, 66 Fordhook Avenue, that our "single" has passed muster. The threat of my balls becoming Christmas jewelry is now a thing of the past. This, as you might imagine, is a relief. But there is even better news. Ken says RCA Records is interested in signing us. We don't have to ask each other who is on RCA. Everybody knows who is on RCA.

Ken has set up a showcase specifically for RCA at the Speakeasy on August 5. Fender Soundhouse is block-booked for rehearsal. We are already rehearsed to death but we go at it for hour after hour and fine-tune the details.

Speakeasy, August 5, 1974. It's bad from the moment we show up in the afternoon. We have been loaned Stray's PA system and roadies for the gig. For some reason they don't seem to like us very much. Just what you want from a road crew. The stage is a postage stamp. It can't handle all our fabulous new equipment.

Louie and Mike are fighting the good fight with Stray's roadies, who are under the impression that they are in charge. Nobody told that to our guys, who are standing their ground. Now, we know Louie's a psycho, but Mike is also showing a heretofore hidden vicious side. Good lad. It is entertaining but this feud cannot bode well for the gig.

Nor can the fact that nobody has seen Brady for three days.

Four hours before showtime, word comes through from the office that Brady is in Pentonville prison. Yeah, not a local nick, but Pentonville. Johnny Cash could sing about this joint. Massive walls, towers, and razor wire. Apparently, Brady attacked a row of Bentleys and Rollers in Belgravia, smashing windshields, ripping off mirrors and aerials, and scratching paint jobs. Thousands of quids' worth of damage, and caught in the act by two coppers on the beat.

Absolute panic. We're fucked. We want to kill him. Ken spends a solid hour on the phone in Mr. O'Leary's office, calling the police, calling lawyers. Then Mr. O'Leary takes over. According to Ken, Mr. O'Leary went into another room, closed the door, made one phone call then hung up, came back out, and ordered coffee for the two of them. Fifteen minutes later the phone rang with news that Brady was free to go. Mr. O'Leary then dispatched a Rolls-Royce to pick him up at the prison gate.

The gig at the Speakeasy, the showcase for RCA Records, is a disaster from the first note. We are terrible and Brady is worse. We are five snails and the audience is one big salt cellar. After the first thirty seconds we're playing entirely for that minuscule knot of fans that still think we're the canine's danglers. These misfits hoot and holler after every song but are immediately, completely, and justifiably drowned out by boos from London's finest music critics.

Strange things are happening during the set, too. The sound is harsh and drenched in feedback that won't quit, microphones keep cutting in and out, and other low-rent happenings. We were better in the old days, when we were operating with exploding rubbish gear. Mysterious. Sabotaged by Stray's vengeful road crew? Perhaps Casino pissing on their beer crates was unwise.

Afterward, the verdict is written all over Ken's pale mug as he approaches us. He says the representatives from RCA not only didn't like us, they hated us. When I press Ken for what they said *exactly,* he replies, "They *exactly* said, 'We hate them.'"

In the dressing room, sitting quietly, lost for words, on the tatty red velveteen bench, we towel off and shake our heads at the insanity of it all. We summon belated sympathy for our, until recently banged-up, guitarist. He was in Pentonville prison, guard towers, razor wire, dogs, the works, for three days and three nights. I ask him, "Brady, what was it like?"

He keeps staring at the floor, shaking his head. Finally, he says, "Sore bum and sixpence."

Later, knocking back a couple of beers at the Speakeasy bar, Casino and I are cursing the fates, waiting for the rest of the lads so we can blow this dump, when we are approached by two guys, midthirties, Top Rank–style threads.

They stick out their paws for a handshake and introduce themselves as two members of the Merseybeats, saying they are now in management and record production. They say that Keith Moon has had a word with them about us. They like what they've just seen onstage. They understand the problems. Do we have a manager at the moment?

"No, as a matter of fact we don't have a manager," Cas and I immediately say. Why not? What's a couple more managers added to our collection. They hand us a business card and tell us to give them a call Monday. Righto Merseys, will do.

Imagine that, the Merseybeats. And after one of the worst gigs we've ever done. And Keith Moon. Well, every cloud and all that. Then Casino says he thinks Mr. O'Leary has been watching us the whole time.

Five minutes later we see both of the friendly, discerning Merseybeats bent backward over a table, being roughed up by Speakeasy bouncers.

On August 14 the highly influential satirical magazine *Private Eye* features an article on Worldwide Artists. It denounces them as "crooks."

That's bound to help matters.

It's August 22, and Ken calls, saying he has good news. He has been in intense negotiations with Bell Records for the last week. He's had four meetings with all the principals and they seem very keen indeed.

Bell Records? That is great news. We run through the known Bell Records roster: Gary Glitter, David Cassidy, Partridge Family, Showaddywaddy, Bay City Rollers. That junk is on a completely different planet to us. With a stable like that, what can Bell Records possibly see in the Hollywood Brats?

Turns out not much. They say no the next morning.

At two o'clock that afternoon Worldwide Artists stop our wages.

The Osmonds are number one in the charts. Again.

On September 1, 1974, just to boost our spirits, Wilf delivers the cheery message that if we don't get a record deal in a week we're out on our ears. Only he doesn't express it in quite such a genteel manner. Ken says not to worry. Our tapes are great and the music business needs the shake-up only we can provide. The charts are long overdue for a massive overhaul, says Ken.

Armed with a diary full of appointments, a sharp suit, Ray-Ban shades, an immaculate head of tousled hair, our tape, and Gered Mankowitz photos, Ken hits the streets of London.

DJM Records
Thurs. Sept. 5 12 noon
Mitchell Hiller
Response?
NO

Warner Bros. Records
Fri. Sept. 6 10:30 a.m.
54 Greek St.
Peter Sweteham
Response?
NO

Bus Stop Records
Mon. Sept. 9 11:30 a.m.
16 Clifford St.
Gary Jones
Response?
NO

Decca Records
Tues. Sept. 10 10:30 a.m.
9 Albert Embankment
Mr. Tauber
Response?
NO

Island Records
Tues. Sept. 10 5 p.m.
22 St. Peter's Square
Richard Withas
Response?
NO

Gull Records
Wed. Sept. 11 3 p.m.
56 South Molton St.
David Howells
Response?
NO

A&M Records
Wed. Sept. 11 4 p.m.
136 New King's Rd.
Mike Noble
Response?
NO

Magnet Records
Thurs. Sept. 12 12 noon
Peter Walton
Response?
NO

RAK Records
Thurs. Sept. 12 3 p.m.
Mickie Most
Response?
"Ken, you're not serious?"

GTO Records
Thurs. Sept. 12 5 p.m.
J. Myers
Response?
NO

Bearsville Records
Fri. Sept. 13 10 a.m.
Ian Kimmet
Response?
NO

CBS Records
Fri. Sept. 13 1 p.m.
17 Soho Square
Response?
NO

Polydor Records
Fri. Sept. 13 3 p.m.
Clive Selwood
Response?
NO

Evolution Records
Mon. Sept. 16 10 a.m.
Martin Saville
Response?
NO

Virgin Records
Mon. Sept. 16 12 noon
Martin Cole
Response?
NO

EMI Records
Mon. Sept. 16 3 p.m.
Rod McSween
Response?
NO

Carlin Music
Mon. Sept. 16 5 p.m.
Savile Row
Freddie Bienstock
Response?
"What the hell is this crap?"

WEA Records
Tues. Sept. 17 11 a.m.
Dave Dee
Response?
NO

EMI Records
(again)
Tues. Sept. 17 3 p.m.
Nick Mobbs
Response?
NO

Elektra Records
Tues. Sept. 17 5 p.m.
Nick Phillips
Response?
NO
Alert the judge. The jury has reached a unanimous verdict:

While Ken is out pounding on bricked-up doors and trying to convince cocked-up ears, the three of us, sometimes four, sometimes five, are kicking around 66 Fordhook Avenue like we're in prison: broke, complaining, waiting, watching TV. Phoning Ken fifty times a day for news. Doing anything but making music.

Films on the Beeb and ITV distract us, save us from punching each other into a raw bloody pulp. We watch *The Alamo* with John Wayne and Laurence (*Expresso Bongo*) Harvey, *Texas Across the River* with Dean Martin and Joey Bishop, *A Day at the Races* with the Marx Brothers, *Sex and the Single Girl* featuring Tony Curtis and everybody knows Natalie not only Wood, but usually did.

Our two favorites, though, are *King Kong vs. Godzilla*, starring King Kong and Godzilla (in his prime), and *Loving You* with Elvis Presley. All of us come to the immediate conclusion that we have ignored Elvis to our embarrassing detriment. He is completely brilliant in *Loving You* and warrants a full re-evaluation on our part.

This isn't fat Vegas Elvis in a white polyester jumpsuit. This isn't even "comeback" Elvis in black leather in '68, the concert that gave Casino that dangerous word. This is the real-deal Presley. He's playing a Gibson J-200, his hair is stunning, the moves are perfect, and the voice is so 1957 it's almost got big fins and a V8. We all agree we need more Elvis records around this joint. We'll get Mike on it tomorrow.

Next day, September 11, 1974, Mike calls. He's been sacked.

Ken calls a meeting at a quintessential English pub in Ealing, just off the Common, on a sunny Sunday afternoon. From the dew-soaked hedge creeps a crawly caterpillar. Cricket match on the green: the thwack of willow on leather. Such a beautiful setting to waste on an autopsy.

Upshot of it all? Upshot is, *c'est tout*. That's it. Ken has run out of doors to knock on. We're stuffed. Nobody out there in the world wants to sign the Hollywood Brats.*

---

* Ken Mewis, Bali, 1989

"Not really sure why the Worldwide connections didn't connect. And I didn't feel like inquiring."

We have just enough collective ego remaining to bristle and be astounded. What do you mean, nobody? Just, nobody. What about . . . ? No. Yeah, but surely . . . ? No. Not even . . . ? No. Just a resounding, definitive "no."

On the jukebox in the background, the Faces sing "What Made Milwaukee Famous (Has Made a Loser Out of Me)."

We drink Guinness and watch the lads in white trousers, caps, and pullovers out there on the green. I've no idea what they are trying to achieve. I don't have a clue about cricket. But they look good doing it. I also have to acknowledge that I don't have a clue about the music business. But we looked good doing it.

I'm sick of it all and I want to smash my fist through a wall. Not a pub wall, mind you. Something less sturdily built, less knuckle-crunching. A Japanese shoji screen, perhaps. Lots of clatter and ripping paper. To make a point.

We're all full of some kind of rage.

The next day, the phone is disconnected at Fordhook Avenue. The day after that, a telegram arrives from Worldwide Artists, Dover Street. We are told to vacate the premises with immediate effect and make arrangements to hand back our instruments and amplifiers. Furthermore, we are informed that the Olympic Studios and Majestic Studios tapes, having failed to garner a deal, are to be taped over.

An hour after the telegram arrives, two journalists show up for a pre-arranged interview with Casino and me. Considering the circumstances I can't decide if the timing is terrible or perfect.

Casino and I have been sharing a bottle of Teacher's whiskey, no glasses, on the couch in the living room, for an hour before the journalists get here. We are each carrying a bushelful of inter-Brat grievances. Truth is, we're barely on speaking terms. It is the Brats' first-ever interview. Luckily, Lou is here to referee.

I'm dressed for the interview in full Cary Grant mode: green silk Chinese bathrobe with accompanying ascot, silver bracelet, and black silk slippers. I have a paring knife and have been using it to slice thin strips off a ripe melon. By the time Jan Friis and his Norse buddy arrive with their notebooks, tape machines, and microphones, the Matheson-Steel Corporation is half-zonked and rapidly closing in on full-zonked status.

The journalists ask a question and we'd both give totally conflicting answers. Then we argue, on tape, about the various points of conflict. Following that, we swear at each other and move farther away on the couch so that they have to reposition the microphones. Then, screw this, I go to sit on the armchair so we can trade insults across the room. What the hell does a piano player know, anyway?

The journalists are looking at each other in astonishment. Finally, Casino staggers from the couch into an upright position and makes some stupid joke. He stands there, laughing. I feel the paring knife in my hand, and he laughs no more.

I wish. Instead, I throw the melon at his head and exit in a huff, stomping, as much as one can in black silk slippers, upstairs, where I slam my bedroom door like Joan Crawford in, well, at least twenty movies.

I am fuming in my attic when there comes a pounding of footsteps up the stairs, and in bursts a rabid Casino followed by a placid Lou followed by a truly interested Jan and his equally fascinated colleague. The room is ten-feet square. There's a woman in there, too. Dressed in lingerie and . . . tidying up, shall we say? It's overcrowded. Casino pushes right up to me and, without saying a Norwegian word, he hauls back and socks me in the jaw. Wow. For a man of modest stature he punches like a stevedore. But, as every man knows, you don't punch another chap in front of a woman dressed in stockings and suspenders. It's just not on.

Hence I immediately throw a right uppercut that catches him on the left side of his mouth. Lou leaps between us to stop further carnage. Cas and I threaten each other with at least death, Lou holding us apart. Snarling and in pain, I am pleased to see Casino's mouth leaking the red stuff. Then I look down and notice that my yap is dripping blood all over my Cary Grant gown.

As if that isn't enough amateur theater for one day, the two journalists go full Viking on each other for failing to get the altercation on tape. I can't understand them, but judging by the hysterics and implied umlauts it seems that they might also start throwing dukes any second.

Lou Sparks is the only sane person in the house.

I slink back to Watford and Carole and Brillo kindly take me in. I'm twenty-one, I'm washed up. Lou goes off to the girl in Clapham. We move all the gear to a garage in Camden and put an ad in the *Melody Maker*: "Great gear, greater prices. Must sell. Being chased by the Mob."

Dozens, maybe hundreds of musicians descend upon Camden and we sell all our lovely equipment to the top bidder. Need a Hammond, squire? Well, surely you could use a Leslie to go along with that? Lou, alias Mr. Chat, is master of ceremonies, arguing, goading, and charming the pound notes out of the wallets and into a pillowcase that fills up to the brim over the course of the day. Just like he did years ago, flogging records outside Bushey station. Casino and I keep watch up and down the street. On the lookout for you know whom.

Next day, Casino and I stake out the Worldwide Artists office at 27 Dover Street from a vantage point a few doors down, and as soon as all dangerous principals have left for lunch I go inside, taking the stairs two at a time. I breeze through the big doors with my best smile directed right at Mandy, as though hunky has just met dory and everything is fine in the world. I walk straight to the shelf where the two-inch tapes are stored, grab ours, and one cheery wave later I'm back out the door. The whole caper takes 45 seconds.

Worldwide Artists (a con, a front, a laundry, who knows?) conveniently chooses this moment to implode, and in the ensuing legal and logistical chaos the Hollywood Brats are forgotten. This is a big relief. We want to be forgotten by them right about now.

Brady goes into a complete sulk and quits the band. I'm losing count but I think it's the third time he's quit. The nerve. Casino and I invented the little prick. He'll never be in anything as good as the Brats again. Trouble is, in the witching hours when sleep won't come I can't escape the nagging, gnawing feeling that none of us will ever be in anything this good again.

Ken remains steadfast in his belief in the Hollywood Brats. He does, however, throw a fit about the gear being "misplaced." His knees may have to pay the price.

Weeks of nothing turn into months of less. The disappointment is crushing and weighs on the heart. We thought we had everything. We thought we had the perfect band. We thought we'd made the perfect record. September goes, followed by October. November says, "Don't look at me, losers."

Derek goes somewhere and does something. We don't know. We don't care.

Turns out he was being paid £50 a week while the rest of us were on a tenner. What a joke.

The Brats are reduced to Me, Lou, and Casino. We meet at pubs to laugh and mope, trying to figure out what to do next. We convene at 17 London Street, where we rage at the fates and play our scratchy acetates over and over. Then Lou, my mate through Cross Road, Aldenham Road, Mill Lane, Bishop's Road, and Fordhook Avenue, decides he's had enough and goes back to the land of the Micmac. This leaves just the two of us, me and Cas. Right back where we started.

Casino and I meet for a Christmas drink at the Sussex Arms. At the end of the evening he sorts it with the barman that we can take a cognac down the street to the derelict huddled up on his cardboard bed outside Ladbrokes. We feel good doing it, giving something from the little we have. The spirit of the season fills our rancid little souls.

We hand the drink to him and wish him a very Happy Christmas. He reaches out of his blankets and takes it, with a look on his face like he's been waiting for it for the last hour and was wondering where we'd got to.

I think we are in rats' alley
Where the dead men
lost their bones

T. S. Eliot, *The Waste Land*

1975

I

One morning in Watford, bringing in the milk bottles, silver foil tops pecked by greedy, opportunistic, cream-sucking sparrows, a song comes on the radio called "Geronimo's Cadillac." It's by Claire Hamill. Now, an Apache in a Cadillac is an interesting concept to me so I give it an ear. Afterward, Tony Blackburn informs us that it is on the Konk label. It hits me that this is a record company we have overlooked—and of all the record companies to overlook. Konk Records is relatively new and was started by Ray and Dave Davies of the Kinks. I love the Kinks. This is perfect.

Later that afternoon I find out the phone number, take a deep breath, and give it a bell. What will I say if Ray answers and says "hello" through that gap in his front teeth? Needn't have worried. A very nice lady answers and says that they are indeed looking for artists and I should drop a tape off at the office. They'll give it a listen.

I have a bath, brush every tooth rigorously, polish my shoes, and generally spruce up to tip-top shape. Just before I leave the house with the Hollywood Brats tape under my arm I wonder, Should I? No, don't be daft, I tell myself. Well, why not? Because it's not the sort of thing you do, I insist. But you could make an exception just this once, couldn't you? Oh, all right then. Stop arguing with me. I suppose I could.

I go to my room overlooking the air-raid shelter and the railroad tracks, and from among my meager possessions I pick out my treasured copy of

Something Else by the Kinks. It is my favorite record, my absolute Desert Island Disc, and this scratchy copy has been with me forever, or at least it seems that way. During all the bleak times this album was the only one I resisted the urge to sell.

Let It Be, *Get Yer Ya-Ya's Out!*, *Back Door Men*, Shangri-Las, all the rest, they've ended up hocked in pawnshops or sold by Lou outside railway stations. But not *Something Else*. I could never part with it. It has seen me through many a dark time—living in a bunkhouse while working in the mine, in the Aussie Ghetto in Earls Court and the curry-stench cell in Harrow—and many a pleasant, sunny time, as well. I'm wondering, Is it possible to get Ray to autograph it? Wouldn't that be something?

It is an expensive hour-and-a-half journey from Watford Junction by Brit Rail, the Tube, and shanks' mare to get to Konk Records in Hornsey. Thankfully, the very nice lady is behind the desk when I get there, and she duly takes the Brats tape. She also gently eases the embarrassment I feel when I ask if I can get *Something Else* autographed.

I walk out feeling quite optimistic on both counts.

Two weeks pass like a particularly jagged gallstone. During that period, for conduct unbecoming a houseguest, I am made to walk the plank at 112 Bradshaw Road for the second time in my career. Eventually, covered in seaweed and ignominy, I wash up on the shores of 17 London Street in Paddington, and my old mate and his lass Sonja very graciously pull me to safety. I interrupt their life and sleep on their couch.

Sonja spends her days working hard from early morning until late in the evening at the Duchy Hotel in Lancaster Gate. Casino and I spend our days burning egg and chips on the stove, griping, drinking, bemoaning our fate, and going to Arsenal football matches.

Around about this time, stuck as we are without a breath of wind in the doldrums, Casino cons his way into writing an entertainment column for a newspaper back in Norway. He files his columns every Friday, which is handy because the London music papers come out on Thursday and that allows him to steal every single sentence, so the wheeze doesn't have to take up a great deal of his time.

What a scam. He gets paid *plus* he gets journalist credentials, so every week the record companies send all their new releases for him to review. This, of course, he never does. Instead, he takes each week's stack down the street and sells them to a record shop.

Another angle he's working is that, since he's using his maiden name for the newspaper byline, he can drop the handle "Casino Steel" into his columns every now and again, mentioning this up-and-coming musician who's really making waves in London. So it turns out Casino Steel is making quite a name for himself, especially for a man who's not making quite a name for himself.

One day, Casino and I come back home after going for a lecture and a free lunch in a hall in Bayswater. There is always one barmy cult or another on Praed Street soliciting society's zombies to come away with them on buses to their communes in the Pennines. We usually ignore them, of course, but this one offered lunch so, since we were hungry, we said, "Sure."

The lecture was short but full of words, something about communism and why the BBC needs more state control and why our possessions aren't making us happy. Fair enough. Then it's on to lunch. The blackboard says gumbo, which I associate with New Orleans or at least Louisiana or Hank's "Jambalaya" but which, whatever the case, I have never eaten. It turns out to be a bowl of gelatinous white plastic squares floating in a weak, milky, spiced porridge. Son of a gun, it ain't big fun. These cults, I tell you.

We arrive back *chez* Steel to find there is a message. Carole, not one to hold a grudge, has called from Watford, saying Konk Records want to see me anytime after 10 a.m. tomorrow.

We are beyond excited. We go through scenario after scenario. The prevailing one being that the Kinks love us and will be releasing our record next week. I told you my Kinks connection meant something. It was fate, always at my elbow, tugging my sleeve, leading us to this very high-rent intersection where Kinks meet Brats.

Next morning, bathed and primped, I set off, on a return ticket from Paddington station. Not to seem overly eager, I present myself at Konk Records in Hornsey at half past ten. A deep breath, a couple of them actually, and through the doors I go. The selfsame very nice lady smiles brightly as I approach the desk. All the way here on the Tube I've been rehearsing the perfect opening line. And I've got a great one. I open my smiley mouth; however, she beats me to it. She reaches behind her, grabs our tape, and hands it to me. "I'm sorry. This is not what we're looking for at the moment."

In that instant, eighteen hours of Matheson-Steel hopes and dreams shatter like a champagne-glass pyramid at a *Penthouse* Christmas party. My smile goes rictus. I summon every reserve I have to try to maintain a modicum of composure.

The very nice lady continues in script form, a script not even personally tailored for me: "We do thank you so much for considering us and we wish you all the best in the future."

I feel nauseous. I reach out my hand, slowly take the tape, and murmur something—"Thanks, oh, okay"—something useless and, wanting nothing more than to disappear into a hole in the floor, I turn to go.

Then I remember. I turn back. God, this is embarrassing. I ask, "Um, I was just wondering . . . about . . . the record I left?"

She looks up from the hugely important task she just had to attend to five-hundredths of a second after that wish-you-all-the-best-in-the-future line. "Sorry?" She's all fluttering eyelashes.

"Yeah. The record. I . . . uh . . . I left a record to be . . . I don't know . . . autographed or something?"

"Record?"

"Yeah, *Something Else*. It's okay if it's not . . . if it couldn't . . . I just want it back."

"Record. You left a record? Here?"

I nod. This is excruciating. If you knew me you'd know just how painful this is. "Yes, I gave it to you and asked if it was possible to have it autographed. It's no big deal now. I just want to get out of here. I'll just take it and go."

"You gave it to *me*? Well, that doesn't ring a bell. Let me just ask if anyone has seen it. What was it called, you said?"

"*Something Else*."

"And it's of course by . . . ?"

"The Kinks."

"Of course. Let me just check."

She calls somebody and somebody checks with another somebody, and through all these torturous somebodies I listen to her say things into the phone like, "No, no neither have I," and, "No, she hasn't seen anything like it," and, "Well, of course. Well, we'd have noticed, wouldn't we?" All of which leads nowhere. She hangs up the phone, sighs politely, and goes back to the script.

"I'm so sorry. Nobody seems to know anything about it. Now, you're sure you . . . yes, yes, of course you're sure. Well, if it turns up I'll let you know."

And then I leave.

I walk aimlessly down some street for a while and then sit down on a bench near a park. It is 10:39 a.m. Nine minutes for that.

Konk Records
Hornsey
Nice lady
Response?
No

How could we be so stupid? How could we get our hopes up like that, after all we've been through? The message "anytime after 10 a.m." said it all. Anytime after 10 a.m. is anytime between 10:00 a.m. and the end of the world. And even then they wouldn't care, would they? "Uh-oh, world's blowing up. Did the Hollywood Brats pick up their tape?"

They didn't care when you got there, idiot. They didn't even care *if* you got there. How could we not see that?

I take my time returning to London Street.

Indefatigable Ken's been working the phones from home. Alice Cooper's producer Bob Ezrin has heard of the Hollywood Brats and wants a meeting with Ken. Trouble is, Ezrin is in Toronto and Ken's in penury. We empty the pillowcase of the last of the Camden quids and Ken flies out of Heathrow.

Nimbus 9 Productions
39 Hazelton Ave.
Toronto, Ontario
Bob Ezrin
Response?
No*

After this final debacle Ken decides he's had enough. He has a wife and child to look after. Reluctantly (so he says), he bows out.

---

* Ken Mewis, Bali, 1989

"I think we'd already sold everything that was movable. I hit the Toronto mattresses. I walked the streets paved with snow. Sundays in Toronto sucked. You couldn't get a drink unless you had a meal. A dozen hamburgers from room service just to get wrecked enough to watch TV.

Bob Ezrin, Alice Cooper's producer, heard 'Sick On You' and, after the coughing, puking bit at the end, says to me, very straight-faced, 'Hey, man, some chick musta really burned that guy.'"

II

Brady's got a brand-new band and he's been beating his gums together around town, yapping about how good they are. They're playing the Marquee so Cas and I pop in for a look. I am now considered so boring and ineffectual even the Marquee lets me in again. Now it's us who are the music police, standing at the back, arms crossed, waiting to be impressed or, as in this case, not.

I understand they're called Violent Lunch. Like a menu item at a caff in Kilburn. They're going nowhere.

Actually, we suffered a bit of trepidation coming in, wondering what the Dublin defector was up to, but in the end we needn't have worried. The band doesn't even qualify as rubbish. More like aural wallpaper. A less-than-ordinary, plodding four-piece playing Chuck Berry and Frankie Miller retreads; a suburban pub-level outfit at best.

And Brady, what's that you're wearing, lad? He's in a pair of trousers that look like something Gary Glitter would put on when he's washing his wigs. Also, he looks weird. He is gaunt, pasty, and cadaver-like. And not in a cute young *Vogue*-model way.

Turns out he's on smack. And not in a cute young *Vogue*-model way.

Backstage in the dressing room at the Marquee, Brady shows us how he gets his kicks these days. Or maybe he doesn't care who is watching, or possibly he doesn't know we are even there. Anyway, it's clear he ain't getting his kicks on Route 66 anymore. He takes a dirty, sweaty scarf in his teeth, wraps it around his upper arm, and pulls tight. Some rat-boy creature is, meanwhile, holding a cigarette lighter under a piece of foil containing what looks like a small pile of crusted brown sugar and baking soda. The flame soon turns it into a cesspool of brown liquid. This is heroin and cocaine: a speedball.

The murky liquid is sucked up into a filthy, blood-specked syringe by yet another twitching mutant who then approaches Brady and searches his pale, scarred, skinny arm for a suitable vein. Then, upon finding just the right blood vessel, he pushes it in, squeezes home the joy juice, and walks away, leaving the spike dangling.

Brady gasps, his eyes roll up under his lids, and he falls backward onto the floor with his arms outstretched, head lolling back and forth, moaning.

Now, that looks like fun. Casino and I say "toodle-oo" and leave. Nobody cares, nobody notices. We're getting a lot of that these days.

We appear to be out of allies and options. Now that the pillowcase money is long gone the two of us spend our days in London Street playing *Dean Martin's Greatest Hits* over and over, and using my putter to smack golf balls across the carpet into a shot glass. Over and over.

One fateful morning, Casino decides to take the tapes to Norway to see what damage he can do there. I don't hold out much hope for what I see as a kamikaze mission, but I wave a hanky from the control tower and wish him banzai as he flies off to his date with destiny at Pearl Fjord. A day that will live in infamy.

A lonesome week without my pal crawls by. It is a week filled with wandering the streets of London, cadging dodgy lunches from even dodgier cults, and enduring the endless, unavoidable sonic torture of "Mandy," by Barry Manilow, and "If," by Telly "Kojak" Savalas, as they duel for the number-one spot in this most wretched of wretched pop charts. Dog days, indeed.

And then, finally, on a Tuesday afternoon, as I'm trying to work out the chords to "Return to Me" by Dino, Casino returns to me, bursting through the door with news that is absolutely staggering. The Hollywood Brats have a record deal with Mercury Records, Norway.

Cas hands over £62.50, my half of the £125 advance, and we immediately head out to the Sussex Arms to invest it in many rounds of celebratory suds.

So, what happened in Norway? The usual and then the startlingly unusual happened. Casino initially met with the anticipated wall of disapproval, the usual "No" at every stop. And then at Mercury/Phonogram, during a meeting with the strikingly prescient gentleman of fine breeding and obvious good taste, the honorable Audun Tylden, he met with the absurdly unusual, a resounding "Ja."

According to Casino, Audun Tylden cranked up the tape machine, heard the first fifteen bars of "Tumble With Me," turned to Cas, and yelled, "I love it!" or, actually, "Jeg elsker det!"

This is stunning news, great news, unbelievable news. The Hollywood Brats finally have a record deal. There's just one slight snag.

The Hollywood Brats no longer exist.

III

We don't have a band. Three-fifths of us—rats, perhaps—have long since left leaking, listing HMS *Brats*. Well, Lou's not a rat, I suppose. He's in Halifax, Nova Scotia, and word has it that the girl in Clapham has joined him. I know that because one afternoon I called her number, 622-1339, thinking that, even though it's south of the river, I'd go down there and offer to throw a quick one into her. But her mum answered and said she'd gone to Canada.

Lou ultimately went back to find a real life. Can't blame him. It must be said that he hung in there to the bitter end, which he then kindly left to us.

Derek? What about him? He was always the hired hand, and at fifty nicker a week he was earning five times what the rest of us were. We tried to accept him, but we could never get over the fact that he originally turned us down and only came aboard when things were rosy, with contracts and TVs and Olympic and fab gear and whatnot. He never adopted the lifestyle, philosophy, and culture of the Brats. An okay bass player, a renowned swordsman, and a good sense of humor, but he could never shake the tag of "opportunist." As Brady always said, "There are only four Hollywood Brats."

Which brings us to Eunan Seamus Brady. A piece of tame, lumpen clay, a mild milquetoast pretend-Keith that even soppy Love Affair instructed to look away from the camera at a stone prison wall. And he did. Or, then again, perhaps he didn't. Maybe he was genuinely looking at the prison wall, thinking, If I play my cards right, I'll be behind one of those one day.

Casino and I had taken him and shaken him, cursed, coerced, and rehearsed him until he had finally started to act like a guitar man the world might take seriously. We'd whipped him into stage form, taught him to sing, taught him to walk and talk like a Hollywood Brat.

We'd teed him up, freed him up, licensed him to let loose in London Town, kick them trash cans down, rip off them Rolls-Royce aerials. Good boy. Have a beer.

We had fried his fingers and beaten him to red pulp in the studio, made him do take after take, and dropped him into solos a dozen times over four bars to create those effortless-seeming, biting, flowing guitar tracks.

We had invented him.

We'd almost electrocuted him.

Hell, we even christened the boy.

And what does he do?

He quits, buys a Hayman, and injects speedballs.

So what do we do? Mercury Records are crying out for artwork, photos, liner notes, and we're sitting on a sofa in London Street, the last two left, bereft. How can we pull this off? We're not Sonny & Cher.

It's not brilliant, but this is what we come up with. We decide to be Andrew Matheson & the Brats. This solution allows some scope for forming a new band. Thus, Casino sets up a photo shoot with his old pal Tony the Italian. On a rainy night in Soho we choose a suitably sleazy street, Rupert Court, full of strip joints and clip joints. I'm wearing a thirties hat, aviator shades, a red-and-white striped top, and ever so slightly tatty formal tails, white silk scarf, white shoes. Anonymous. Could be anybody. But it ain't.

For the back cover we throw in live shots and a couple of other random photos. A quick call to Ken and, once he recovers from the shock of us having garnered a record deal, he agrees to pen some liner notes.

I suggest to Casino that we call the album "Grown Up Wrong," after the title of a song on the *12 x 5* album by the Stones. He said yeah (bom-doo-be-doo-bom-bom), he said yeah.

Next day, the piano player and I are scoffing the full English at Bela's greasy spoon in Fulham Broadway. On a stool in a corner in a stack of old newspapers I find a beat-up, dog-eared *Batman* comic. I haven't read a *Batman* comic since I was a lad, and even back then all those caped crusaders weren't really my cup of tea. I was more of a *Beano, Lone Ranger, Classics Illustrated* type of lad. But this is Wednesday, not Thursday, and there's no music press. Casino is reading last night's *Evening Standard*, but who wants yesterday's papers?

I flick through the pages of the comic but my heart's just not in this Gotham wheeze. Batman has a great set of wheels, but what else? A suspect relationship with Robin, who makes Superman's pal Jimmy Olsen seem like a positively suave career man. In fact, the only thing Batman's got that I covet, other than the car, is his mansion. This place, complete with butler, is just the kind of digs I intend to, one day, stride about in, whacking a riding crop against my leather boots and terrorizing the servants. Not to mention rogering the more comely of them. Batman's mansion even has a great name, Wayne Manor.

Ultimately, there were three bass players on the Hollywood Brats album. By the end of breakfast Casino and I agree that Wayne Manor is their name.

IV

Next, we take the tapes (the nicked tapes; the tapes that were hours away from being taped over by those wisest of wise guys) on the bus to Phonogram Studios on Stanhope Place, Marble Arch, where Mercury Records have set up a session for us to sequence the record: "Chez Maximes" first, "Sick On You" last, and so on. Also, I've got an idea I want to try.

"Ain't We Got Fun?" is a song from the twenties. The lyrics denote a life wherein not much is right with the world—no money, rent's due, that sort of thing—but despite it all, baby, ain't we got fun? It seems a perfect motif for the Brats, not to mention Casino and me at this strange juncture in our lives. I want it to lead off the album, played dead simple, a one-finger, kitten-on-the-keys sort of thing. Just eight bars, but at the end I want a jagged, fractured note. A fractured note that hints, dear listener, that maybe this is a ruse, a con, a Burmese tiger pit. Maybe we ain't got fun after all. Maybe you should just brace yourself. Then—wham!—straight into "Chez Maximes."

I want it on the outro, too. At the end of "Sick On You," right after the last piece of falling sheet-metal sky and cough-choke chaos, I want that piano to incongruously reappear, monotonous, eerie, and echoing as it slinks off into the ether, dragging your battered preconceptions behind it. Anyway, some rubbish like that.

Cas says, "Okay."

Phonogram Studios, grand piano, lights dim, Casino leaning over the keyboard, right forefinger poised. I hit the talk-back button and remind him of the mission. Twelve notes, repeat, then mess up the last one, please. Got it? Of course I've got it. Simple? Couldn't be simpler. Fine. Roll tape. Tape rolling.

Take one. Just one slight problem: he can't do it. Take two. Uh, let's take it again. Take three. He still can't do it. His tempo is perfect, his feel is perfect, but his plinking finger just refuses to hit that bad note at the end. The engineers look at me nervously. They've only known us for forty-three minutes. It occurs to me that there's a good chance they might think we're slightly drunk interlopers who've wandered in off the street and are having a laugh. After all, Phonogram Studios costs hundreds of quid an hour, and there's a guy out in the studio, giggling quietly and playing a Bösendorfer grand piano with one finger.

And screwing it up.

I, however, do not panic. I've heard Casino hit a thousand duff notes before, so I *know* that if he really concentrates he can screw that note up royally.

I go out into the studio, where he and I have a two-minute laugh disguised as a consultation, after which I return to the control room and tell two wide-eyed engineers to roll tape for take four. Casino, summoning all of the inspirational ghosts of his former piano teachers, finally hits the required fractured note, the note that we hope will introduce the Hollywood Brats to the ears of the world.

Afterward, following the sequencing of the tracks, while sitting in the Sussex Arms knocking back a polite one, we can't help wonder, for the umpteenth time, why, after relying so heavily on "Melinda Lee" for so long, after it rescued us in all those dodgy situations, did we not record the damned song? A mystery, wrapped in a conundrum, stuck through with voodoo pins.

Anyway, next morning, we put the photos and fiction together with the tapes in a brown box and send it to Mercury Records.

A month of hopeful boredom later, a box duly arrived at 17 London Street, Paddington. We opened it and there it was, *Grown Up Wrong* on Mercury Records. Five copies. We examined the front and back covers, devouring every word. We remarked on the dozy pencil-and-eraser school motif that the art department, obviously leaning on the *Grown Up Wrong* aspect, came up with.

We stared at the label and saw the Matheson-Steel writing credit in actual print under the song titles. There it was. We were real writers. It says so. We saw "Southern Belles," our first song, written a thousand lifetimes ago, and "Sick On You," the most troublesome of our compositions. It was there on the label. Real.

We took the vinyl out of the inner sleeve, held it at an angle to the light, and stared in wonder at the black plastic width of each song. There it all was, deep in those mysterious grooves, the noise that was the Hollywood Brats. That's what "Chez Maximes" looked like and "Tumble with Me" and "Drowning Sorrows" and all the rest. It was wondrous.

I put on the black leather jacket that I had bought at Kensington Market with twenty-two quid of my advance money and we strolled down the street for a pint.

This was the first time we had walked down London Street as recording artists, and back in the bedsit we had black vinyl on a Mercury label to prove it. And we didn't know it then, walking down London Street to the Sussex Arms, walking with unstoppable smiles yanking our lower faces apart, walking two feet off the pavement past the derelict down there on his cardboard carpet with his plastic snifter of Brut. We didn't know it then but that was it. That moment on London Street was the pinnacle, because nothing else happened. The record was released in Norway and did not unduly drain *Norske* wallets. In fact, it went utterly unnoticed. There was no marketing budget. We didn't even know what marketing was. The record was never advertised. It was never reviewed in print. It was never played on the radio. It came and went, shyly, politely, anonymously, with a minimum of fuss. The antithesis of the Hollywood Brats.

We were informed three months later that, before it died its meek death, it had sold precisely five-hundred-and-sixty-three copies. Five-hundred-and-sixty-three people bought the Hollywood Brats album. Five-hundred-and-sixty-three wonderful people.

I got sick, sick, sick, sick to death of having long hair, so I gave Ken a call. When he first hit swinging London, long before he became a music bizzer with Immediate Records, Ken was a hairdresser of some renown. So he came over with his blades and a three-quarters-full bottle of vodka. We had a laugh and, while we listened to the Shangri-Las' *Greatest Hits*, he chopped my locks off, doing his customary, flamboyant Warren-Beatty-in-*Shampoo* performance.

Afterward, I stared at the mirror and a pale Elvis in *Clambake* stared back at me.

The Hollywood Brats were dead.

EPILOGUE

I

Months later, following the unseemly plummet and Technicolor splat of the Hollywood Brats, Casino and I had only just about scraped ourselves off the pavement. But still, our collective soul (recently redeemed from Sad Sack's hockshop) was cracked and leaking heartbreak fluid.

The two of us were lounging horizontally, cheap limbs draped over cheaper furniture, drinking schnapps freshly nicked from a shop in Holloway, watching *Match of the Day* on telly. And then, right at that juncture, right at that moment when these weird happenings are most required, a tentative but insistent knock came on the door two flights below.

We tried to ignore it but it became less tentative and more insistent so, reluctantly, Cas got off the couch and looked out the window. On the street below were two hippy types (massive hair, trouser flares flapping proudly in the draft of the passing traffic) staring beseechingly up and waving. Soft-hearted Cas looked at them kindly for a moment and then shouted, "Fuck off," closed the curtains, and came back to the Arsenal–Leeds match.

We didn't check but, since there was no further knocking and yelping, off they presumably had fucked.

Annoyingly, though, they repeated the process, same time, the next night. So, giving them two points for persistence, Cas clomped down three flights of stairs and, without opening the door, lifted up the letter-box flap and once again suggested that off was the desired direction in which they should still fuck, and posthaste, if you don't mind. Once again, they duly, though reluctantly, did. Only this time, with no football on our black-and-white telly to distract us, they had got our attention. Just who were these two coves?

The next night these longhairs reappeared, but this time with a handwritten sign that said "PLEASE?" Given the sign and the imploring looks on the faces of the two hairy hopefuls, we wilted. Also, we were bored, curious, and in need of light entertainment, so we thought what the hell and let them in.

They introduced themselves as Mick Jones and Tony James. Their hair was long, lank, and stiff with hairspray. They had painted fingernails, mascara, and eyeliner. They sported bangles and necklaces and various items from the women's department of Debenhams. In short, they looked like the Hollywood Brats circa not that long ago.

Mick and Tony then went on to say that they were huge Hollywood Brats fans and that they had a copy of the record. If this was a shock to me, they in turn seemed shocked yet fascinated by my now-spiky *Clambake* hair arrangement, and stared as though I was Samson recently returned from an iffy afternoon at Delilah's Barbershop & Barbiturates Emporium.

Then they said, "Behold, for we bring tidings of great joy," or words to that effect. "Yeah, what tidings would they be?" we asked, all tingly with curiosity. The tidings were these: some impresario named Malcolm McLaren wants to manage the Hollywood Brats. Malcolm McLaren. Now, where had we heard that name before?

Oh, yeah. He had recently managed the New York Dolls (already on life support and nearly flatlined) straight into the grave. Under McLaren's bogus-Svengali miss-molly management, he and his seamstress spinster auntie, Vivisect Westwood, had dressed the Dolls in ludicrous red patent-leather outfits, adorned the stage with a veritable miasma of left-wing commie tossery, replete with hammer-and-sickle motif, and pushed them out into the world in a puff-pop of publicity, where they were snickered at, briefly pitied, and then ignored. In short, McLaren had ushered the Dolls all the way to true mock-rock status, thereby belatedly, pathetically rendering *Old Grey Whistle Pest* Bob correct after all. Cripes. Wake me, shake me when it's over.

Well done, Malcolm. And now he wants to manage us? Well, hammer and sickle on you, mate. Why not? Let's go meet him. So we donned the finery and slapped on the face paint. Just like old times. And yet, not like old times at all. This time it felt like dressing up, like playing a role. Like a false little ghostly stab at old times, really. Just messing about, not living a lifestyle.

As a last-minute "up yours" I strapped on one of my two swastika armbands (the real thing, bought for 50p each at a charity shop in West Hampstead). Mick Jones was rather taken with the look and asked to borrow the other one. Soon afterward, the four of us were parading through Soho looking like the Weimar wing of the National Front, disturbing the delicate sensibilities of the hookers, wide boys, and tourists until we arrived at an address on Denmark Street.

We entered to find, sitting primly on a sofa, what looked like four trainee accountants staring at us, bug-eyed as lemurs and speechless. I felt like matron walking in and catching four public-school boys, trousers round their ankles in the first getting-to-know-you communal wank of the new term. We didn't know it at the time, but these were John Lydon (not yet Rotten but quite obviously Rotting), Glen Matlock, and the other two whose monikers escape me, collectively the Sex Pistols.

An awkward silence ensued, broken by Mick, who picked up a guitar from the floor and said, like the Grateful Dead–type council-flat hippy he was, "Let's jam, man."

At this point, our eyes rolling like pinballs, Casino and I were halfway out the door to find the nearest pub when down the stairs came a chap who was clearly barking mad—indeed, he looked like a caricaturist's idea of the bonkers scientist: bulging eyes, unwashed hair mud-red and curly (the hair nobody wants), skinny arms sticking out of a faded T-shirt, wrists flapping and fey—beckoning us to come upstairs: come, come.

Malcolm McLaren was a slippery sort, alternately louche, bored, and slo-mo, the next second spouting staccato rubbish, jittery as a speed freak. Eye contact minimal and a handshake like a half-opened tin of sardines.

So things looked quite promising.

Downstairs, Mick had enticed the lemurs/accountants to plug in, and they were all blasting away, out of time and tune, playing what sounded like five different songs in four different keys and tempos. Malcolm, looking disconcertingly reminiscent of Ken Mewis, uncoiled himself from the couch, sashayed over to the door like a drag queen trying to butch it up in front of the cops, and slammed it shut.

Coming right to the point, he said, "I'll come right to the point. I want to manage the Hollywood Brats."

I said the first thing that came into my mind: "It stinks in here."

"Oh, does it? Fuck, let me open the window." He wrestled with the window like a famine victim trying to bench-press a two-hundred-pound barbell. The window eventually squealed open a few inches, which only rendered the fug stench mobile and brought new varieties of pong to our olfactory receptors. McLaren drew a deep breath, coughed it out, and continued.

"There, that's much better. Anyway, Brady was saying that the four of you were looking for management, and I've heard the record and I like it so . . ." At this point I held my arm (the one with the swastika armband) straight out, with my palm at a right angle in the "stop" position. Sort of like a cross between an *Obersturmführer* and Diana Ross.

"Wait a minute. Did you say Brady? What's Brady got to do with anything?" Tony James was frantically trying to get my attention, but he's the kind of chap that makes me frantically hit the "ignore" button.

McLaren shrugged. "Well, Brady came to see me, with this idea . . ."

"When?"

"When? Well, last week, maybe Tuesday."

"I haven't clapped peepers on Brady in months."

"What are you talking about? He's downstairs, you came in with him."

Well, what do you know? Turns out Mick Jones has been poncing around town telling everyone he is Brady from the Hollywood Brats. While I was digesting this bit of monumental weirdness, McLaren was outlining his plan for world domination. Apparently, the centerpiece of said plan was "Sick On You." While struggling to keep up with his flailing limbs and even more flailing syntax, I gathered that he envisaged something along the lines of a snotty musical revolution, with the attack and sonic snarl of "Sick On You" being the template. Oh, brilliant idea, Braino. Except for the fact that everybody hates "Sick On You," remember?

Sometime during McLaren's mouthy manifesto, Mick "Brady" Jones stopped the repetitive thrashing of "E," the one chord with which he was comfortably familiar, and came upstairs to join us. Casino and I lay back in rock 'n' roll's time-honored couch-slouch, while Mick and Tony leaned forward on the edge of their seats, nodding and drooling at every adjective, enthralled by every point-emphasizing cigarette stab, entranced by every promise of a promise that came from the thin dry lips of Malcolm Mac.

Then Casino Steel, Mick Jones, Tony James, and I were "treated" to the first-ever public performance by the Sex Pistols. The first time they had played in front of humans that weren't named Malcolm or McLaren.

Nine minutes. Four songs. Three chords. One verdict: dentist drill in molar, sans novocaine. They even did a song by the Monkees. *The Monkees.* Made me yearn for Micky Dolenz.

Very early in the tenth minute we left. As the four of us trudged through Soho trying to find a pub that would accept patrons in swastikas and lipstick, I thought the Sex Pistols were substandard, derivative posers and I thought Malcolm McLaren was a weak-minded, possibly insane, fantasist.

I was completely right about the Sex Pistols.

I was completely wrong about Malcolm McLaren.

But, more importantly . . . we missed *Coronation Street* for this?

II

A few days later came a further knock on the door at 17 London Street. Casino went down, peered through the letter box, and spied Glen Matlock, one of the Pistols, and his manager Bernie Rhodes (McLaren's partner at the time). They said, "Malcolm wants another meeting. And is Brady here?"

Casino replied, "Which one?"

"Either one will do. We're not fussy."

"What's in it for me?"

They couldn't come up with a satisfactory answer, so Cas said, "Fuck off," slammed down the letter-box lid, and came back upstairs.

We did meet with McLaren again, this time on our turf, the Sussex Arms. Once again, he was a fidgety ball of twitching nerves. He acted like he had missed his last three appointments with his parole officer and was expecting the rozzers to pounce on him at any moment and drag him back to Wormwood Scrubs.

He brought his girlfriend Vivisect with him and introduced her as a clothing designer. I had never met one before and I was not convinced that this was what they looked like. She was cadaver pale and wore an orange silk frock that had obviously been run over by a lawnmower a few times. Perched on her hairdo was a pillbox hat with a strip of mosquito netting stapled to the front. She had a severe expression on her face, as though she had been condemned to perpetually gnaw a mouthful of thistles. She plucked a piece of blue chalk from behind her ear and drew annoyed A-line dresses on the tabletop.

Malcolm explained, to the wall five inches above my head due to his continued aversion to eye contact, that the percentage he would require from us for his managerial expertise was so high because it included Vivisect designing clothes for us.

I said I liked my own clothes. Vivisect snorted and turned away in disgust. Malcolm implored her to "Tell them what you told me."

Sighing a sigh that indicated that she thought any sentence directed at me would be a colossal waste of her precious time (which was, in fact, true), she explained that it was all about T-shirts. The future of fashion was a T-shirt, and if we got with the program we could have all the T-shirts we wanted. McLaren added, "T-shirts and 'Sick On You.' That is the future, boys."

We drained our drinks and left before I could get stabbed with a hatpin.

Two nights later, Mick Jones and Tony James came back to see us and, after a glance through the letter box, Casino begrudgingly let them in. This time Mick and Tony entirely ignored the McLaren gambit. This time they told tales of an exotic oasis, a haven, a mecca for convivial Hollywood Brats types.

"Hollywood Brats types? What on earth are you two rabbiting on about?"

"Yes, yes," they said. "Come, we will guide you. We will take your hand and lead you to a special environs where 'Sick On You' is the anthem and they play *Grown Up Wrong* into the wee hours."

Okay. I decide to indulge. I ask, "Kindly tell, enlightened stranger . . . what is the name of this sacred place?"

"Verily it is known colloquially as, and I must shield my eyes as I murmur the words, Maida Vale."

Maida Vale? Cor, it does sound magical. Makes Camelot seem like a housing estate in Lambeth. I swear, I think I saw the lights dim as he mentioned the name.

I inquire further. "And where, fair knights Sir Mick and Sir Tone, in the exalted environs of Maida Vale is the exact locale of which you trill so enthrallingly? In other words, can you be more specific as to the fucking address?"

"Yeah, sure, 47 Warrington Crescent."

Well. Let me take you down, cos I'm going to . . . Warrington Crescent.

Next day, bored stiffer than Bob Guccione's penile implant, Casino and I got out our London *A–Z* and located this mysterious outpost of empire called Maida Vale. It was right over there, where it had always been. We checked our schedules and, noting that we had nothing pressing for the next five years or so, brushed our teeth, hit the street, leaped a Tube turnstile, and duly arrived at our destination: 47 Warrington Crescent, Maida Vale.

What a sight! Spacious, subterranean pad with coal-scullery studio, pool table, more good-looking babes than was strictly necessary (including a soon-to-be *Penthouse* Pet of the Year, Jane Hargrave), various lurking musicians making with the furtive sidelong glances, a nervous, blond fake-singer fellow, and a black chap, sort of a good-looking Curtis Mayfield, who looked like, in the event of a funk emergency, he could immediately step into Kool & the Gang.

And, true to rumor, the Hollywood Brats LP was playing, cranked up.

Six of us peeled off from the crowd, cracked lagers, and had a chat: me (vocals), Geir Waade (drums), Casino Steel (keyboards), Matt Dangerfield (guitar), Mick Jones (guitar), and Tony James (bass).

Geir, a mate of Casino's from Norway (good-looking lad, bags of style, erratic talent), suggested we call ourselves the London SS. Great name, I thought, and we all kicked around ideas for a stage set: lighting naturally nicked from *Cabaret*, coils of barbed wire strung in front of the stage, sirens, light towers on each side, and maybe just a hint, a whiff, the merest puff of Zyklon B to knock out the first two rows.

But enough chat. We plugged in and had a bash. A crucial mistake. Things were going so well.

I was a member of the London SS for a grand total of fourteen minutes. Just long enough to be part of an ensemble that massacred "Bad Boy" (Larry Williams song/Fabs version) three times. This wasn't a band, this was an insult to instruments. Geir and Tony (the so-called rhythm section) played as though they hated each other and couldn't wait for the rest of us to leave so they could fight. Mick Jones was apparently under the illusion that volume, distortion, and bouncing up and down could paper over glacial, ham-fingered chord changes (turns out he was right, actually; he built a career out of it). Through the chaotic cacophony I swear I could hear Harry Moss calling me back to the management-trainee program at Moss Bros. It was that bad—that hopeless.

As the last weak, flat, desultory note of attempt number three whined its discordant way into a dank corner of the one-time coal scullery, I ditched the microphone, drained a can of Long Life, wrapped a scarf noose-like around my throat, and stalked out in a huff (a '59 Huff with big fins and velvet dice hanging from the rearview mirror) into the Maida Vale night, taking a sharp right at the top of the steps and heading to the blessed environs of the sacred Warrington pub, where all ills are nursed, all wounds salved, and all grievances tut-tutted.

Later, back at the Paddington ranch, Casino and I had a word and we both agreed that the prize pig at the fair was the guy called Matt. Stick a blue ribbon on this boy's rump, we decided. He was quiet, well, let me rephrase that, he was reserved and cool. He wasn't all that quiet. He had suggestions but he was the consummate gentleman when it came to voicing them.

And he could play, which put him in the top 50 percent of the chaps in the room. Much more importantly, Matt looked good. The biggest mystery of all was how this guy had avoided our net all these years. Had he shown up at any Hollywood Brats audition he would have been in before he even stuck a plug in an amp.

And it turned out that 47 Warrington Crescent was his digs.

The two of us went back and met with Matt. We had a laugh and a pint or ten.

But my heart just wasn't in it. Not to use too emotive a term, but my spirit was in tatters. The failure and demise of the Hollywood Brats had brought me to my knees, figuratively most nights, literally on some. I thought that band was perfection and it quite patently wasn't. It died a death. Thus my dalliance with the Warrington Crescent experiment was doomed from the start, regardless of the potential.

So, much like Captain Oates with the Scott expedition or Mick Groome back on Bishop's Road, I walked off into the night, never to return.

III

Whatever Happened to . . .

Casino Steel

Casino flourished. He formed the Boys with Matt Dangerfield, Honest John Plain, Duncan Reid, and Jack Black, and under the wine-soaked tutelage of former Brats manager Ken Mewis signed with NEMS Records. "The Beatles of Punk," as some lazy, talentless hack dubbed them, purely because they could actually play their instruments, sing harmonies, and write real songs. They recorded the Hollywood Brats' "Tumble with Me" and "Sick On You" on their debut album *The Boys*. Wise Boys.

Casino went on to even greater success in the early eighties with Gary *Auf Wiedersehen, Pet* Holton (soon to die tragically), and then to a solo career, to jail and back.

He has played the *Grand Ole Opry*, backed by Elvis's singers, the Jordanaires.

He is as he was, a one-off, a classic, the real thing.

Brady

Brady toured and recorded with something called Wreckless Eric, on Stiff Records, kicked heroin, embraced cocaine, emigrated to Australia, came back in tears, and launched a spectacularly unsuccessful solo career. He played, brilliantly, on both of my solo albums.

An amateur cross-dresser, he can be spied most nights in flamboyant garb, plying his left-handed trade in some of the less reputable pubs and clubs in London Town. He is always entertaining, always thirsty, and quite often in tune.

Lou Sparks

Lou married the girl in Clapham. They moved to the ancient land of the Micmacs and lived ever after.

Roger Cooper

Married Rosie and lived in Kings Langley, Hertfordshire. Became a dad and a granddad. Played the blues. In 2012, sadly, the Grim Reaper knocked.

Mal & Yosemite

Returned to Australia and faded effortlessly into an arid background.

American Brian

Followed his dad's patent-leather footsteps into the polyester/plaid world of mid-level Yankee political chicanery. Played bass in the office band. Sent plaintive e-mails to unresponsive websites. Has either died or moved to Sacramento. It's not easy to tell the difference.

Slats Silverstein

Failed impresario, octogenarian, amateur philatelist, former "acquaintance" of Barbara Windsor. Currently living in Golders Green, wading through knee-high stacks of writs and tortes, nursing grievances and plotting revenge.

Brillo

Lifelong pal, japester, father, and grandfather. The Grim Reaper knocked at his door, as well.

Carole

Still a friend, still lives in Watford, still looking for that kimono.

Zlatan the Mysterious

Became a property magnate in North and East London. Currently retired, practicing Buddhism and exotic horticulture in Doddington, Kent.

Queen

Ancient Marquee slap-fest seen as the folly of youth, the chaps invited Casino and me to the launch party for *A Night at the Opera*. We quaffed champers with the delectable Lynsey de Paul, and at the end of the evening the exalted Ringo Starr hailed us a cab.

Mick Jones

Formed the Clash and enjoyed great commercial success, at the height of which he stunned fans and critics alike by recording the hilarious comedy album *Sandinista!*. In the eighties Mick continued to flout convention by going defiantly bald. Can be seen perambulating the Portobello Road, pondering his deathless existential beatnik question: "Should I cool it or should I blow?"

You know the answer, Mick.

Tony James

Formed Generation X with Bone Idol, recording the hiccuping gay anthem "Dancing with Myself." Went on to form something called Spug Spug Sitcom in the eighties. Can be seen these days doing absolutely nothing.

Malcolm McLaren

Managed the Dolls, the Pistols, Adam and a couple of his Ants, plus Mom Mom Mob, which, upside down and backward, is Bow Wow Wow. Reputed to have met his frankly scary missus, Vivisect Westwood, at the Railway Hotel in Harrow. Buried in Highgate Cemetery, not far from his idol Karl Marx.

11 Mill Lane, West Hampstead

Former rat-infested, petri-dish squat has recently been appraised at over £2 million. Despite literally dozens of signatures on an obviously poorly worded petition, there are no plans, as of yet, for a Hollywood Brats English Heritage blue plaque.

Ken Mewis

Managed the Hollywood Brats, then the Boys, then, of course, a nightclub in Bali. When asked to sum up his life he said, "I manage." All too soon the unwelcome spook with the big black scythe knocked. Brady attended the funeral. Eulogies written by Andrew Loog Oldham and Andrew Matheson. The Brats sent a wreath shaped like a musical note along with these words, semi-nicked from his favorite film, *Casablanca* . . .

> *Of all the gin-joints in the world*
> *You had to walk into the Speak.*

Mick Groome

Went on to play with many artists, including Robert Plant. Currently plays with the Barron Knights. And back in the Brats fold.

Sometime after the demise of the Brats, he saw Keith Moon enter a tailor shop with two blondes. Upon being told his garment wasn't ready, Moon wrecked the shop, stormed out, went to a pub nearby, and ordered a pint of brandy. Mick followed and summoned the nerve to ask Moon about the Hollywood Brats. He hadn't a clue.

Andrew Loog Oldham

Married Miss Colombia and currently resides in Bogotá. Well, who wouldn't?

Wilf Pine

A true hard man in a world of so many fakes and posers. A "trusted lieutenant of the Krays" who, as Wilf said, kept their violence and mayhem "among consenting adults," unlike today's gutless yardies and hoodies. Wilf is the subject of the book *One of the Family: An Englishman in the Mafia.* Clunky, fifteen-syllable title, but what the hell. I've got an autographed copy.

Thanks for not killing me, Wilf.

IV

Time ticked and tocked.

Years went by, five of them to be exact, and by then the Hollywood Brats were the furthest thing from my thoughts, though there had been periodical murmurs, vague dispatches from the front, hints and notions.

In 1979 a writer named Julie Burchill wrote a couple of paragraphs in the music press about witnessing Marianne Faithfull singing a song called "Sick On You," from a lyric sheet, at the Marquee.

Odd.

And, while the Brats were a million miles from my thoughts, unbeknownst to me they were quite at the forefront of the thoughts of Iain McNay and Richard Branson.

Iain had just started a new label, Cherry Red Records.

> *Richard Jones, who was one third of Cherry Red, had a copy of the Hollywood Brats album. It had originally come out in Norway. He really liked it and said, "Why don't we have a go with it?" I was nervous about putting the album out as I didn't know how it would sell. Also that it was my first deal with Richard Branson and his company Caroline Exports.*
>
> *Richard said, "Why don't we do a deal on the Hollywood Brats?" He thought it would export quite well. He said, "Give us an exclusive three-month export period at a decent price and we'll guarantee to buy so many albums." I thought, that's great.*
>
> *The funny thing is that, years earlier, when I worked at Bell*

*Records, we almost signed the Hollywood Brats. We were going to
put out "Then He Kissed Me." It was on the release schedule. Then
Clive Davis came over from America and said, "Don't be stupid,
this isn't the kind of act we want on Bell Records." So it never got
released.*

*But I knew of the band from back then. I'd seen them play a
couple of times in a club in Piccadilly. That was the coincidence.
I thought they were amazing.*

Iain McNay, London, 2013

The four of us, of course, were blissfully ignorant regarding all these
machinations. As far as we were concerned, the Brats were dusty, painful
history. We had no clue about Cherry Red Records or the fact that Ken Mewis
had done a deal with them to release the album.

Pocketed the cash, too, the scoundrel.

Then, one morning in 1980, the phone rang. It was my manager at the
time, alerting me to a review in the *Record Mirror*.

Peter Coyne, *Record Mirror*, March 15, 1980

*Too much, too soon. Casino Steel's purposely discordant piano that
introduces both "The Hollywood Brats" and "Chez Maximes"
hardly prepares for the brilliant rock 'n' roll onslaught that is to be
found on this excellent record.*

*Back in '73 the Hollywood Brats were Britain's answer to
Staten Island's finest, the New York Dolls. Like the Dolls, the
Hollywood Brats (Andrew Matheson on vocals, Casino Steel on
piano, Lou Sparks on drums, Wayne Manor on bass, Brady on
guitar) employed a similar use of glam and musical aggression.
Also like the Dolls, they were light years ahead of their time and
destined to be doomed.*

*Managing to record only this album, which was released only
in Scandinavia, the Hollywood Brats eventually disbanded in '75
and the Brats were sadly scattered here, there and everywhere.*

In no respect does this record sound five years old when you compare the Brats' sheer teenage brilliance with what passes for rock 'n' roll now.

"Chez Maximes," a naughty rocker concerning a high-class brothel, explodes (the only descriptive term possible) in fine style from the speakers, kneeing the listener immediately in the groin and at the same time kissing him/her on both cheeks. Matheson exploits his perfect Jagger simper from the outré opening line of "My daddy was a sailor in the Second World War" all the way to the album's dynamic conclusion on "Sick On You."

If it means anything, this is the greatest album I've ever had the pleasure to review, so let's kiss and make up with the Hollywood Brats. Long live rock 'n' roll.

Acknowledgments

I unreservedly thank the following individuals for all the help, expertise, and kindness extended to me.

If I have omitted anybody the oversight is either inadvertent or with damned good reason.

Jake Lingwood

Anna Mrowiec

Hilary McMahon

Amber Matheson

Honest John Plain

Terry Chamberlain

Richard Chamberlain

Ken Mewis

Andrew Loog Oldham

Gered Mankowitz

Marcus Gray

Alwyn Turner

Roger Cooper

Mick Groome

And most importantly

My Blood Brothers:

Casino Steel

Lou Sparks

Brady

Andrew Matheson

Of late, I've been minding my own business, walking the grounds with my vicious but faithful Irish wolfhound Rommel, reading Gibbon's *Decline and Fall of the Roman Empire*, shooting rats with a .22, drinking cognac, staring into the stark embers of life's fire, and generally wondering why everything is so undeniably naff.

I didn't ask to be disturbed.